The Evolution
of the
United Nations
System

The Evolution
of the
United Nations
System

Second Edition

Amos Yoder

Taylor & Francis

USA	Publishing Office:	Taylor & Francis
		1101 Vermont Avenue, NW, Suite 200
		Washington, DC 20005-3521
		Tel: (202) 289-2174
		Fax: (202) 289-3665
	Distribution Center:	Taylor & Francis
		1900 Frost Road, Suite 101
		Bristol, PA 19007-1598
		Tel: (215) 785-5800
		Fax: (215) 785-5515
UK		Taylor & Francis Ltd.
		4 John St.
		London WC1N 2ET
		Tel: 071 405 2237
		Fax: 071 831 2035

THE EVOLUTION OF THE UNITED NATIONS SYSTEM, Second Edition

1 2 3 4 5 6 7 8 9 0 E B E B 9 8 7 6 5 4 3

This book was set in Times Roman by Taylor & Francis. The production supervisor was Peggy M. Rote; and the typesetters were Wayne Hutchins and Miriam Gonzalez. Printing and binding by Edwards Brothers, Inc.

A CIP catalog record for this book is available from the British Library.
∞ The paper in this publication meets the requirements of the ANSI Standard Z39.48-1984(Permanence of Paper)

Library of Congress Cataloging-in-Publication Data

Yoder, Amos.
    The evolution of the United Nations system / Amos Yoder.—2nd ed.
      p. cm.
    Includes bibliographical references and index.

    1. United Nations. 2. International agencies. I. Title.
II. Title: Evolution of the UN system.
JX1977.Y6 1992
341.23—dc20
92-40144
CIP

ISBN 0-8448-1740-6 (case)
ISBN 0-8448-1741-4 (paper)

Contents

Preface

A major aim of this book is to bridge the gap between the liberal internationalists and the advocates of power politics, who believe that only material power counts in international relations. It is particularly important today as the United Nations takes center stage in international crises to understand how power can be used to support international law and order.

After World War II many internationalists had unrealistic hopes of what the United Nations could accomplish, and many were disillusioned when it failed to prevent major wars. The power brokers, on the other hand, have underestimated the importance of UN actions when internationalists like Presidents Truman and Eisenhower and other world leaders supported it.

I describe in this book how leaders have effectively used power, including military strength, within a framework of international law in support of the United Nations. I do not expect to convert those who believe leaders should support with power what they define as the national interest, and believe that they should not be hindered by international law. I do hope to help them understand the liberal internationalists' point of view that the interests of nations converge in supporting the United Nations and the rule of international law.

Before World War II, in particular, some internationalists relied too much on international agreements and were afraid to challenge aggressors. In this way they created a belief that all internationalists were "appeasers" in the worst sense of the word. However, an examination of the Axis aggression in the 1930s indicates that power brokers as well as internationalists were appeasers, and that some internationalists were more ready to oppose aggression than some of the diplomats.

Men and women of good intention have worked for peace on both sides of this argument, and I hope I can help build a bridge of understanding between them, although a bridge of agreement may not be possible.

In the economic and social realm, I believe that texts tend to give too little attention to the important work of the International Bank and the International Monetary Fund and to the UN Development Program. As the world grows more interdependent, the network of UN Specialized Agencies also has been addressing global economic challenges, including health and environmental problems. This work is seldom reported because it is unexciting and routine, and I hope to provide perspective on these accomplishments.

It is important to take a new look at the United Nations System because there have been dramatic changes in the attitudes of the two superpowers toward supporting the United Nations since 1988. This book evaluates these changes in the perspective of the past criticisms and achievements of the UN System.

I would like to call attention to the Security Council exercise described in Appendix D. It gives students a chance to attempt to solve real problems addressed by the United Nations, and at the same time shows them how hard it is to get an agreement on a resolution, if they accurately represent the position of their country. Students often get hooked on this exercise in preparing speeches, and they realistically debate and argue over issues as their counterparts do in the United Nations.

An alternative is to write the United Nations Association of the United States of America, 485 Fifth Avenue, New York, NY 10017 for their kits for United Nations exercises. Also, the Public Inquiries Unit, Room GA-57, United Nations, New York 10017 can provide useful documents.

United Nations Headquarters, New York, New York, 1985. (*Courtesy:* UN Photo 165070/Louis Conner)

Chapter I

INTRODUCTION

At the beginning of the 1990s the United Nations enjoyed a revival of prestige, particularly in the United States. The UN Security Council in 1990 and 1991 issued ultimatums to Iraq to end its aggression in Kuwait, and when these were ignored, the Security Council authorized the use of force against Iraq. Iraq was defeated by a UN coalition in a short, decisive war. Also, the UN secretary general and his representatives had mediated a withdrawal of Soviet forces from Afghanistan, helped end the Iran-Iraq war, and helped mediate a peace in Nicaragua and El Salvador. Many pundits suggested that the United Nations was finally beginning to function as its founders had intended.

The United Nations had regained much of the prestige that it had enjoyed at the close of World War II, but U.S. support was still not firm. In 1992 the United States was still over $600 million in arrears to the budgets of the UN System.

Critics and supporters of the United Nations had divided along two lines of arguments. Before 1988 the supporters of power politics derided the UN for its weakness. Criticisms in the U.S. news media were widespread. The United States had ignored the condemnation of the International Court of Justice for supporting attacks against the government of Nicaragua. The Soviet Union had violated the UN charter and ignored its resolutions by suppressing dissent in Eastern Europe and by invading Afghanistan.

Academics who supported the United Nations noted that the world is becoming interdependent and that countries are relying more and more on international organizations for economic and social services. David Mitrany called this "functionalism." This theory stated that as the world becomes more interdependent and people depend more on organizations involving other countries, this will spill over into the political field and increase activities and influence of international organizations such as the United Nations. This would act as a self-reinforcing process. Internationalist supporters of the United Nations asserted that if the world is to avoid wars and a nuclear holocaust, governments should promote respect for the United Nations and international law. However, they seldom noted how the UN System had settled international crises and alleviated economic and social problems, but instead they would blame the superpowers for failing to support the UN System.

Because the United Nations was based on the League of Nations, we will review the League's successes and its failures. The review of its history notes the contests between internationalists of the League and power brokers outside the League. We will review how the power brokers acted outside the League to undermine its initial actions against the aggressors. This helps us understand the Soviet's and the United States' initial support for the United Nations. At first the United Nations was able to take decisive actions against aggression in Korea. However, in the following decade this support weakened and the United States went to war in Vietnam without UN support. Strangely, the U.S. defeat in Vietnam helped increase disillusionment about the United Nations. The United Nations continued to function despite the lack of cooperation of the two superpowers, and we examine what it accomplished despite this handicap.

In 1989 President Bush ignored international law and the United Nations by an attack on Panama to arrest its leader, General Noriega, on drug charges. In the following years, however, Bush reverted to being one of the strongest supporters of the United Nations, confining U.S. action against Iraq to actions authorized by UN resolutions. We will try to understand these twists and turns in policy.

A major focus in this book is the importance of the United Nations and international law for war and peace issues. This includes an assessment of the Security Council's actions to try to end or contain conflicts, and an evaluation of the network of nuclear arms control agreements. Many of them were sponsored by the United Nations, while other major ones are related to the UN agreements. We will also review major economic and social activities of the UN System, emphasizing the operations of the International Monetary Fund (IMF) and International Bank (IBRD), which is also known as the World Bank.

The long first sentences of the preamble of the League of Nations Convenant and of the UN Charter state that their founders are determined to prevent war and respect international law. The UN Charter added an affirmation of a belief in human rights. Philosophers and statesmen had affirmed these ideas in previous centuries, and it is revealing briefly to examine ideas and institutions for preventing war that influenced the drafters of the League Covenant and of the UN Charter.

One of the most influential writers was Hugo Grotius, whom many point to as the father of international law. Grotius was a lawyer, diplomat, and theologian of the seventeenth century who wrote the classic treatise concerning the law of war and peace when he was in jail after trying to mediate in the Thirty Years War. In this work he tried to set forth the rules by which states should be governed, deriving these rules from natural law and reason, and the consent of nations as set forth by philosophers and other writers. The fundamental principle of his writings was that the sovereignty of states should be respected. His aim was to mitigate the horrors of war by international law, whether it was derived from nature, divine command, or custom and compact.[1]

Subsequently, international lawyers built on these foundations, and many scholars followed with their learned works. Their writings have been of practical importance, not only in settling disputes between individuals in domestic courts, but also in settling disputes among nations. It is estimated that between 1816 and 1900 about 200 disputes and differences between states were submitted to arbitration, and in the vast majority of these cases the awards of the arbitrator were accepted.[2]

This idea of settling disputes by international law was further developed in world conferences before World War I. The First Hague Conference in 1899 was called by the tsar of Russia with the aim of establishing peace and ending the arms race. This world conference failed to limit armaments, but with the help of the Interparliamentary Union and the International Law Association the conference adopted a convention committing signatories to use mediation in international disputes "as far as circumstances allow" and establishing the Permanent Court of Arbitration at the Hague. This institution was neither permanent nor a court, but it consisted of panels of arbitrators who would be called on to settle disputes.

The tsar called the Second Hague Conference eight years later in 1907 with 44 nations attending. Ominously, the major efforts of the delegates were to elaborate the laws of war. This conference made no further progress in getting a permanent international court or getting states to make a meaningful commitment to arbitration, but it did call for another conference in eight years with a committee to be established two years in advance to prepare proposals for settling international disputes. World War I, of course, intervened to prevent the third conference.

The above moves toward establishing an international system to prevent war had been reinforced during the previous century by a growth of international organizations in the economic and social fields, which Mitrany would call functionalism. The revolutionary growth of technology in commerce brought about by the Industrial Revolution stimulated the growth of these organizations. By 1914 there were over 30, including the Danube Commission (1856), the International Telegraphic Union (1865), the Universal Postal Union (1874), the International Health Office in Paris (1907), and others. Along with these were a number of influential nongovernment organizations such as the International Law Association, and the Interparliamentary Union mentioned above.

Although the Hague Conference and these organizations were devoted to the idea of promoting international organization and international peace, they failed to prevent World War I. Out of this catastrophe came a determination of world leaders to create a strong international institution devoted to preventing war. By the close of the war there was overwhelming popular support for the League of Nations.

Some writers have suggested that the Concert of Europe of a previous century was a forerunner of the League of Nations. The Concert was a meeting of the great powers to divide up colonies, territories, and spheres of interest on the basis of power factors, rather than on the basis of international law and democratic procedures as reflected in the League Covenant and the UN Charter. During the nineteenth century the great powers in the Concert partitioned Asia and Africa, while Chancellor Bismarck acted to prevent the building of alliances that would threaten the new German nation. Bismarck was so skillful in the use of power politics, including three international wars to unify Germany from a group of over 200 small states, that many diplomats tried to follow his example rather than be guided by international law. Liberal internationalists would say that the Concert of Europe, without a secretariat or rules of conduct, was the opposite of an international organization trying to work within limits of international law.[3]

The Concert of Europe was so weak by 1914 that Lord Edward Grey, the British foreign minister, was not able to convene it to try to head off World War I. It was this failure that led to his determination and that of others to establish the League of Nations as a permanent institution that at least could call a meeting of major powers on short notice to try to prevent war. As we see in the next chapter, the power brokers and the liberal internationalists came together to agree on the League of Nations Convenant.

The Soviet Union at first was excluded from the League of Nations. Later, it was admitted, but after a decade it became disillusioned. The Soviet's historic suspicion of the United Nations is relatively easy to understand. Its Marxist-Leninist philosophy, growing out of its materialistic, revolutionary origin, holds that international politics reflect attempts of capitalist states to dominate the world. The communist philosophy supported revolution and the use of military and political means to oppose capitalist imperialism. In this view, the League of Nations and other international organizations would be useful only as they contributed to the defense of Russia and to communism's historic struggles.

The Soviet Union's suspicion was reinforced by the historic failure of the League of Nations to oppose Hitler's aggression, and the Soviet belief that the West tried to turn Hitler against the Soviet Union before World War II. During World War II Stalin decided to support the idea of the United Nations with the aim of maintaining the wartime alliance to prevent a resurgence of Germany and probably to prevent the capitalist nations from ganging up on Russia.[4] However, the Western nations tended to dominate the United Nations, and until 1988 the Soviets participated but contributed a minimum to it because it was of little use in achieving the aims of Russian foreign policy.

President Woodrow Wilson, a liberal internationalist, had unsuccessfully tried to obtain the support for the League of Nations against U.S. opponents, some of whom had previously favored the idea. Secretary of State Cordell Hull and president Truman learned from this experience and successfully fathered the United Nations. President Truman and Eisenhower gave relatively strong support to the United Nations, but later U.S. support faded, and erosion of support for the United Nations was pronounced under most of the Reagan administration.

The hypotheses that I use in trying to explain the varying fortunes of the United Nations System are the following:

1. Strong leaders like President Truman and President Eisenhower successfully worked through the United Nations after World War II. These liberal internationalists were working toward the goal of creating a respect for the United Nations and for international law so that eventually wars would be eliminated.[5]

2. The United Nations, as was the League, is not an independent power that can be blamed or praised for actions in international affairs. At the present state of international development, nationalism still commands the actions of states. The United Nations is mainly a forum and an instrument that depends on the support of its members, particularly the powerful United States.

3. Reporting on the United Nations has been unfavorably distorted, particu-

larly in the United States. There is a natural bias of the news media to report the dramatic, bad news rather than the relatively dull news of constructive action in the United Nations System. Power politics always get the headlines. The day-to-day constructive operation of the UN's family of agencies in the fields of international finance, development, health, and many other areas receive virtually no attention in the news media. This reporting affects the evaluations of historians and political scientists. This book tries to assess these activities with a more balanced perspective.

4. This view of the lack of importance of the United Nations has been transferred back in history as if the United Nations never was of much importance. Yet, following World War II, we will see how the United Nations was regarded by many as humanity's best hope for peace, and it was used to settle important conflicts. The distortions of looking backward from a current perspective have also created negative perceptions of the League of Nations despite its accomplishments in the 1920s, and most observers remember only that nations in the 1930s under the League failed to rally against the Fascist aggressors.

5. Unilateral actions of power brokers before and after World War II have shown little success in comparison with the actions within the framework of the United Nations. This is a controversial hypothesis, but I believe it is supported, particularly in Chapters IV and V.

6. UN institutions including the International Monetary Fund which was established to prevent the type of economic chaos that occurred after World War I, have been relatively successful and are preparing to meet global challenges.

The above are initial hypotheses as I analyze why the League failed in its major task of preventing World War II and how the United Nations has met the challenges of the post-World War II era.

I begin with examining how the United Nations evolved from the experience of the League of Nations. I then evaluate how the United Nations moved from center stage in preserving peace after World War II to a less important role in international crises. I next look at the important but underestimated network of agreements to control nuclear weapons, many of which originated in the United Nations. I also examine the recent revival of the United Nations in mediating and peacekeeping and also its growing importance in economic and social issues. The conclusion evaluates the potential for the United Nations System to help solve the many problems of a troubled world.

Notes to Chapter 1

1. A. Campbell, *The Rights of War and Peace* (Washington, DC: M. Walter Dunne, 1981), Chapter 1.

2. F.P. Walters, *A History of the League of Nations* (London: Oxford University Press, 1973), Vol. I, p. 9.

3. F. S. Northedge, *The League of Nations* (New York: Holms and Meier, 1986), pp. 9–10.

4. J. Stalin, *The Great Patriotic War* (Moscow: Novosty Press Agency Publishing House, 1945).

5. The term *liberal internationalist* is appropriate for distinguishing these leaders from power brokers. The term *liberal* is associated with English "liberals" of the 19th century who supported extending democracy beyond propertied classes. They were also anti-imperialist. Prime Minister Lloyd George of the Liberal Party helped found the League of Nations. However, in the heat of U.S. presidential campaigns, *liberal* is applied to those who advocate increased government spending. The opposite is true in international affairs. Liberal internationalists would rely more on the United Nations, whose programs cost the United States less than one % of the U.S. military budget, which is the basis of power politics.

Chapter II

THE LEAGUE OF NATIONS EXPERIMENT

THE BIRTH OF THE LEAGUE

After World War 1, the liberal internationalists favoring international cooperation and the power brokers of Europe cooperated to form the League of Nations. President Woodrow Wilson took the lead in proposing a framework for collective security, arbitration of disputes, and limitation of armaments—ideas that had been expressed in the Hague conferences. The victims of the war, who wanted to ensure that Germany would not again threaten the peace, joined in support of the League of Nations. The French, particularly, were determined to use the League to exact reparations from Germany and disarm the foe that had warred against them twice in the lifetime of many French leaders. Supporters included members of many international organizations that were cooperating in the fields of mail, electronic communications, health, and other areas. Finally, many diplomats supported the idea of a league to maintain peace. Lord Grey, the British foreign secretary who had vainly tried to call the leaders of Europe together to prevent World War I in 1914, was determined that after the war there should be a system where such a conference could readily be called.

Lord Grey, Prime Minister Lloyd George, and some of the leading diplomats, as well as historians who later examined the records of World War I, were convinced that the war could have been avoided by a conference of the powers.[1] The Serbian government did not support the assassination by Serb nationalists that triggered the war. Austria-Hungary, however, attacked Serbia in order to punish it to prevent that kind of terrorism from happening again—Austria-Hungary was not trying to conquer Serbia. Germany gave a "blank check" of support to Austria-Hungary mainly to reinforce Austria-Hungary as its only reliable ally. Germany did not have aggressive designs on Europe then as Hitler did 30 years later. Russia then stumbled into a mobilization to support Serbia—this mobilization threatened Germany and triggered its attack against France, the major ally of Russia. Russia did not realize how its mobilization appeared to Germany as a threat from both Russia and France. Although during World War I and after, observers accused Germany of aggression, in reality mistakes and poor communication were mostly to blame.[2]

Lord Grey, Sir Robert Cecil, and Woodrow Wilson, strong supporters of the League of Nations, realized how a world organization might have prevented the war. Others such as Clemenceau, the bulldog leader of France, and Lloyd George, the British prime minister, wanted to use the League of Nations to prevent Germany from becoming a threat again. Finally, there was a widespread yearning for peace and for an end to war from the many millions who had lost family and friends in the fight. This idea of a world organization was promoted by the many peace organizations. During the war lawyers and others in the United States and Britain had drafted plans for a world organization that incorporated features that later were incorporated in the League Covenant.

The League to Enforce Peace held its first meeting in Washington, DC, in 1916. Its main speakers were President Wilson, head of the Democrats, and Henry Cabot Lodge, leader of the Republicans in the Senate. Both men that day called for a new international system to maintain peace under a rule of international law. They stated if necessary that the armed forces of the major powers, including those of the United States, should be a full partner in a future league of nations. (By this time the idea of a league of nations had become prevalent.) At this point Wilson was still hoping that the United States would be able to stay out of the war and use its strength and influence to mediate and help bring about a peace.

Ironically, the United States was drawn into World War I by insisting on its rights under international law—that is, the right to supply England with peaceful commerce as long as Germany did not mount an effective blockade by surface ships. The Hague conferences had helped work out these principles. When Germany sank U.S. merchant ships without warning, it triggered outrage in the United States and contributed to the decision by Wilson to ask Congress to declare war on Germany.

This was an agonizing decision for Wilson. He reasoned that he could use the war to "make the world safe for democracy" and establish a system to maintain peace. In his April 2, 1917, address to Congress calling for war against Germany, he said, "We shall fight for the things which we have always carried near our hearts—for democracy . . . for a universal dominion of rights by such a concert of free peoples that shall bring peace and safety to all nations and make the world at last free. To such a task we can dedicate our lives and our fortunes." Wilson spelled out American war aims in the famous Fourteen Points in his address to Congress on January 9, 1918. The following relate to the League of Nations: (1) open covenants, openly arrived at, (2) absolute freedom of navigation of the seas, (3) removal of trade barriers, (4) reduction of armaments, (5) free, open-minded, and impartial adjustment of all colonial claims, and (6) "a general association of nations must be formed . . . for the purpose of affording mutual guarantees of political independence to territories of great and small states alike." After the war Wilson went to the Versailles Peace Conference determined to establish a league of nations to enforce peace.

Wilson was welcomed with enthusiastic parades in Europe, where his Fourteen Points had struck a chord of public approval. He used this public support effectively to press for his views at the peace settlement. He was determined that the League of Nations would be an integral part of the peace settlement, and to his surprise he found no opposition. Wilson's proposal that the League be the first business of the peace conference was adopted, and a commission was appointed to draft the covenant. The president was made chairman of the committee, which included Bourgeois, a French internationalist, Ian Christian Smuts of South Africa, and Sir Robert Cecil of Britain, all supporters of the League idea. The committee included the major powers plus five minor powers—Belgium, Brazil, China, Portugal, and Serbia. The minor powers insisted on additional representation, so Greece, Poland, Czechoslovakia, and Romania were added. An Anglo-American draft worked out by Colonel House and Lord Cecil and incorporating basic ideas of Smuts was used as the basis for drafting the League Covenant. In 11 days the committee came up with the first draft.

What then happened to Wilson's beautiful dream? Why was it rejected by the U.S. Senate, including senators such as Senator Lodge who originally supported the idea? Most historians blamed Wilson's bad political tactics. He made the League the major issue of the Democratic congressional campaign in 1918, asking the voters to give the Democrats a strong majority to enable him to speak with authority at the forthcoming peace negotiations. This aroused the violent resentment of the Republican opponents, and Senator Lodge, a former supporter of a league, led the opposition. Wilson's appeal was counterproductive with the Republicans winning control of both houses. Moreover, Wilson kept his draft of the proposed league secret and only produced it officially at the Peace Conference itself. Wilson did not consult with the Republicans, and at no stage did the draft have the "benefit of criticisms of a clear-headed opposition."[4] As we see later, when President Truman was in a similar position, he consulted fully with Republican congressman on the UN Charter.

Wilson returned to the United States after a few weeks at the Versailles Conference to defend the Covenant against growing criticism. After returning to Paris and incorporating in the new draft suggestions by some opponents, he returned again to the United States to sell the idea to the American people. By this time, the strain of the war and the negotiations at Versailles had taken their toll, and Wilson was very ill. During the campaign to sell the League, he had a stroke and returned to Washington a broken man. Colonel House himself was also ill, too ill to testify before the Senate. In November 1919 the treaty was rejected by the Senate and then again in March 1920 by a vote of 49 in favor and 35 against. With the two-thirds constitutional requirement, a vote of 56 would have been required. Actually, by this time the Senate opponents had made such drastic amendments to the treaty that Wilson himself asked supporters to vote against it.

Wilson's last public words on November 11, 1923, were prophetic. He said: "I cannot refrain from saying it: I am not one of those who have the least anxiety about the triumph of the principles I stood for. I've seen fools resist providence before and I've seen their destruction, as will come upon these again—utter destruction. That we shall prevail is as sure as that God reigns."

If he had lived, Wilson would have blamed Hitler's rise to power before World War II on the failure of the United States to support collective security under the League of Nations, and he would have pointed to the formation of the United Nations as a fulfillment of his dream. Critics of Wilson would blame weakness and a reliance on international law instead of strength as the cause of World War II. There is truth in both sets of criticisms.[5]

THE LEAGUE COVENANT

The League of Nations Covenant was put in effect by the other major powers without the United States (see Appendix I.) Its major provisions were the following:

1. The preamble emphasizes the aim to achieve international peace, not to resort to war, and to establish international law as a rule of conduct among governments.
2. Major organs of the League were an assembly, council, and permanent

secretariat. The Assembly consisted of representatives of all members of the League; the Council consisted of representatives of members of the principal powers together with nine representatives of other members of the League. The Assembly and the Council had overlapping authority, and a clear line was never drawn on their respective functions.[6]

3. The Assembly decided how the expenses of the League would be shared.
4. The secretary general was appointed by the Council with the approval of a majority of the Assembly.
5. A 1926 amendment to the Covenant called for a vote of two-thirds of the Assembly to elect new members to the League.
6. Article 8 called for the reduction of national armaments and designated the Council to formulate plans for reducing armaments.
7. Article 10 called for members of the League to "respect and preserve as against external aggression the territorial integrity and the existing political independence of all members of the League." It added an escape clause for the Council to advise the means by which this obligation should be fulfilled.
8. Article 18 called on the members of the League to register treaties and international agreements with the League of Nations.
9. Article 24 called for the international bureaux to be placed under the direction of the League. (When the United Nations was founded, these international agencies were called Specialized Agencies and placed under its direction.)

The aims and structure of the League of Nations were used as a model for the United Nations, with modifications by the drafters of the UN Charter to correct the weaknesses of the League Covenant. The Covenant and the Charter share the same stated aim—to achieve international peace and support international law as the rule of conduct among governments. Both the League and the United Nations have an assembly, a council, and a secretariat. Both the League and the UN Council are primarily concerned with crises and give the big powers a major voice. The assemblies are like a legislature with every member nation having one vote. The secretariats arrange the meetings and provide all the services including interpreters and reports in many languages.

The International Court of Justice, established by the League of Nations shortly after it was formed, is an integral part of the UN Charter. Another major UN organ, the Trusteeship Council, corresponds to the Mandates Commission under the League of Nations. Just before World War II, a

League committee considered creating a major body for economic and social affairs. This idea was picked up and used in establishing the UN Economic and Social Council, which is the other major organ of the United Nations (see Fig. 1 in Chapter III).

There are, however, important differences between the League and the United Nations. The League of Nations worked by unanimity on all but procedural matters. The politicians of the League managed to get around this by making approval of reports with recommendations a procedural matter, so that the views of the League could not be vetoed by one member. This, of course, did not bind those who disagreed. Another major difference was that the mandates system in Article 22 of the League Covenant called for the well-being and development of colonies and territories as being a "sacred trust." The UN Charter went beyond this in Article 1 calling for friendly relations among nations based on "self-determination" of peoples. Moreover, the UN articles under the chapter on the trusteeships plainly call for the United Nations to promote "progressive development towards self-government or independence." Since World War II these aims have been dramatically carried out by the achievement of independence by about 100 nations. Moreover, paragraph three of Article 1 of the UN Charter calls for promoting and encouraging respect for human rights and for fundamental freedoms without distinction as to race, sex, language, or religion. This was not included in the League Covenant, and the United Nations has been much more of an activist in this regard than the League was.

The League like the United Nations coordinated the activities of the "bureaux," which today are called the Specialized Agencies. Some of the major activities of the League of Nations were carried out by special committees and commissions that later became international organizations in their own right, such as the World Health Organization.

Probably the most important difference between the League and the United Nations is that the League Covenant was less flexible than the UN Charter for settling disputes or containing a war. The United Nations is more of a political institution. Articles 15 and 16 of the League Covenant stated that disputes not submitted to arbitration or judicial settlement should be submitted to the Council. If the Council could not settle the dispute, it unanimously or by majority vote should make and publish a report. If there was unanimous agreement on the report, other than the votes of the parties to the dispute, the members of the League would not go to war with any party to the dispute that complied with the recommendations. They then reserved to themselves the right to take such action as they considered necessary for the maintenance of right and justice. If any member of the League resorted to war in disregard of its agreements under this procedure, it should be deemed to have committed an act of war against all other members of the League, which then were required to sever economic and financial relations and other contacts with the guilty state. It was the Council's duty, then, to recommend what armed forces should be used to protect the covenants of the League. The members of the League also agreed to cooperate in the financial and economic measures taken under this article. Under the Covenant these acts would be automatic; under the UN Charter there are almost an infinite number of options for ways to settle disputes. We now look at how the League applied the above provisions.

THE LEAGUE IN ACTION

For 10 years the League of Nations was the center of action for cleaning up the mess left by World War I, but it was not called upon to settle major disputes between the great powers. It helped reconcile Germany and France in the late 1920s, but by the 1930s it did not obtain the support necessary to handle the world economic crisis of that decade or to meet the challenges of powerful Fascist aggressors.

Let us first list the important successes of the League in the 1920s and then turn to two major crises of the 1930s—Manchuria and Ethiopia—where major powers failed to use the League or other instruments to stop the Axis powers on their way to World War II.

The accomplishments of the League listed below have received little attention from historians, who naturally focus on the tragic events of the 1930s. The first group of important activities arose out of the destruction and disorder of World War I, and the League set up and supported the following activities to alleviate the distress:

1. Fridtjof Nansen of the Red Cross under the authority of the League restored more than 425,000 prisoners of 27 nationalities to their home countries from Russia; these people were without means of subsistence. The League then conferred the title of High Commissioner for Refugees upon Nansen. Although it gave him little additional help, with assistance from private sources his organization helped resettle millions of Russians, Armenians, and Greeks, and alleviated famine.

2. Ludwik Rajchman, a Polish doctor and secretary of the Health Organization of the League, headed the League's Epidemic Commission,

which in 1920 prevented the spread of typhus, cholera, and typhoid from Russia and Poland into the rest of Europe.

3. The Health Section of the League's Secretariat under Rajchman also did outstanding work in combating epidemics in the Middle East, Far East, and throughout the world, enlisting support of leading scientific experts. The organization was later transformed into the World Health Organization (WHO).

4. The League's finance committee worked out a plan for loans and reconstruction of Austria, a defeated country, and by 1925 it left Austria with a recovered economy. In 1923 and 1924 another League committee helped rehabilitate Hungarian finances.

The League Council also settled a number of difficult boundary disputes, some of which involved conflicts. It got off to an inauspicious start by allowing Belgium to keep Eupen and Malmedy, areas disputed by Belgium and Germany, by refusing to challenge Belgium's plebiscite, which allowed its authorities to put pressure on the voters. The League then asserted its authority and settled the following territorial issues:

1. In 1921 League commissioners awarded the Aaland Islands to Finland with guarantees for the Swedish inhabitants.

2. The League Council in 1921 carried out a plebiscite in Silesia and drew a frontier line between Germany and Poland in the area. The Council then established a joint commission that managed relations along the border and settled grievances during the next 15 years.

3. In 1921 the Council with British support helped preserve Albania from being carved up by Yugoslavia, Italy, and Greece.

4. The League successfully administered the Saar until 1935, when it carried out a plebiscite that overwhelmingly indicated that the inhabitants of this rich coal-mining area wanted to return to Germany, and subsequently they were returned.

5. The League helped settle a major dispute between Greece and Italy over the murder of an Italian diplomat and Italy's occupation of the Greek island of Corfu. The Council was reluctant to confront Mussolini, but it eventually overcame the dictator's initial defiance of the League.

6. The Council settled the difficult problem of Memel, which had been turned over to Lithuania by Versailles, by protecting the right of German citizens there. League supervision lasted until Hitler took Memel in 1939.

7. The Locarno Pacts, which established normal international relations between Germany and France in 1925, were tied into the League as the ultimate authority. If the guarantees of those agreements had been honored by the major powers, the German aggression of the 1930s could have been contained.

8. The League Council during the 1920s also settled other frontier disputes, including those between Germany and Poland, Lithuania and Poland, Finland and Russia, Bulgaria and Greece, Bulgaria and Yugoslavia, Hungary and Rumania, Hungary and Yugoslavia, Poland and Czechoslovakia, and Turkey and Iraq. In certain of the disputes such as those between Bulgaria and Greece, and between Poland and Lithuania, hostilities broke out and the Council was able to stop them by exerting pressure and offering mediation.

In the above disputes the League did not act like a policeman or judge imposing a solution. Rather it acted as a forum, an investigative body, and as a conciliator or arbitrator, allowing passions to cool and recommending solutions. Although neither side was happy about the solution, they were solutions that both sides could accept.

The League failed to give more than rhetorical support against repression by Turkey of the Armenians in 1920. It did not rewrite the Treaty of Versailles with its harsh territorial provisions that Hitler later exploited. It was saddled with administering entities created by this treaty such as imposing an international administration on the city of Danzig. Hitler demanded the return of Danzig and used this as a pretext for his invasion of Poland that triggered World War II. The League failed to oppose France in 1922 when French troops occupied the Ruhr in demanding Germany meet reparations payments. The resulting disruption of the German economy laid the basis for the rise of the Nazi party, but it also resulted in a reparations settlement outside the League that permitted a temporary German economic revival until the Great Depression of the 1930s.

In acting as a political body, including avoiding some of the above major international issues, the League disappointed those who hoped it would assert more authority in its role.[7] At the end of the 1920s, however, the League's prestige was high and Geneva was a center of diplomatic action for solving issues other than the demands of radical German parties to again redraw the map of Europe. Prime ministers and heads of state regularly attended the League meetings to discuss major international issues. We now look at the crises of the following decade when the Fascist aggressors led by Germany destroyed the League, and when the League's accomplishments were largely forgotten.

THE LEAGUE IN RETREAT

In the second decade of the League's existence, Germany, Japan, and Italy, the Axis powers, surged toward world empire and World War II, and in the process destroyed the League. After the stock market crash in the fall of 1929, the malaise spread to Europe, and the cycle of debt repudiation, runs on banks, and financial crises grew until in 1931 the world was in the grip of the Great Depression. The economic chaos that followed gave Hitler and the aggressive leaders of Japan the opportunity to take control and lead their governments into World War II. Many economic observers believe that it was the burden of reparations and war debts that was a fundamental cause of the international economic crisis of the 1930s. If the United States had been an active participant in the League's activities, it would have been easier to address the world economic crisis, and action could have been taken more quickly. The world's leaders were not able to cope with the economic and political crises in Europe or with the events in Manchuria, where Japan began aggression that led it to direct confrontation with the United States and the attack on Pearl Harbor.

The Manchurian Incident

In 1928 the Japanese army blew up a train to kill a local Manchurian warlord who would not cooperate with it. The new emperor, the late Hirohito, demanded of Prime Minister General Tanaka that the officers be disciplined. The army refused because it would damage its prestige and its leaders would not take orders from the civil government. At that time, the army showed that it could defy the government, and the emperor was put in his place as a figurehead.

The Japanese military took control of Manchuria in 1931. At that time Manchuria was the industrial heart of China. Russia had dominated it at the beginning of the century, but Japan challenged it and by 1930 had achieved economic dominance. By 1931 Japan's investment in Manchuria of $1.1 billion represented over 80 percent of the total Japanese overseas investments.[8] Japan's colonial ambitions ran head-on into the desire of the new nationalist government of Chiang Kai-shek to reassert control over Chinese territory. His programs of boycotting Japanese goods and of building a rail-road competitive to the Japanese rail line stimulated Japanese opposition, particularly among the military.

The boycott hurt because Japanese industry, like others, was suffering from the drop in trade from the Great Depression. There were numerous disputes concerning trade, rights of Japan to settle in China, and functions of Japanese administrators and teachers, but the Japanese military was de-termined to impose its will without stooping to negotiate these complex is-sues. The military brought the situation to a head in September 1931 by secretly blowing up a small section of railroad and blaming it on the Chinese. They then moved in to "restore order."

The Japanese prime minister, who opposed the action, was assassinated by a group of nationalistic naval officers on May 15, 1932. The Japanese then set up a puppet emperor ("The Last Emperor" of China) and took over control of what they called the new state of Manchukuo. This was open aggression in defiance of the League.

President Chiang Kai-shek called on the Chinese people to remain calm, and appealed to the League. On September 21, 1931, soon after the news of the attack arrived, the League was distracted that same day by the Eu-ropean financial crisis with Britain going off the gold standard. The Japanese representative on the League Council assured it that Japan wanted to ne-gotiate the issue with China, and backed by pressure from the United States to permit negotiation and not to weaken the position of the Japanese civilian prime minister against the military, the League merely called on both sides to contain the conflict. The Japanese army, however, pressed forward. Over a month later the United States changed its position and called on the League to assert pressure and announced that the American government, acting in-dependently, would reinforce what the League did. On October 16, Prentiss Gilbert, the American consul in Geneva, took a seat at the Council table. Secretary of State Stimson, under attack by the isolationist press, however, withdrew Gilbert from the last meeting of the League sessions.

Meanwhile, Japan was in the grip of war fever with troop trains being surrounded by cheering crowds. The great powers were reluctant to chal-lenge the other great power on the other side of the world. When the Council met again, the Japanese delegate, apparently stalling, proposed an investi-gation, which was in line with the regular procedures of Article 15 in such a crisis. This proposal was supported by the Chinese delegate.

On December 10 the Council adopted a unanimous resolution to send a League Commission of Inquiry to the Far East. On February 3, 1932, the commission with Lord Lytton at its head left for the Far East, but it did not arrive in Manchuria until April, traveling through Japan to Shanghai and then north to Manchuria.

Meanwhile, on January 7, 1932 the United States sent a note to China and Japan, later called the Stimson Doctrine, asserting that the United States would not recognize any situation that would impair American treaty rights or that was brought about by means contrary to the Kellog Pact of 1929, in which nations had agreed to outlaw war. Stimson was concerned that the attack would cause "incalculable" damage to the structure of international societies provided by postwar treaties.[9] A few weeks later the Council adopted a statement similar to the Stimson Doctrine that refused to recognize Manchukuo. Severe fighting continued with the Chinese troops resisting the Japanese. In March 1932 an armistice was arranged.

At the end of February, Secretary of State Stimson published a letter to Senator Borah of Idaho, which was communicated to the League. Borah was a strong opponent of Japanese aggression in China. The letter suggested that the Assembly adopt the principle of nonrecognition as set forth in the January 7 note. The Assembly accepted the suggestion and also formed a committee, which participated along with the great powers, to arrange the truce between Japan and China. Meanwhile, Japan consolidated its hold on Manchuria.

In September 1932 the Lytton Report was finally published, one year after the Japanese attack. It vindicated the Chinese position. The Council passed the report to the Assembly, which debated it at length. It soon became apparent that the small powers of the Assembly were calling on the great powers to take an action that would involve them in the dispute with Japan. On February 24, 1933 the Assembly adopted the report of its Special Committee affirming that the members would not recognize the new state of Manchukuo or do anything to prejudice a settlement consistent with the sovereignty and administrative integrity of China. The Japanese delegation dramatically left the Assembly, and a month later, on March 27, 1933, Japan formally withdrew from the League.

This was the end of "action" by the League on this issue. On May 31, 1933 Chiang Kai-shek accepted an armistice with Japan controlling Manchuria, and for the next four years there was relative peace.

The outcome was not all bad, considering that the major powers were reeling from the Great Depression. Although Japan had taken control of Manchuria, China gained time to prepare for the final showdown, beginning about five years later. Japan was condemned and forced to withdraw from the League. This was painful because it had been a useful and cooperative member before the military took control of policy. It is also noteworthy that the Assembly, which represented the small powers, took a more forthright stand against aggression than the Council, which was dominated by the major powers. But the members of the League had failed to maintain the territorial integrity of one of its members, or impose the sanctions called for in Articles 15 and 16.

China was so far away from Europe, where the League's center of power rested, and Japan's military strength so dominant in Eastern Asia, that none of the League members seriously considered military or even economic confrontation with Japan.[10]

Italy Attacks Ethiopia

Benito Mussolini, the Italian dictator, made the next attack against the League with a drive to expand a colonial empire. Mussolini was the father of fascism, an extreme nationalistic, totalitarian philosophy that places the welfare of its own state above other values, and particularly above the values of international law that would try to protect the weaker nations. Hitler supported Mussolini until the end, rescuing Mussolini from Italian partisan forces in the final days of World War II.

At the end of the nineteenth century, Britain, France, and Italy had staked out claims around Abyssinia (Ethiopia), with Italy getting the poor and barren areas of Eritrea and Somalia on the northern and southeastern boundaries of Ethiopia. In 1935 all a weak Ethiopia could muster for defense were primitive weapons such as matchlock rifles. By 1933 Mussolini began to plan his attack with the aim of obtaining colonies like other major world powers.[11]

Italy worked out military and intelligence plans to create disorder in Ethiopia, and on December 5, 1934 the opportunity occurred with a clash between the forces of Ethiopia and Italy in a disputed area between Italian Somaliland and the Ogaden province of Ethiopia. Italy had occupied a border area since 1928 claimed by Ethiopia, and the clash occurred between troop units in the area. It was settled by the arrival of a few tanks and airplanes supporting the Italian garrison. The Italians widened the attack and positioned troops to threaten a major Ethiopian military post. Ethiopia brought the matter before the League Council in December 1934 and January 1935.

The Council and the Secretariat looked to London and Paris to take the lead. Although the two powers were bound by a 1906 treaty to maintain the independence of Ethiopia, the natural tendency of the foreign offices was to settle the dispute at the expense of the weak and relatively defenseless Ethiopia. This was a great temptation because Mussolini had originally opposed Hitler's attempt to take control of Austria in 1934, and Britain and France hoped to use Italy to offset the threat of German aggression in central Europe. There is a "painful doubt" that by this time France's foreign minister had promised Italy "a free hand for military action in Ethiopia."[12] The Council stalled while the Ethiopians pressed their case during the next nine months. Meanwhile, the League Assembly met and took up the case.

In June 1935 the results of a "Peace Ballot" of about 12 million British persons were published showing an overwhelming support for League membership and fulfillment of the Covenant's provisions for collective security by economic and military sanctions. This initially stiffened the British policy toward Italy.

During the crisis the Russian representative Litvinov spoke out strongly for the League to uphold the principle of collective security, pointing out that Italian claims that Ethiopia was backward and oppressive were not relevant. Pressures in the Assembly and by outside groups finally had an impact on the Council.

In October 1935 just as the Italian army mounted a major attack, the Council issued a report supporting the Ethiopian case. The report stated in the language of Article 15 of the Covenant that Italy had resorted to war in violation of its pledges under the Covenant. Council President Benes of Czechoslovakia then directed the Assembly's attention to the issue, and after a three-day debate, 50 of the 54 members accepted the report of the Council calling for a ban on exports of key commodities to Italy. Since Albania, Austria, and Hungary did not make the acceptance unanimous, Benes announced that sanctions were up to the decision of the individual members of the League. It then set up a Coordination Committee that drew up proposals that could be accepted or rejected by the individual states. It is significant that in this crisis the Assembly overcame the handicap of the unanimity requirement.

Anthony Eden, the British representative, led the debate with proposals to stop additional loans to Italy, already heavily in debt, and to stop imports from Italy. However, agreement could not be reached on stopping exports of oil and other essential commodities. Meanwhile, the conservative government of Britain had just been returned to power after an election in which it received support as result of its pledges to support the League.

Under the threat of war from Italy, British Foreign Secretary Hoare met with French Foreign Secretary Laval secretly in December 1935 to propose the cession to Italy of 60,000 square miles of Ethiopia and to mark off a further zone of 160,000 square miles for economic expansion exclusively for Italy. Ethiopia was to receive only about 3,000 square miles. The Hoare-

Laval plan, which was leaked to the French press, was received with shock by League members, because the French and British on the record had supported sanctions against Italy.[13] On December 16 Emperor Haile Selassie rejected the British and French plan in a historic speech, warning that the plan would encourage aggressors.

The uproar in Britain over the Hoare-Laval plan was so strong that the prime minister accepted Hoare's resignation after only six months in office. The issue was carried back to the League, but in January and February 1936 Mussolini's troops used the dread weapon of mustard gas and won important military victories.

At the beginning of March 1936, Hitler's troops marched into the Rhineland, putting great pressure on Britain and France to liquidate the Ethiopian crisis so they could face the greater threat from Hitler, and possibly enlist Italy in the effort. The Council stalled and failed to intensify the sanctions against Italy. At the end of June it finally turned the matter over to the Assembly. Prime Minister Chamberlain expressed the view there that to continue sanctions would be madness. This effectively pulled the rug on sanctions, and despite an eloquent plea from Emperor Haile Selassie, only two nations voted to continue the sanctions.

There has been confusion about the role of the United States, with some writers suggesting that it undermined the League effort to apply sanctions. The U.S. Congress was opposed to trade sanctions because it had been drawn into World War I on the principle of maintaining trade to England—freedom of the seas. U.S. neutrality legislation in 1936 prohibited trade with any belligerent country. However, in response to the League's October 1935 appeal, President Roosevelt said that the United States would issue moral appeals to American oil producers, and in response major oil suppliers said they would cooperate. However, the League committee stalled on implementing the oil sanctions for several months, and the Hoare-Laval plan and Hitler's invasion of the Rhineland destroyed the chances for implementing the oil embargo.[14]

The denouement of this tragedy occurred when Italy intervened on the side of Nazi Germany in the Spanish Civil War, joined Germany and Japan in the Axis, and did not oppose Germany's conquest of Austria in 1938. The Axis powers pictured their actions as crusades against communism and concluded the Anti-Comintern Pact of November 25, 1936. The Axis then mounted a major propaganda campaign against the League as an agent of communism, and continued along the path of aggression that led to World War II.

WHO WERE AT FAULT?

Professors and practitioners of the power-politics school, like Professors Hans Morgenthau, George Kennan, and Zbigniew Brzezinski, blame supporters of the League for encouraging governments to rely on international law and the League of Nations to stop aggression in the 1930s, when actually the aggressors of that era would only respect power. The above account suggests that this is not a fair appraisal. The League institutions were actually taking a stronger stand against Mussolini and the Japanese aggressors than the power brokers in control of foreign policy, who were acting outside the League framework to muddle through and to appease Mussolini and the Japanese. Partly these diplomats realized their position was weak against these aggressors, partly they hoped to get Mussolini to help stop Hitler, and partly they wanted to protect their economic and military assets from attack by the aggressors. At the time, these appeared to them to be compelling reasons, although the diplomats' solution was not supported by the British people, at least those who demonstrated support for the League and collective security by a decisive majority in the 1936 Peace Ballot. In retrospect, the world would have been better off and World War II perhaps avoided if the power brokers had backed the instincts of the British people and the League's Assembly during this period, which was calling on the major powers to support the collective security provisions of the League Covenant.

The Axis and particularly Hitler, of course, were primarily to blame for the final demise of the League, which was incidental to the shattering of the Versailles Treaty system. Many also fault the United States for not joining the League and for thereby weakening it from the beginning. F. P. Walters, formerly deputy secretary general of the League, stated the following:

> The immediate loss in power and influence of the Council and Assembly, due to the absence of the United States was great; it was destined to show itself in a hundred ways as the years went by. The indirect effects were no less calamitous. Within each member-state anti-League elements were encouraged. . . . Again with the United States outside the League, any dissatisfied member could henceforth make effective use of the threat to withdraw. To leave the League was not to isolate oneself, but to follow an illustrious example.[15]

Walters could also have noted at this point the disastrous effect of the U.S. failure to cooperate in the world economic conference in 1933 that tried to address the causes of the Great Depression.

It is not the purpose here to make another judgment on that complicated question. Hopefully, this chapter puts the positive contributions of the League in clearer perspective and shows the record that helped shape the minds of those who gathered in San Francisco in 1945 to draft the charter of a more powerful international organization designed to prevent a third world war. Public opinion polls at the time confirmed that there was overwhelming support for the idea of establishing an organization like the United Nations after the war was over. In addition, it was clear that colonialism was dying and that new nations would be born to take part in the new world organization.

Ironically, the attempts of Japan to control its enlarged empire acquired at the beginning of World War II led to a surge for independence in the closing months of the war by colonies formerly controlled by the West. Pearl Harbor had grown out of the Japanese drive for empire—the Greater East Asian Co-Prosperity Sphere—plus its slogan of Asia for the Asians. During the war, Japan proved to be a harsher colonial master than the Western powers. In the closing days of World War II, Japan attempted to rally support from its new possessions by granting them more independence. When the Western victors came back to their colonies, they found that the people had had a taste of independence and self-government and were demanding that the Western allies make good on their wartime pledges for democracy and self-government. The move of the colonies for independence strengthened the drive for a universal world organization based on collective security and on self-determination.

Notes to Chapter 2

1. B. Scott, *The Rise and Fall of the United Nations* (New York: Macmillan, 1973), p. 33.

2. A. Yoder, *World Politics and the Causes of War* (Landham, MD: University Press of America, 1983), Chapter III.

3. *New York Times,* May 28, 1916, pp. 1–2.

4. J. Bassett, *The League of Nations* (New York: Longmann, Green, 1930), p. 2.

5. R. Baker, *Woodrow Wilson: Life and Letters* (Doubleday: New York).

6. P. Walp, *Constitutional Development of the League of Nations* (Lexington: University of Kentucky, 1931), pp. 77–81.

7. F.P. Walters, *A History of the League of Nations* (London: Oxford University Press, 1952); League of Nations Secretariat, *Ten Years of World Cooperation Geneva: League of Nations,* (1930); G. Scott, *The Rise and Fall of the United Nations* (New York: Macmillan, 1973); E. Berdiner, *A Time for Angels* (New York: Knopf, 1975); Bassett, *League of Nations.*

8. T. Takeuchi, *Amerasia.* July 1938.

9. H. Stimson and M. Bundy, *On Active Service in Peace and War* (New York: Harper, 1948), p. 227.

10. Walters, *League,* pp. 466–496; F.S. Northedge, *The League of Nations* (New York: Holms and Meier, 1986), pp. 137–164.

11. Walters, *League,* p. 624.

12. Ibid., p. 830.

13. F. Hardie, *The Abyssinian Crisis* (Hamdon, CT: Archon, 1976), pp. 164–200; G.W. Bair, *Test Case: Italy, Ethiopia and the League of Nations* (Stanford: Hoover Institution Press, 1976), pp. 95–155.

14. Northedge, *League,* pp. 224–225.

15. Walters, *League,* pp. 72–78.

Chapter III

THE BIRTH OF THE UNITED NATIONS

DRAFTING THE CHARTER

Cordell Hull, the American secretary of state, more than any other official, helped nurture the birth of the United Nations. In the mists of history, he is not regarded by Americans as a strong secretary of state, but he received the honor of a Nobel Prize for his efforts to create the United Nations. President Roosevelt supported the idea of the United Nations, but he was preoccupied with winning the war against the Axis, and in the early stages of the war Roosevelt was afraid that his obvious support might stir up isolationism, the type that had defeated President Wilson's League of Nations. A few months before Pearl Harbor, Roosevelt and Prime Minister Churchill of Britain met out in the Atlantic Ocean to draft the Atlantic Charter, which set forth their goals for which the United States would provide material support to Britain against Nazi aggression. One of the points won in the negotiation by Roosevelt was Britain's pledge to respect the right of people to choose the form of government under which they live, which foreshadowed the end of the colonial system.

There was also a relatively weak statement about setting up a world organization. Churchill supported a stronger wording of this phrase of the Atlantic Charter than did Roosevelt. Originally the phrase read, "They (United States and Britain) seek a peace which will not only cast down forever the Nazi tyranny, but *by effective international organization* will afford to all states and people the means of dwelling in security." Roosevelt insisted on striking the italicized words because of the fear that it would stir up isolationist opposition in the United States. At that time Roosevelt said he would not favor creating a new assembly of the League of Nations after the war until "an international police force composed of the United States and Great Britain had had an opportunity to function."[1]

Soon after Pearl Harbor the Atlantic Charter became "the United Nations Declaration" that was subscribed by 26 "United Nations" fighting the Axis. Later, the name "United Nations Organization" or "United Nations" was adopted for the new world organization.

In a meeting in Moscow in November 1943, Secretary of State Hull got Russian and British representatives to agree to establish "a general international organization based on the principles of the sovereign equality of all peace-loving states and open to membership by all such states, large and small, for the maintenance of international peace and security." This was the first wartime conference of the three foreign secretaries, Secretary of State Hull, Secretary Anthony Eden, and Foreign Minister V. M. Molotov.

Shortly after that, Senator Connally obtained the endorsement of the Senate of this wording by a vote of 85 to 5. This gave a green light to the executive branch for drafting a charter and the calling of the Dumbarton Oaks conference to approve a first draft of the United Nations Charter. Meanwhile, Secretary of State Hull set up a series of committees including members of Congress and public leaders to discuss and make proposals for a world organization.[2]

Cordell Hull, who was head of the Democratic party of World War I, had tried to get President Wilson to stay home and not go to Paris because Hull feared Senate opposition to the League would gain strength. As we have noted, Wilson ignored this advice, went to Paris, and failed to get the League of Nations Covenant ratified by the U.S. Senate. Secretary of State Hull's careful preparation by congressional and other conferences during World War II was instrumental in getting the UN Charter ratified by an overwhelming vote.

In August 1944 the United States convened "conversations" with the Soviet Union and Britain, and later China, at Dumbarton Oaks, a mansion in Washington, DC. The State Department was still afraid of stimulating isolationist sentiment in Congress, so it called the meeting "conversations" instead of a conference, which would have been more descriptive. Russia did not participate with China during the second part of the conference because China was at war with Japan, and Russia wanted to maintain its neutrality. There had been general agreement on the responsibilities of the Security Council, General Assembly, and Secretariat in the preconference consultations, so the conference was able to agree on a rough draft of the "charter." During the first part of the conference, the United States consulted with China, so that the second part with China and without the Soviets went smoothly. The draft charter was then circulated among the "United Nations," the name given to the alliance fighting the Axis. At Roosevelt's insistence, the name United Nations was also proposed for the new organization.

The major issue not settled at Dumbarton Oaks concerned voting, in particular the "veto" in the Security Council. Russia wanted a chance to veto all resolutions, whereas the United States wanted a provision that a party to a dispute could not vote on recommendations, but a permanent member of the Security Council could veto enforcement action. Also, the Soviets wanted a vote in the General Assembly for each of their 15 republics. These issues were resolved at the beginning of 1945 in the Yalta Conference in Russia when Roosevelt, Churchill, and Stalin agreed that any of the five permanent members of the Security Council (United States, Britain, Russia, France, and China) could veto action by the Security Council; however, a party to a dispute could not veto a discussion of an issue or attempts at peaceful settlement that did not involve action or measures to restore peace. In return for yielding on this issue, the Soviets insisted on three votes in the General Assembly. Although it had first insisted on 15 votes, after hard bargaining, including a counterproposal by President Roosevelt for the United States to have a vote for each of the then 48 states, the Russians settled for three votes—Russia, Belorussia, and the Ukraine. President Roosevelt was convinced that membership of the Soviet Union was essential, so he agreed to the request, while refusing its offer that the United States also get three votes. The Soviet demand did not appear unreasonable to Churchill, who perceived England as getting a vote for each of its dominions. Until the revolutions of 1989 the Ukraine and Byleorussia automatically voted with the Soviets on important issues. Ironically, their facade of independence then helped them achieve real independence as the Soviet Union broke apart.

Senator Vandenburg, the Republican Senate leader, in a letter suggested that congressional consent should be required if the Security Council used forces outside this hemisphere against aggression. He suggested that use of U.S. forces in a worldwide war should require a congressional declaration of war. Secretary Hull replied with a memorandum suggesting that the U.S. representative on the Security Council would be under instructions by the president and that our commitment was controlled by a U.S. veto. He added that the president had the authority to involve the United States in a war in any one of a number of ways. A limitation of a declaration of war by Congress would cause the safeguards under the United Nations to lose much of their force. Vandenburg dropped the issue. Six years later President Truman committed U.S. forces in a war to defend Korea under a Security Council request and without a declaration of war. This was not challenged by the Congress.[3]

After the voting formula and membership issues were resolved at Yalta, the three leaders of the Western alliance decided to call the United Nations Conference on April 25, 1945, and the United States, as host, selected San Francisco as the site.

Truman's first announcement as president after Franklin Roosevelt died was that the UN Conference in San Francisco would be held as planned. "It is of supreme importance" he said, "that we build an organization to help keep the future peace of the world." In his memoirs, Truman stated that it had always been his hope that independent nations would some time work out a world parliament set up along the lines of the Senate and House of Representatives of the United States.[4] He knew this was not possible at the current stage of national rivalry, so he wanted to find a way to pool what power nations were willing to delegate to prevent aggression and keep the peace. Truman was convinced that without Russia in the pool there would be no United Nations, so he made strenuous efforts to compromise UN charter issues with the Soviets.[5]

Truman followed up his initial decision to support the UN by meeting with the American UN delegation, which included Republican and Democratic leaders. He kept in touch with them daily by telephone. In going over their instructions with Secretary of State Stettinius, moreover, Truman insisted that if the veto were to be used in the UN Security Council, some way should be found to let the General Assembly consider the question. This provision was incorporated in the UN Charter. Later, in Truman's administration, the United States used this provision to permit the UN General Assembly to supervise the war in Korea after Russia blocked action in the Security Council.

The San Francisco Conference met on April 25, 1945, before the end of the war. Fifty nations attended, including Byleorussia and the Ukraine. It was a major conference with 282 delegates from 50 countries plus 1,500 staff and a 1,000-person secretariat to translate the documents in the five official languages. About 2,600 reporters from the press and world media attended. Within two days the conference agreed to negotiate on the basis of the Dumbarton Oaks draft, and one week was set for submitting amendments of the draft except on trusteeship matters, which involved former colonies. The principal committees on the General Assembly, the Security Council, and the World Court were open to the public. There were 12 other committees on drafting and ironing out differences on the draft charter that were not open to the public.

One of the most controversial issues at the conference concerned the veto of any of the five great powers in the Security Council. Australia led the charge to modify the Yalta formula and prevent the veto from being exercised against attempts at peaceful settlement. Under Article 27, finally approved by the conference, a party to a dispute could not block discussion and proposals by the Security Council for peaceful settlement, but beyond that one of the permanent members could veto proposals for action. The Russians were adamant, and Stalin rejected a special appeal, so the smaller nations reluctantly gave up the attempt, and Article 27 was approved.[6] There was a similar attempt by the Soviets to limit discussion of the General Assembly, but this was finally settled by the Russians agreeing to Article 10, which permits the Assembly to discuss any matter within the scope of the charter, except those being considered by the Security Council and to make recommendations on such matters.

Within two months the conference had approved the charter. It is notable that all provisions were approved by at least a two-thirds vote in committee.

By July 28, 1945 the U.S. Senate had approved the charter by a vote of 89 to 2; the United States was the first nation to ratify it. By October 24 the five big powers and a majority of nations at the conference had ratified, so October 24 is considered as the birthday of the United Nations. John D. Rockefeller donated land in the middle of New York City along the East River for the headquarters. This helped the nations of the world to agree that the United States would be the headquarters. Most nations were convinced that one reason for the failure of the League of Nations had been U.S. nonparticipation, so there was little opposition to locating the headquarters in New York City. Moreover, the United States granted the United Nations a $65 million interest-free loan to start building the headquarters building. The point is, at this time President Truman and the Americans were strong supporters of the UN.

Although the UN Charter avoided reference to, and language of, the League of Nations Covenant, there were basic similarities: (1) the major purpose was to maintain peace and security and to take collective measures to implement that aim, (2) its basic organization consisted of a concert of great powers in the council, an assembly of all members, and a permanent secretariat, (3) the United Nations coordinated international economic and social activities and specialized agencies as the League did.

The basic differences were: (1) the UN membership is "universal" and not dominated by Europe, (2) voting in the Security Council and other UN organs is not by unanimity but by majority or qualified majority, (3) the UN is more political and flexible than the League, (4) the UN has more emphasis on economic and social affairs and on self-determination for nations, (5) human rights are emphasized, and (6) there is somewhat more power for the secretary general.

MAJOR PROVISIONS

It is useful to summarize the following major provisions of the United Nations Charter in order to understand its operation (see Fig. 1, also Appendix II for the text of the UN Charter).

Purposes and Principles

The preamble and Articles I and II set forth the following major purposes and commitments:

1. To maintain peace and prevent war by collective measures and a re-

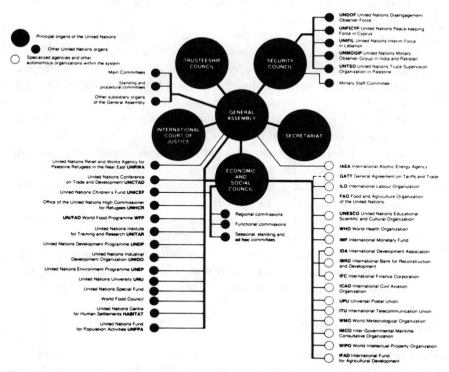

Figure 1. The United Nations System (*Courtesy:* The United Nations Association of the United States)

spect for international law and to refrain from the use of force against another state.

2. To develop friendly relations and a respect for self-determination of peoples.
3. To achieve international cooperation in economic, social, and cultural matters including a respect for human rights.
4. Not to intervene in matters essentially of domestic jurisdiction (this includes civil wars).

The General Assembly

Major provisions for the General Assembly are listed below. The proposals in the economic and social fields for the most part are considered initially by the Economic and Social Council, which reports to the General Assembly.

1. The General Assembly shall consist of all of the members of the United Nations; under Article 10 it may take recommendations on any matters within the scope of the Charter.
2. It may discuss and make recommendations on any questions relating to the maintenance of international peace and security under Article 12 provided that the General Assembly shall not make recommendations when that dispute is being considered by the Security Council, unless the Security Council so requests.
3. Article 11 gives it responsibility for regulation of armaments and making recommendations on them.
4. Article 13 indicates it should make recommendations on promoting international cooperation in economic, social, and related fields.
5. Article 15 states that it shall receive and consider annual reports from the Security Council and other organs of the United Nations.
6. Article 17 delegates the Assembly the power to approve the budget and to apportion expenses.
7. Decisions of the General Assembly on important questions including the budget are made by a two-thirds majority, with decisions on other questions by a majority of members present and voting (Figure 2).

The Security Council

The UN Charter confers on the Security Council the primary responsibility for the maintenance of international peace and obligates members to submit

Figure 2. The General Assembly—September 20, 1988 (*Courtesy:* UN Photo 172.801/Yutaka Nagata)

disputes to it if they cannot settle them peacefully. The Security Council originally consisted of 11 members, but the Charter has been amended to increase the membership to 15 members. The permanent members are the Republic of China (now the People's Republic of China), France, the Union of Soviet Socialist Republics (presently Russia), the United Kingdom, and the United States. The 10 nonpermanent members, according to a General Assembly resolution, are to consist of five from Africa and Asia, two from Latin America, one from Eastern Europe, and two from Western Europe and other areas (Figure 3).

The major provisions of the Charter for the Security Council are:

1. The Security Council is organized as to be able to function continuously.
2. Chapter VI gives detailed provisions for its pacific settlement of disputes, including negotiation and judicial settlement.
3. Articles 30 to 42 (see Chapter VII) provide for deciding on measures including economic and military pressure to maintain and restore international peace and security. Members of the United Nations agreed to make available armed forces and facilities for this purpose, but the

Figure 3. The Security Council Voting on a Resolution to Deplore Israel's Invasion of Lebanon—December 14, 1988 (*Courtesy:* UN Photo 173852/M. Grant)

agreements are negotiated with the Security Council and are subject to ratification by the states involved. This latter provision reflected the insistence of the U.S. Congress that it not give up its constitutional rights to approve the president's use of armed force.

4. It also is responsible for establishing a system for regulating armaments.

5. Article 47 provides for a military staff committee under the Security Council for strategic direction of any armed forces placed at the disposal of the Security Council. The catch was that establishment of this committee was subject to a veto. With the deterioration of the relations between the Soviet Union and the Western Powers in the Cold War, this committee never functioned as it was intended.

6. Article 51 is a key article stating that nothing in the Charter shall impair a member's inherent right of individual or collective self defense if an attack occurs against a member of the United Nations, but this does not affect the authority of the Security Council.

7. Regional arrangements may be used for maintaining international peace

or even enforcement action. (Regional arrangements include the Organization of American States. Military alliances such as NATO and the Warsaw Pact have not been considered as "regional arrangements.")

The principle purpose of the United Nations is to maintain peace and security and to take collective measures to that end. The next two chapters evaluate how successful it has been in achieving this goal. However, about 90 percent of the budgets of the United Nations System is spent for economic and social development, so we also examine its activities in those fields. In assessing its peacemaking function, keep in mind one of our initial hypotheses—that the United Nations is basically a forum and an instrument to be used rather than a supranational authority to enforce the peace.

MEMBERSHIP ISSUES

The drafters of the UN Charter were convinced that the United Nations would have to include the major powers of the world if it were to be a success. The leaders of the wartime alliance against the Axis wanted to preserve it to help keep the peace, and many of those involved in the tragic events of the 1930s believed that the rise of Hitler could have been prevented by cooperation of major powers within the League of Nations. It was also commonly believed that the failure of the United States to join the League seriously hindered its efforts to oppose the aggression of the Axis powers.

Secretary of State Cordell Hull, in making plans for drafting the UN Charter, sold President Roosevelt on the principle of a "universal" organization rather than an association of the victorious powers, which would divide the world up into spheres of influence. The universality principle was not strictly observed immediately after World War II because the enemy states were not admitted. The United Nations idea and name came out of the 1940 United Nations Declaration of the wartime alliance against the Axis. This in turn was based on Roosevelt's and Churchill's Atlantic Charter of the year before. Article 4 of the UN Charter stated that it was open to all "peace-loving" states, and this article was used to exclude the defeated enemy powers until their occupation ended and new states were set up. Within 10 years the enemy states had received their own constitutions, and moves were underway to admit them.

Article 4 also states that members will be admitted by a decision of the

General Assembly upon recommendation of the Security Council. This meant that this action was subject to a veto in the Security Council. This lent itself to Cold War politics with the Soviets advocating membership for the Eastern European states under its domination, whereas the Western powers supported the membership of Italy, Germany, and Japan as well as other friendly states. The log jam was finally broken in 1955 with a package deal in which 16 states were admitted simultaneously, including four Eastern European states and 12 non-Communist states. (Poland and Yugoslavia were admitted in 1946 as original members.) The two Germany's were admitted many years later. By 1992 there were 175 members.

The major issue of Chinese representation in the United Nations was not a "membership" but a credentials issue. The Republic of China as a major ally against the Axis was one of the original permanent members of the United Nations with a right of veto. The Soviet Union maintained correct relations with the Republic of China until 1949, when the Communist government took control of Mainland China, while the Nationalist government fled to the island of Taiwan (Formosa). The new Communist government was officially recognized by only 15 members; the Nationalist government on Taiwan at that time continued to be recognized by 43 members. Moreover, the year after its establishment, the People's Republic of China became involved in the war in Korea opposing the UN forces under the command of the United States. For the next 20 years the United States successfully led the effort to isolate China in punishment for its participation in the Korean War and to keep it out of the United Nations.

The major elements of this complicated legalistic-political issue are as follows. Both the People's Republic of China and the government on Taiwan insisted that they alone represented China, and neither would accept the idea of two Chinas. The United States succeeded in getting approval of a resolution designating the China issue as an "important question"; this procedural resolution requires a majority vote. This meant that the vote on the substantive issue—the "important question" of accepting the credentials of The People's Republic of China—would require an affirmative vote of two-thirds in the General Assembly. Some nations respected the Charter enough to vote the China issue as an "important question," even though they would vote for accepting the credentials of the People's Republic of China while it was not able to obtain a two-thirds vote.

The U.S. efforts to keep the People's Republic of China out of the United Nations, and later to admit it only if it allowed the Republic of China to stay in the General Assembly, failed in 1971 after Henry Kissinger had flown to Peking to arrange a visit by President Nixon to the People's Republic of China. With this informal recognition of the People's Republic, it was obvious from informal tallies that the votes could no longer be mobilized to block its admission. In 1971, therefore, the representatives of the government on Taiwan walked out of the General Assembly when they saw their cause was lost. The General Assembly then voted to expel the Republic of China representative and admit the delegate of the People's Republic of China. Similar action eventually followed in the Specialized Agencies as their governing boards followed the political lead of the UN General Assembly. (To confuse the issue further, the Charter still reads as if the "Republic of China" is a permanent member, but that is interpreted to mean the People's Republic of China, because it is so cumbersome to amend the Charter.)

With the admission of Vietnam in 1977 and the two Koreas in 1992, all major states had become members. The Democratic Republic of Vietnam (North Vietnam) after its victory in the Vietnam War in 1975, had tried to get two Vietnams admitted to the United Nations, but this was vetoed by the United States. After Vietnam's official unification in 1977, it applied for membership as one state, and the United States did not veto its membership. The two Germanies were admitted in 1975 after Chancellor Willy Brandt succeeded in West Germany's initiative to formally recognize the boundaries remaining after World War II.

Until 1991 North Korea had refused to recognize splitting Korea into two governments. In 1948 after a free election in South Korea (The Republic of Korea), the General Assembly had recognized it as the only legitimate government in Korea, but the Soviets vetoed its membership in the United Nations. South Korea, nevertheless, was able to join UN subsidiary bodies like the UN Conference on Trade and Development (UNCTAD) and the Specialized Agencies. However, responding to the threat of the Soviets to allow South Korea to enter the UN, North Korea agreed that both could become members, and they were admitted in July 1991. Switzerland for many years did not join the UN because of a strict policy of neutrality, although it joined UN Specialized Agencies. In 1992 it, too, applied for membership.

The major change in UN membership is which Russia took over the seat of the former Soviet Union was accomplished with amazing ease. In the fall of 1991 after the Eastern European satellites attained independence, the internal empire of the Soviet Union split apart into 15 independent republics. Russia remained as the largest republic with about half of the population and 70 percent of the land area. On December 24, 1991, after the General Assembly had finished its fall business, President Boris Yeltsin of Russia in a letter to the

United Nations stated that Russia as the "continuing state" of the former Union of Soviet Socialist Republics would now occupy its seat in the United Nations; this included its seat as a permanent member of the Security Council. He was following the precedent of British India which took over India's seat after it split into Pakistan and India in 1947. The letter was not challenged. President Yeltsin and his foreign minister pledged to promote the United Nations in every way.

The Ukraine and Belorussia, which had been members since the UN's birth, began to assert independence from Russia's positions. Latvia, Estonia, and Lithuania, which had been taken over by the Soviet Union at the beginning of World War II, after they were admitted as members, at every opportunity demanded the withdrawal of Soviet troops from their territory.[7]

To sum up, for practical purposes the United Nations is now a universal organization organized to meet and consider world crises. In a sense, this makes it stronger than the League of Nations, but as we see in the next chapter, there is a price for this. The United Nations, in order to maintain universal membership, refused to take important enforcement action against a major power such as the Soviet Union when it violated the Charter by its invasion of Afghanistan. In the eye of some critics, this seriously compromised the usefulness of the United Nations. However, we will see that there was a happy ending to this story when the Soviets withdrew as a result of negotiations under United Nations auspices.

Notes to Chapter 3

1. R. Sherwood, *Roosevelt and Hopkins* (New York: Harper, 1948), p. 359.

2. As a college student I participated in one such conference at Ohio Wesleyan University in the spring of 1942. This was sponsored by the Federal Council of Churches of Christ and included Dr. Leo Pasvolsky from the Department of State, John Foster Dulles, later Secretary of State, and Karl J. Hambro, president of the Assembly of the League of Nations. Their proposals stressed the interdependence of nations and need for a world organization after the war (see *Time*, March 13, 1942, pp. 44–48).

3. R. Russell, *A History of the United Nations Charter* (Washington, DC: Brookings, 1958), pp. 469–470.

4. H. Truman, *Years of Decision* (New York: Doubleday, 1956), p. 280.

5. W. Harriman and E. Abel. *Special Envoy to Churchill* (New York: Random House, 1979), p. 448.

6. Russell, *History*, pp. 719–742.

7. J. Tessitore and S. Woolfson (eds.), *A Global Agenda* (New York: University Press of America, 1992), pp. 16–19.

Chapter IV

THE UNITED NATIONS AND THE UNITED STATES: SUPPORTING COLLECTIVE SECURITY

THE FIRST MAJOR CRISES

The founders of the United Nations set as its major purpose to maintain international peace and to settle disputes peacefully in conformity with international law. To evaluate the effectiveness of the United Nations, we first examine cases in early years where the United States worked there to maintain peace within the framework of international law. Later, power politics dominated the world scene, and the United Nations tended to be used as an instrument in the Cold War. However, it still operated effectively. After the end of the Cold War, in the 1990s, the United Nations took over the role envisaged by its founders. We then examine the international agreements for nuclear arms control, many of which reflect initiatives of UN bodies. Next we evaluate the work of the World Court. Finally, we examine patterns of successes and failures to determine why, in recent years, there has been a dramatic revival of peacemaking and other activities of the United Nations.

The Iranian Dispute

The Iranian dispute came before the Security Council in January 1946 in its first meeting after the United Nations was founded. Early in World War II the Soviets and British invaded Iran to establish a supply route to Russia, since Hitler's forces blocked the normal European supply routes. Reza Shah was deposed and his son installed as the new Shah. The United States, as the main supplier of war materiel, had considerable leverage to put pressure on the Soviets and Britain to sign a treaty committing them to withdraw after the war. This was in line with the traditional U.S. policy of supporting the sovereignty of Iran. The Russians suspected American intentions, however, because Iran had offered oil concessions in the north to U.S. firms. (Incidentally, oil was never found there.)

After the war, in September 1945 President Truman received reports that Russian army units were preventing Iranian police and its military from moving into the area of Azerbaijan in a section of Iran along the Soviet border, where the Iranian Communist party (Tudeh) was promoting a rebellion of Azerbaijan to achieve independence. The Russians at first refused to discuss withdrawing their forces. Iran, therefore, brought the matter up before the Security Council at its first meeting, charging Russia with interfering in Iran's internal affairs. The Security Council could not pass a resolution supporting the charge because of the Soviet veto, but it was able to pass one calling on the parties to negotiate the issue.

Iran, the United States, and others on the Security Council raised a major fuss, with the news media giving the crisis wide publicity. In addition, President Truman sent a stiff note in March 1946 expressing the earnest hope that the Soviets would withdraw troops as had been promised in the 1942 treaty. Meanwhile, the Iranian prime minister indicated that the Soviets also could obtain an oil concession in northern Iran. Finally, several weeks after the deadline, the Soviets announced that they would withdraw. They left advisers there, and the Iranian government was not fully able to exercise its authority until the end of 1946 when it moved its troops into the area.[1]

The fuss raised in the United Nations, which embarrassed the Soviet Union, was an obvious factor in its decision to withdraw. Moreover, at this time it was still hoping to preserve the United Nations as an instrument to prevent future German aggression, and, even more important, to maintain a relationship with the United States that would permit Russia to share in the control of Germany. Thus Iran was successful in using the United Nations, accompanied by U.S. diplomatic pressure, to preserve Iran's sovereignty in the first major crisis faced by the Security Council.

The Greek Crisis

At the end of 1946 and during 1947, Greece, the United States, and others also raised a hue and cry about Communist countries' support of a rebellion in Greece. British troops had liberated Greece after World War II and stayed on to maintain order—that is, to prevent a Communist movement from taking control of the country. The Soviets and other Communist countries complained to the Security Council, but Britain replied that its troops were there on the invitation of the Greek government. The Greek government denied any interference, which put British action within a framework of international law since they were there with the consent of the Greek government.

After the British troops withdrew, Greece asked the Security Council, on December 3, 1946, to consider the situation caused by aid provided to Greek guerrillas from its northern neighbors, Albania, Yugoslavia, and Bulgaria. These countries denied the charges. On December 19 the Council established a commission with one representative of each member of the Council to investigate. The commission submitted a report approved by nine of the 11 members confirming the charges. The Security Council was blocked by a Russian veto from accepting the report, so it passed the issue to the General Assembly. In 1947 and 1948 the Assembly called on Albania, Bulgaria, and Yugoslavia to stop aiding the rebels. The General Assembly, moreover, established a UN Special Committee on the Balkans (UNSCOB) to investigate. In the course of the investigations by the Security Council and General Assembly, volumes of evidence were obtained proving without a doubt that the Communist countries were supporting the rebellion against the Greek government. The General Assembly passed resolutions every year until 1954 condemning this intervention.

Meanwhile, the United States provided massive aid to Greece in the forerunner of the Marshall Plan of aid to Europe, and Yugoslavia broke out of the East European bloc, expelled Russian advisors, and asserted its independence. These developments, plus the UN actions to observe the Greek border and report on violations of international law, brought an end to the intervention by Greece's Communist neighbors, and in 1954 the General Assembly dropped the matter. Greece has been a full member of NATO since 1980 and of the European Economic Community since 1981, and there has been no question of its independence from the Soviet Bloc.

THE KOREAN WAR

The UN was a center of action for the Korean War. This conflict was long, costly, and unpopular, but it could have been much worse. The United States played the leading role through the United Nations in accordance with international law to mobilize support for South Korea against aggression by North Korea. Despite the terrible cost, the aggressor was defeated and the principle of collective security was upheld. President Truman played a leading role in using the United Nations to contain the conflict.

At the beginning of this century, Japan won the colonial competition for

Korea and formally annexed it in 1910. Subsequently, a strong independence movement arose, and in the 1930s Syngman Rhee, a Korean who had
studied at Harvard, took over the movement's leadership from abroad.

In line with the principles of the Atlantic Charter, the United States and
the Soviet Union agreed that Korea would be given its independence after
the war. The Soviets proposed a four-power trusteeship with no foreign troops,
but the United States did not accept this proposal, in part because the Chinese
government informed it that Russia had been training two Korean divisions
in Siberia during the war, as well as political personnel who could be brought
into Korea to set up a Communist government. The United States and the
Soviet Union could not agree on four-power control, so at Potsdam they
agreed to divide Korea at the 38th parallel with the Soviets temporarily occupying the North and the United States the South. Kim Il Sung and his
followers came in with the Soviet troops and took over control of the Korean
Communist Party in North Korea, just after the party leader was conve-
niently assassinated.

It seemed clear to U.S. observers that the Soviets were consolidating their
control of the North with their military and political advisers. President Truman decided, therefore, in November 1947 to turn the issue over to the UN
General Assembly. The General Assembly with the nonparticipation of the
Communist bloc created a nine-member commission to establish an all-Ko-
rean government. The commission was opposed by the Soviets, who refused
to permit it to enter North Korea. The commission, therefore, turned its
attention to the South and arranged for elections to a national assembly in
1948. Syngman Rhee was elected president, and the UN General Assembly
recognized the Republic of Korea as the only "lawful government." The
General Assembly then established a seven-member commission to bring
about unification, which stayed on to observe developments. This was important, because it confirmed that one aim of the United Nations was to
unify Korea. It was also an important action in recognizing South Korea as
a state, so that the later attack by North Korea was an international war
under the jurisdiction of the United Nations and not a civil war of only local
concern.

In 1949 following the withdrawal of Soviet troops from the North, the
U.S. National Security Council (NSC) in line with a recommendation of
General MacArthur proposed the withdrawal of U.S. forces from South Korea. The withdrawal was accomplished in 1949, and only 500 officers of
the U.S. military advisory group remained behind.

General MacArthur, on March 1, 1949 in a speech that left out Korea,
stated that the U.S. defense perimeter included the Philippines, Okinawa,

and Japan, and the Aleutian Islands. About a year later Secretary of State Acheson drew a similar line but added:

> . . . so far as the military security of other areas of the Pacific is concerned, it must be clear that no person can guarantee these islands against miliatry attack. . . . Should such an attack occur. . . . the initial reliance must be on the people attacked to resist it and then upon the commitments of the entire civilized world under the Charter of the UN, which has so far not proved a weak reed to lean on by any people who are determined to protect their independence against outside aggression. (Acheson 1969, 357)

The statements by MacArthur and Acheson leaving South Korea out of the U.S. defense perimeter may have played a part in encouraging Stalin and Kim Il Sung to attack the south on June 25, 1950. Khrushchev's memoirs, which describe the meetings between Kim Il Sung, Stalin, and Mao, who together planned the war, were confident that the United States would not come to South Korea's assistance. Khrushchev's memoirs indicate that Kim's aim was to start a war of liberation to liberate all of South Korea and bring it under North Korea's control.[2]

The United Nations commission was uneasy about reports of North Korea's aggressive intentions, and in the months before the war it expanded observation teams along the 38th parallel, the dividing line at the time between North and South Korea.[3]

On June 25, 1950 UN Secretary General Trygve Lie was informed by the United States and the UN Commission on Korea that North Korean forces had attacked the Republic of Korea all along the 38th parallel. In view of the UN role in helping form the South Korean government, the June 1950 invasion was an attack on the United Nations as well as South Korea. On that same day the UN Security Council, at the request of the United States, by a vote of 9 to 0 with one abstention (Yugoslavia) and one absent (the USSR), stated that an "armed attack" had occurred, called for immediate cessation of the hostilities, the withdrawal of North Korean forces, and assistance of UN members in carrying out the resolution. Two days later the UN Security Council by a vote of 7 to 1 adopted a U.S. resolution calling on all members to furnish such assistance as necessary to repel the armed attack. On that same day the United States announced that it had ordered land and sea forces to support the Republic of Korea (map 1). Although the announcement of U.S. assistance took place a few hours before the second resolution was passed, the first resolution by calling North Korea's action an "armed attack" made clear that collective self-defense was justified under Article 51 of the Charter.

Subsequently, 51 UN members supported the Security Council's action; five, including the USSR, said it was illegal because it had been adopted in the absence of two permanent members of the Security Council, the USSR and the Peoples' Republic of China. The Soviet Union was absent during the first meetings of the Security Council because it objected to the Republic of China representing China on the Security Council instead of the People's Republic of China.

The Soviet Union argued that a strict interpretation of Article 27 indicated action beyond procedural matters required the presence of the Soviet Union. On the other hand, the Security Council had passed a number of resolutions previously when a permanent member had "abstained" from voting and had passed two resolutions in 1946 when the Soviets were absent. Since the 1950 war the practice has been accepted that absence or abstention does not constitute a veto.[4] The Russians returned to the Council on August 1, but the Security Council in accordance with Article 11 of the Charter in a procedural vote passed action to the General Assembly, which authorized continuing military support for South Korea.

On July 8 the Security Council in line with the secretary general's suggestion passed a resolution requesting the United States to command the UN forces, and authorizing them to use the UN flag under a Unified Command, which was not under the authority of the secretary general.[5] The United States designated General MacArthur as the commander. Combat units for the Unified Command were provided by Australia, Canada, Belgium, Colombia, Ethiopia, France, Greece, Luxembourg, the Netherlands, New Zealand, the Philippines, Thailand, Turkey, the Union of South Africa, the United Kingdom, and the United States. Denmark, Italy, India, Norway, and Sweden supplied medical units, However, it took time to mobilize these forces, and the North Korean forces had swept through Seoul and down through the end of the Korean peninsula to Pusan before U.S. and UN assistance became effective. While UN forces held on to a small defense perimeter in Pusan, General MacArthur carried out a surprise amphibious landing at Inchon near Seoul. This caught the North Koreans off balance, and they fell back from the Pusan perimeter in a disorderly retreat (Map 1).

President Truman had reacted quickly to the challenge of the North Korean attack. In his memoirs he points out the heavy influence in his thinking of Hitler's aggression in World War II:

> There was no suggestion from anyone that either the United Nations or the United States could back away from it. This was a test of all the last five years of collective security . . . Communism was acting in Korea just as

Hitler, Mussolini, and the Japanese had acted 10, 15, or 20 years earlier. If the Communists were permitted to force their entry into the Republic of Korea without opposition of the free world, no small nation would have the courage to resist threats and aggression by stronger Communist neighbors. If this was allowed to go unchallenged, it would mean a third world war, just as similar instances had brought on the Second World War. It was also clear to me that the foundations and principles of the United Nations were at stake unless this unprovoked attack on Korea could be stopped.[6]

Secretary of State Acheson came to the same conclusion, but he reached it by a different philosophy, that of power politics. Nevertheless he was loyal to Truman and he recognized the usefulness of the United Nations. He regarded it as an:

open, undisguised challenge to our internationally accepted position as protector of South Korea, an area of great importance to the security to American-occupied Japan. To back away from this challenge in view of our capacity for meeting it, would be highly destructive of the power and prestige of the United States. By prestige, I mean the shadow cast by power, which is of great deterrent importance.[7]

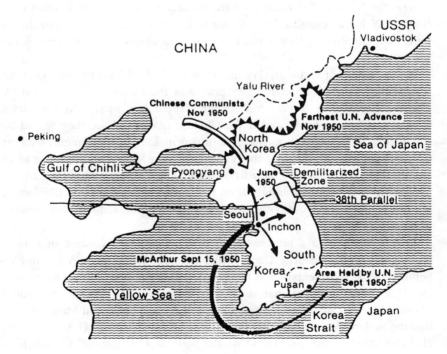

Map 1. The Korean War

These statements show how supporters of international law and those using power politics can unite to support collective security.[8]

China did not participate in the Korean attack initially, but at the time it
seemed to be preparing to attack Taiwan and this helped convince Truman
and Acheson to take a strong stand against Communist aggression in Korea.

The China issue soon became a major issue in the Korean War. On September 27, 1950, Truman approved instructions to MacArthur, which included as an objective "the destruction of the North Korean armed forces."
MacArthur was authorized to conduct military operations north of the 38th
parallel as long as there was no threat of Chinese or Soviet intervention. A
few days later the United States obtained UN General Assembly authorization in a resolution that recommended that "all appropriate steps be taken
to insure conditions of stability throughout Korea." The resolution established the UN Commission for the Unification and Rehabilitation of Korea
(UNCURK) of seven states to establish a unified, democratic, and independent government of all Korea. The UN delegates in discussing this issue
realized that this was authorizing operations north of the 38th parallel.[9] On
October 2, as the first South Korean units crossed north of the 38th parallel,
the State Department received a number of messages all reporting the same
thing—the Chinese Communists were threatening to enter the Korean conflict if UN forces crossed the 38th parallel. However, Truman chose to ignore this, thinking it was a bluff designed to affect the UN vote on the
resolution.[10]

In the middle of October, Truman flew to Wake Island to meet General
MacArthur. One of Truman's concerns was the threat of intervention by
Chinese Communist forces. MacArthur assured him there was very little
chance of Chinese entry, and if the Chinese troops did so, they would be
easily defeated. However, as MacArthur was making this statement, the first
Chinese troops were crossing the Yalu River into Korea, and by the end of
October they had mounted their first attack. The Chinese called their troops
"volunteers" to avoid declaring war on the United States and other UN forces,
but the volunteers were obviously those of the Communist Chinese government.

After November 6 a representative of the People's Republic of China,
participated in the Security Council discussion of the Korean War. On November 28 the representative of the People's Republic of China asserted that
the U.S. announcement that its navy would protect Taiwan constituted
"aggression" because Taiwan was a part of China. The United States replied
that the action was designed to keep the peace and that the U.S. navy was
also instructed to prevent attacks on the mainland by Marshal Chiang Kai-
shek's forces.

At the beginning of November, the General Assembly institutionalized its authority to supervise collective security when the Security Council is tied up with a veto. The General Assembly adopted the Uniting for Peace Resolution calling for the Assembly to meet in an emergency session when a veto prevents action to meet a threat to the peace. The resolution established a Peace Observation Commission of 14 members including the five permanent members of the Security Council to report on the situation. Also, a Collective Measures Committee of 14 members was established to report on methods that might be used to maintain peace. In the Korean War this committee consisted of those who provided troops to Korea.

MacArthur's troops pressed on toward the Yalu with the expressed hope of ending the war by Christmas. On November 28, 1950 the Chinese volunteers mounted mass attacks. As the UN troops fell back into disorderly retreat, MacArthur indicated that he might have to evacuate his forces from the Korean peninsula unless he was authorized to attack and blockade China, to obtain reinforcements from Formosa, and to have the option of using atomic weapons against North Korea.[11] Despite this statement of near panic, General Ridgeway, MacArthur's field commander, was able to establish a line below Seoul and then fight back to the 38th parallel north of Seoul.

The General Assembly, in considering the "intervention" of the People's Republic of China in Korea, established a Cease-Fire Group of the president of the Assembly, Canada, and India to arrange a cease-fire. On January 31 the Security Council, stymied by a Soviet veto, again removed the Korean War from its agenda, leaving the way for General Assembly actions. China rejected the Cease-Fire Group's proposals, and on May 18, 1951 the Assembly recommended an embargo against China of all shipments of arms and items useful for war.

Meanwhile, U.S. officials were carrying out a series of delicate negotiations for a truce that eventually succeeded but only after the firing of General MacArthur. Publicly, and in a letter to the House of Representatives minority leader, MacArthur called for the use of Chinese Nationalist troops in the war. This was directly in opposition to the president's view and that of the United Nations, which did not want to expand the nature of the war to a war against China by such a step. Truman asked for and obtained MacArthur's resignation in April 1951.

The secretary general maneuvered cease-fire negotiations to the military commanders to avoid political demands such as the admission of China into the United Nations. The armistice negotiations formally began between the military commanders of the opposing sides on July 10, 1951. The main stumbling block preventing agreement was what to do with about 25,000

Chinese and North Korean prisoners of war. Difficult negotiations were carried out by the military commanders of both sides and in the United Nations. Finally agreement was reached providing for a UN Repatriation Commission including Czechoslovakia, India (chairman), Poland, Sweden, and Switzerland to interview the prisoners. Some observers suggest that Eisenhower's veiled threat to use nuclear weapons played a part in reaching agreement on this final issue holding up the armistice.[12]

The Armistice Agreement was signed on July 27, 1953. It established a cease-fire zone between the two sides, and a Military Armistice Commission with representatives of the two sides was set up to supervise the agreement. Subsequently, the Geneva Conference of 1954 failed to reach agreement on a peace treaty, but it agreed that failure to reach this agreement did not prejudice the armistice. Since the truce there have been tension and incidents along the demilitarized zone, and there has been no permanent settlement. The United States maintains a sizable number of troops along the northern border of Korea, and periodic verbal conflicts take place in the Mixed Armistice Commission. The United States continued to report periodically to the Security Council on the implementation of the 1958 Armistice Agreement.

The cease-fire has held with minor exceptions, and there has been no war. South Korea has prospered. With a larger population it appears capable of defending against any renewed threat from the North, particularly since it is buttressed by thousands of U.S. troops still stationed in South Korea. There has never been a peace treaty, and Korea has not been unified. There have been periodic attacks and even terrorist incidents instigated by North Korea against the South. However, most observers regard the UN action to defend Korea as a high point of supporting collective security under the United Nations Charter. Some suggest that this was an accident due to Russia's absence from the Security Council, but others note that the General Assembly during this crisis established the machinery and precedents for it to act when the Security Council is stymied by a veto. It is true that the United States dominated the military action, but this reflects a fact of life in the United Nations that it needs the support of major powers, and particularly the United States.

THE ARAB-ISRAELI WARS

The Middle East is a highly strategic area that has been a cockpit of power politics since the beginning of written history. Even before the Suez Canal was built, it was a corridor to Africa and Asia. Since the Suez Canal, Britain and France have regarded the area as a lifeline to their colonies and former colonies in Asia and Africa. Since World War II airlines have used the Middle East airspace for their routes. In recent decades the Middle East has become a major source of oil and the world's energy. It is ironic that the United Nations, which is based on international law, inherited the Palestine issue and was thrust into the middle of the power politics and conflicts of this strategic region.

The depth of feeling in the conflicts of the Middle East reflects thousands of years of religious history. The tribes of the area have been fighting for thousands of years over historical and religious claims. The book of Genesis tells of God's covenant with Abraham to give him and his descendants the land of Canaan, which later became known as Palestine. The problem is that Arabs, Jews, and Christians claim Abraham as their father and also claim his inheritance. The Jewish Zionist movement, stimulated by persecution of Jews in France, began to reassert the Jews' claim to Palestine at the end of the last century.

During World War I the British Cabinet approved a statement called the Balfour Declaration, which read as follows: "His Majesty's Government views with favor the establishment in Palestine of a national home for the Jewish people, and will use its best endeavors to facilitate the achievement of this object, it being clearly understood that nothing may be done which may prejudice the civil and religious rights of existing non-Jewish communities in Palestine, or the rights and political status enjoyed by Jews in any other country." This declaration was later accepted by the League of Nations as part of the British Mandate for Palestine.

Different British officials had different reasons for encouraging Jewish immigration into Palestine by granting the Balfour Declaration to the British/Jewish community. Some officials favored it for religious reasons, believing that such a refuge was ordained in the Bible. Others wanted to use the declaration to get more enthusiastic support for World War I from the Jewish communities in Britain, and also in the United States and Russia. Other British officials probably wanted to create a rationale for continued British rule over the area of Palestine, which was close to the vital Suez Canal link to Britain's colonial empire in Asia and Africa. The declaration did promote unrest in the mandate, and Arab terrorists attacked the Jews to discourage their immigration into Palestine, forcing Britain to act as a referee.

In 1922 Britain defined the area of the Palestine Mandate as separate from TransJordan, and since that time the area of Palestine has generally been regarded as west of the Jordan River. At the time of the Balfour Declaration, Jews made up about 10 percent of the population of the Palestinian Mandate. During the 1920s and 1930s, limited immigration was permitted and Jews managed to buy up a considerable part of Arab farmlands in Palestine. By World War II Jews constituted about 30 percent of Palestine's population.

The First Arab-Israeli War

The Arab-Israeli conflict in Palestine came to a boil after the end of World War II. At that time the world was horrified by the reports of the Nazi extermination of 6 million Jews in the Holocaust. This gave a tremendous momentum to attempts of the Zionists to establish a refuge in Palestine for the remaining hundreds of thousands of Jews left in Europe. The Arabs of Palestine, however, were determined that their land should not be used to repay the Jews for the horrors suffered under Hitler. As fighting broke out, Britain was left holding the bag with the Palestine mandate, and it tried to keep the lid on by limiting the immigration of Jews into Palestine. The British policy was opposed violently by Menachim Begin's Irgun, which attacked the British military for its policies of restricting Jewish immigration. A surge of opposition to British policy occurred after the British sent the ship *Exodus*, with 4,493 Jews, back to Germany after it tried illegally to discharge its passengers in Palestine. In frustration the British Cabinet, on April 2, 1947, approved a letter to the secretary general of the United Nations stating that Britain would withdraw within a year and asking that the question of Palestine be placed on the agenda of a regular session of the General Assembly, at which time Britain would submit a report of its administration of the mandate. Britain also asked that the General Assembly session appoint and instruct a special committee to make a study with recommendations on the issue. This was an orderly way to dispose of this issue because the United Nations had inherited the League of Nation's responsibilities for mandates.

On May 15, 1947 the special session of the General Assembly established a UN Special Committee of 11 members—Australia, Canada, Czechoslovakia, Guatamala, India, Iran, the Netherlands, Peru, Sweden, Uruguay, and Yugoslavia—to study the issues. Note that none of the great powers were included. The Jewish Agency maintained liaison with this committee, but the Arab Higher Committee refused to cooperate. The Arab states objected to the fact that no reference was made in the covering resolution to the interests of the inhabitants of Palestine. The committee visited Palestine, Lebanon, Syria, and TransJordan, and also displaced persons camps in Germany and Austria. Representatives of the Arab states presented their views in hearings in Lebanon.[13] On August 31, 1947 it reported to the General Assembly with two sets of proposals, both recommending partition of Palestine. The majority recommendation by Canada, Czechoslovakia, Guatamala, the Netherlands, Peru, Sweden, and Uruguay, was that two separate states be established with Jerusalem as the capital under international trusteeship. India, Iran, and Yugoslavia proposed a federal state of an Arab state and a Jewish state with Jerusalem as the federal capital. Australia abstained, stating that the proposal went beyond the terms of reference of the committee. On September 23, 1947 a special ad hoc committee of the General Assembly, composed of all member states, heard the three parties. The General Assembly then adopted the majority plan by a vote of 33 to 13 with 10 abstentions.[14]

The Assembly resolution provided for the Trusteeship Council to prepare a statute for the city of Jerusalem and for the UN Palestine Commission to carry out the recommendations of the General Assembly. Following this resolution, the Arab states began preparing for war. By April the Security Council established a Truce Commission to try to prevent war between the Arab and Jewish communities. Violence increased in Palestine as the end of the mandate drew near.

During this period the U.S. position was confused, with President Truman for a while losing control of U.S. policy. The United States approved the partition, but it refused to support it with a UN force, although the Soviets probably would have agreed. Then as violence increased and war threatened, the United States UN delegation proposed a trusteeship for Palestine, apparently trying to stop the partition from going into effect. The Arabs were delighted at this proposal, but it did not garner support. On the day the British withdrew, the Jews declared Israel as a state, and the United States from the White House immediately gave it *de facto* recognition. The next day the Arab states attacked. The Jews managed to hold on to Jerusalem, although their forces were greatly outnumbered by the armies of their Arab neighbors. Jews had manufactured a number of small arms and managed to buy other arms on the black markets of the world.

The Security Council established a Truce Commission for Palestine consisting of Belgium, France, and the United States. It initially worked closely with UN mediator of Palestine, Count Folke Bernadotte, the head of the Swedish Red Cross, to establish a truce.

There were so many rivalries among the Arab states that they were not able to get their act together to defeat Israel. On June 11 with the support of a Security Council resolution that threatened sanctions, Count Bernadotte was able to arrange a cease-fire for only 30 days. During this period the Jewish forces were able to regroup and get more supplies into Jerusalem. Fighting broke out again, but by July 15 the Security Council obtained another truce. By this time the Jews had gained an area more than double the size of the original UN partition plan.[15]

The Security Council established the UN Truce Supervision Organization (UNTSO), a team of 63 U.S., Belgian, French, and Swedish military observers to help the mediator. In September 1948 Count Bernadotte was killed by Jewish terrorists. The Council appointed another mediator, Ralph Bunche, a black American, and reinforced UNTSO under him. By a series of bilateral negotiations he got Israel and Egypt to sign a general armistice agreement in February 1949. Agreements followed with Israel and Lebanon on March 23, Jordan and Israel on April 3, and Syria and Israel on July 20.

Meanwhile UNTSO was increased to a strength of 700 to observe the armistices and report back to the Council. It was assisted by Mixed Armistice Commissions chosen by both sides and chaired by the chief of staff of UNTSO. In August 1949 the Security Council ended the role of the mediator and made UNTSO an autonomous organ of the Security Council with the UNTSO chief of staff in command. It still operates in the area with a force of about 300 from Argentina, Australia, Austria, Belgium, Canada, Chile, Denmark, Finland, France, Ireland, Italy, the Netherlands, New Zealand, Norway, Sweden, Russia, and the United States. The participation of many countries in UNTSO and other organs of the United Nations in the Middle East gives the organs a genuine international character, which obtains respect that would not be given to groups made up of parties who take sides in the conflicts. It suffers casualties, which are incurred as a result of high-risk patrols and mediating in the area (Table 1).

It is important to note that the new state of Israel was recognized by action of the Security Council and by over a two-thirds vote of the General Assembly. Israel was formally admitted to the United Nations on May 11, 1949. (At that time, the Soviet Union supported Israel and did not veto its admission.) The Arab nations were furious and frustrated, but they have not been able to turn back the clock and get the world community to withdraw recognition of the state of Israel.

The 1956 War

The principal events leading to the 1956 Suez War were the decision of President Nasser of Egypt to nationalize the Suez Canal Company, which managed the operation of the canal, and the violent response of the British and French to this act. As a prelude to this crisis, the United States and the International Bank had engaged in a long, complicated negotiation to help Nasser finance building the Aswan Dam, a huge project on the Nile that Nasser hoped would bring power and irrigation to Egypt, permitting it to enter the twentieth century. At the last minute, however, the United States, in July 1956, withdrew its offer in frustration over the antagonistic policies of Egypt, which opposed U.S. efforts to build an alliance against the Soviet Union in the Middle East. Nasser had openly courted the Soviet Union and arranged to buy arms from Czechoslovakia, at the same time supporting nationalist rebels in Algeria against France.

Nasser had added to the tensions by preventing Israeli ships from going through the Suez Canal and by supporting fedayeen raids from Gaza into Israel.[16] As the raids and reprisals had mounted, the UNTSO chief of staff had warned the Security Council that such incidents could spread like brushfire. The UN secretary general had undertaken extensive negotiations in the spring of 1956 and had managed to get an uneasy cease-fire along the armistice lines, but the withdrawal of the offer to finance the Aswan Dam and the nationalization of the Suez Canal completely undermined these efforts.[17]

After Nasser nationalized the Suez Canal Company on July 26, 1956, the

Table 1
UN Peacekeeping Operations (September 1992)

Name	Date Established	Number of Personnel
UN Operation in Somalia (UNOSOM)	4/24/1992	550
UN Transitional Authority in Cambodia (UNTAC)	2/28/1992	15,000
UN Protection Force (Yugoslavia) (UNPROFOR)	2/21/1992	13,000
UN Angola Verification Mission (UNAVEM II)	5/30/1991	750
UN Observer Mission in El Salvador (UNUSAL)	5/20/1991	625
UN Mission for the Referendum in Western Sahara	4/29/1991	350
UN Iraq-Kuwait Observer Mission (UNIKOM)	4/9/1991	460
UN Interim Force in Lebanon (UNIFIL)	3/19/1978	5,854
UN Disengagement Observer Force (UNDOF)	5/31/1974	1,293
UN Peacekeeping Force in Cyprus (UNFICYP)	3/4/1964	2,200
UN Military Observer Group in India and Pakistan	1/24/1949	39
UN Truce Supervision Organization (UNTSO)	6/11/1948	290

Source: UN Chronicle, September 1992, p. 17.

French and British secretly began to plan with Israel to attack the canal and re-establish British troops in the canal zone. Meanwhile, American Secretary of State John Foster Dulles attempted to mediate the controversy by establishing a "users committee" of major nations using the Suez Canal that would oversee Egyptian management of the canal and insure that this vital transportation link would not be closed. Dulles appeared on the verge of getting final approval, when, on October 29, Israel in a secret league with France and Britain, attacked Egyptian forces in the canal zone. In accordance with their plan, British and French troops moved in to "protect" the Suez Canal. This was in line with a 1954 treaty that permitted them to protect it in the event of war.

President Eisenhower and Dulles saw through the scheme and were furious with the British and French for having misled the United States on this issue. Eisenhower took the high road of international law in supporting the U.S. position. He explained his position in his memoirs by stating that Nasser was within his rights in nationalizing the canal company, since it lay completely within Egyptian territory. He added that Egypt had an inherent right to do so provided that just compensation was paid to the owners of the property so expropriated. Moreover, he added, resort to force was unjustified. During the crisis, he made these views known in strong terms to British Prime Minister Eden.

The day before the British and French and Israeli attack, the Soviets moved to suppress a rebellion in Hungary. The United States condemned this Soviet move. Eisenhower, in the middle of a presidential campaign, explained that "we cannot—in the world, any more than in our own nation—subscribe to one law for the weak, and another for the strong." The United States immediately asked for a meeting of the Security Council on the Suez question. General Burns, the chief of staff of UNTSO, in the early hours of October 30 requested Israel to withdraw its troops from the Sinai and stop firing.[18]

The British and French vetoed a Security Council resolution to oppose their aggression. The Council then passed the issue to the General Assembly under the "Uniting for Peace Procedure." On November 2 the General Assembly at 4:20 A.M. approved a U.S. cease-fire resolution by a vote of 64 to 5, opposed only by Britain, France, Australia, New Zealand, and Israel. Also, by a vote of 50 to 8, the General Assembly demanded that the Soviets withdraw their troops from Hungary. Under strong pressure from the United Nations, supported by economic pressure from the United States, the fighting in the Sinai and the Canal area came to an end within a few days.

Meanwhile, on November 4 the General Assembly asked the secretary general to form an emergency force supervised by the chief of the UN Truce

Supervision Organization. By November 6 Secretary General Hammarskjold had negotiated the arrangements for a cease-fire and international force to supervise the withdrawal of Israeli, French, and British forces. He accepted offers from 10 states—Brazil, Canada, Columbia, Denmark, Finland, India, Indonesia, Norway, Sweden, and Yugoslavia—to provide contingents. The United States offered the airlift. By November 7 the fighting had stopped. By early 1957 the UN Emergency Force (UNEF I) had been brought to its full complement of 6,000 officers and men. In connection with pressuring Israel to withdraw, the force undertook to patrol the border between Egypt and Israel in order to prevent terrorist raids against Israel.

Britain, France, and Israel completed evacuation of all occupied areas by March 8, 1957. During the next 10 years, UNEF I maintained peace along these borders. It was lightly armed, whereas UNTSO observers are never armed. It is important to note in connection with the 1967 war that Hammarskjold, in setting up UNEF I in 1956, pledged that it was stationed on Egyptian territory only with Egyptian consent.[19] With the putting into effect of the agreements for the UNEF I, the reputation of the secretary general reached an all-time high. He had arranged a face-saving device for three major powers for withdrawing their forces from the Suez Canal and established a basis of cooperation of Egypt with UNEF patrols that worked smoothly for a decade.

The negotiations for clearing the canal of ships sunk by the Egyptians were difficult because of Egypt's initial objections to accept British salvage ships. The canal was cleared by March 29, 1957. The arrangements for occupying Gaza were even more difficult because of Israel's insistence that the United Nations administer Gaza and that Egypt not take over control, whereas Egypt insisted on administering the area. Israel finally accepted a minimum Egyptian presence in Gaza.

The secretary general maintained that the expenses of the UN Emergency Force were expenses of "the organization," according to Article 17, paragraph 2 of the Charter. However, the Soviets and their Eastern European allies did not agree, claiming that the force under the General Assembly was established in violation of the Charter provisions, which required that such force be a responsibility of the Security Council. The General Assembly and the secretary general obtained an advisory opinion from the International Court supporting their position that the cost of this force should be borne by the UN members according to the general provisions for financing UN expenses. (The Court ruled, however, that UNEF had no power of "enforcement"; such powers are reserved for a force of the Security Council.) The Soviets still refused to pay, and as the total expenditures of the UN

Emergency Force mounted, the United Nations faced a major financial crisis. The UN nations were reluctant to try to force the Soviet Union to back down. The financial crisis was alleviated ultimately only by voluntary contributions and the issuance of UN bonds to pay the expenses of the emergency force. The UN Emergency Force I kept the peace for over 10 years, but it was terminated as a result of the 1967 war, as indicated below. At its peak it consisted of 6,000 officers and men. It suffered 89 fatalities. Its total cost over 10 years was $213 million, which was microscopic in comparison with the military budgets of major powers during those years. However, its Achilles heel was revealed in the 1967 crisis when Egypt requested it to leave.

The 1967 War

The 1967 war was a major disaster that laid the basis for the 1973 war and created lasting impediments to achieving peace in the area. In the spring of 1967 there were increased fedayeen raids against Israel encouraged by Nasser's *Voice of Cairo*, a radio that blanketed the Middle East. Israel retaliated with raids against Syria and Jordan. This added to the pressures against the moderate pro-Western governments of Jordan and Lebanon, which refused to ally with Nasser and accept his leadership. Israel's relations with Syria were particularly bad. Syrians had fired into Galilee from the Golan Heights, and Israel retaliated in dog fights in which six Syrian planes were shot down. The radical Arab press made sarcastic remarks about the inaction of President Nasser, who had a defense pact with Syria. In this explosive atmosphere the Soviets spread rumors that Israel was about to attack Syria. This added to the tension even though the United States investigated and found the report untrue. Israel proposed that the Russian ambassador tour the northern part of the country to confirm that the Israelis were not mobilizing forces, but he refused. The cynicism of the Soviet Union, after spreading rumors about Israel preparing an attack, was demonstrated when it said on May 24 that the situation was not serious enough to warrant convening the Security Council. Russia and Egypt apparently were overconfident of the latter's military power.[20]

Within the Egyptian government, General Amer put increasing political pressure on Nasser to act against Israel, and on May 16 Nasser declared a state of emergency for the Egyptian armed forces. The Egyptian government then requested General Rikyhe, the United Nations Emergency Force commander, to withdraw his forces. Secretary General U Thant called an advisory committee meeting of the countries that provided the force. Opinion was divided between India, Pakistan, and Yugoslavia, which wanted immediate withdrawal, and Canada, Denmark, Norway, Sweden, and Brazil, which wanted to appeal to Egypt to change its mind and then to put the question to the General Assembly. However, the committee did not propose to convene the General Assembly to consider the crisis. The legal validity of Egypt's demand to withdraw UN forces was recognized since those forces were stationed there with the consent of that government.[21] It will be recalled that UNEF forces were under the General Assembly, which did not have the authority to put troops in Egypt without its agreement. Under the UN Charter, Security Council forces would have had that authority, since the Council acts on behalf of the entire membership on such issues (Article 25, Chapter VII).

U Thant tried without success to get Egypt to withdraw its demand and to get UNEF forces stationed in Israel. On May 18 he expressed deep anxiety to the UN Advisory Committee for UNEF I about the dangerous deterioration of the situation, but he continued with the evacuation of the 3,378 troops of the UN Emergency Force.[22] He replaced them with a few UNTSO observers to maintain a UN presence.

Anwar Sadat's memoirs report that Nasser knew that his actions were being provocative. On May 22 Nasser declared the blockade of the Strait of Tiran, and in a cabinet meeting he admitted that this action made war "100 percent" certain. Nasser asked if General Amer was prepared, and Amer answered that everything was in tip-top shape.[23] During this tense period Egyptian spokesmen made threats about destroying Israel.

Britain proposed to the United States that a naval task force he establisheed to keep the strait open. On May 30 Israeli Prime Minister Eshkol told the United States through the Israeli ambassador that it was essential that a naval escort move through the strait "within a week or two." Meanwhile President Johnson, who was embroiled in the escalation of the war in Vietnam, asserts in his memoirs that he was trying to get congressional and UN support for such a commitment of forces to the strait. With his immersion in Vietnam, Johnson refused to give a clear commitment to keep the strait open without strong allied and congressional support.

The secretary general in his report to the Security Council of May 26 said that he had expressed his "deep concern" about Egypt's restricting innocent passage through the Strait of Tiran. In the Security Council debates Ambassador Goldberg of the United States also pleaded with Egypt to forego the act of belligerence of closing the Strait of Tiran, but in vain. This belligerence gave Israel the excuse that Egypt had committed the first warlike act, even though in the 10 years the strait had been open only five Israeli ships had used it.[24] The Council debates asked for restraint, but it made no move to establish the international naval escort the Israelis had demanded.

On June 5 Israel attacked, wiping out the Egyptian and Syrian air forces, and Israeli forces drove into the Sinai. Within a week the Israelis had taken the Sinai, the Golan Heights, Gaza, and the West Bank. By June 10 the way was open to Damascus, but the Israelis called a halt. The Security Council in a series of meetings and resolutions demanded a cease-fire. By June 10 fighting had stopped, and the UN Truce Supervisory Organization (UNTSO) was observing a cease-fire under instructions of the Security Council. Israel now controlled the Sinai, the Gaza Strip, the West Bank including Jerusalem, and the Golan Heights (see Map 2).

The Security Council met in July and October to consider complaints by both Israel and Egypt about violations of the cease-fire. In November the Council considered Egyptian complaints of Israel's failure to withdraw its forces from the occupied territory.

On November 22 the Security Council unanimously passed Resolution 242, a landmark. Lord Caradon of Great Britain drafted it after months of discussion in the Council and General Assembly, and after extensive discussion with the Arabs, Israelis, and other delegates. It was later accepted as a basis for the Camp David negotiations that established peace between Egypt and Israel. At the same time, the Security Council appointed a special representative to assist in efforts at a peaceful settlement.

The major points of the resolution, whose full text is in Appendix C, are as follows:

> 1. The Security Council: affirms that fulfillment of charter principles requires the establishment of a just and lasting peace which should include the application of both the following principles:
>
> (i) Withdrawal of Israeli armed forces from territories occupied in the recent conflict;
>
> (ii) Termination of all claims or states of belligerency and respect for and acknowledgment of the sovereignty, territorial integrity and political independence of every State in the area and their right to live in peace within secure and recognized boundaries free from threats or acts of force;
>
> 2. Affirms further the necessity
>
> (a) For guaranteeing freedom of navigation through international waterways in the area;
>
> (b) For achieving a just settlement of the refugee problem;
>
> (c) For guaranteeing the territorial inviolatiblity and political independence of every State in the area, through measures including the establishment of demilitarized zones;

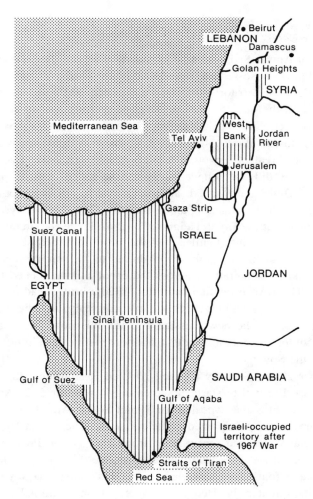

Map 2. Israel after the 1967 War

Resolution 242 is intentionally vague about whether Israel should return *all* territories that it occupied in the 1967 war, with the Arabs insisting it should and Israel refusing to agree. The Palestinians object to the resolution because it does not mention the rights of the Palestinian people. Nevertheless, the resolution has stood the test of time and was still being used as the basis of the U.S. initiative in 1992 to try to bring about a settlement of the basic causes of the Palestinian uprising against the Israeli ocupation of the West Bank and Gaza.

The 1973 War

Vice President Anwar Sadat became president of Egypt after Nasser's death in 1970. Sadat was obsessed and humiliated by the 1967 war and determined to get back Egyptian territory. In 1971 he expelled 20,000 Russian military advisors because the Soviets were involved in plotting a coup against him. However, Sadat continued to get military equipment from the Soviet Union to replace that lost in 1967. After the loss of Russian military advisors, few if any took the threat of Egyptian military action seriously. Even Sadat's own commanders did not believe him when he asked them to prepare to attack Israel.[25] But Sadat insisted, and on October 6, 1973 Egyptian forces surprised the Israelis by attacking along the Suez Canal, while Syrian forces mounted an attack at the Golan Heights. For a while the Syrian tanks threatened to break through into Galilee, but the Israeli air force and defenders turned back the attack. Then the action shifted to the south where General Aric Sharon led a counterattack across the canal and threatened to cut off the Egyptian Third Army, which had established a bridgehead in the Sinai. This fighting recorded the biggest tank battle in history, and the Israelis lost hundreds of tanks to the new Russian antitank missiles. The Israelis also suffered heavy losses to their aircraft from new mobile antiaircraft weapons provided by the Soviets.

On October 22 the Security Council adopted Resolution 338 calling on parties to cease fire and to start implementing Resolution 242. As fighting continued President Sadat appealed for a joint Soviet-American force to be sent to the area. This precipitated a nuclear crisis. The Soviet Union in response to Sadat's plea had sent a letter from Brezhnev to President Nixon calling for joint Soviet-U.S. contingents to police the truce, adding that if the United States found it impossible to act in this matter, the Soviets would consider acting unilaterally. Henry Kissinger, Nixon's national security adviser, interpreted this in the worst way because he did not want Soviet troops in the area, and his fears were increased by intelligence that the Soviets were alerting airborne divisions. With a phone call to the president, who was in the middle of the Watergate crisis, and to the secretary of defense, Kissinger raised the alert status of U.S. nuclear forces from a normal DEF-CON 4 or 5 to a DEFCON 3. Soldiers were called back from leave and B-52 bombers were put on emergency alert. These signals were received in the Kremlin, but fortunately the crisis did not escalate further.

The next day the UN Security Council approved establishing UN Emergency Force II, without soldiers from the superpowers. The force, which eventually numbered about 7,000 soldiers, was sent promptly to monitor the truce. Since the Security Council set up this force, it could have been authorized to take enforcement action, in contrast to UNEF I set up under the General Assembly, which did not have this power. The acceptance of this UN force without question contrasted with the nuclear crisis that occurred when the Russians proposed a Russian-U.S. force, and the incident demonstrates the neutral nature of the United Nations as a source of peacekeeping units.

Secretary of State Kissinger began shuttling back and forth between Cairo, Jerusalem, and Damascus to try to achieve a cease-fire. These efforts succeeded, and the cease-fire was formally endorsed by the Peace Conference on the Middle East under the cochairmanship of the Soviet Union and the United States on December 21, 1973. This conference was under the auspices of the United Nations. Egypt, Israel, and Jordan attended, but Syria refused.

During the crisis the Arab states had put pressure on the United States by cutting back on their oil exports, while insisting that there be a withdrawal of Israeli forces. This helped motivate Kissinger in his shuttle efforts. Also, a military working group under the chairmanship of the UN Emergency Force commander in December 1973 and January 1974 reached agreement on provisions for the disengagement of forces from the Sinai and establishing a buffer zone between Egyptian and Israeli troops. This disengagement was supported within Israel by General Dayan, now the foreign minister, and by the efforts of Secretary of State Kissinger.

UN military observers in October began observing the cease-fire in the Golan Heights. On May 31, 1974 an agreement mediated by Kissinger was signed on the disengagement of forces between Israel and Syria along that border. The Security Council on May 21 then set up the UN Disengagement Observer Forces of UN members (UNDOF) to patrol a cease-fire line and neutral zone. This consisted of about 1,250 lightly armed military personnel at a cost about $1.7 million a month. Both the UNDOF and the UNEF II forces were renewed periodically by the Security Council. They were responsible to it and the secretary general.

On September 4, 1975 Kissinger succeeded in mediating a second disengagement agreement between Egypt and Israel providing for futher withdrawal of Israeli forces to east of the Gidi-Mitla passes in the Sinai and from the oilfields along the Red Sea. This agreement established a large buffer zone between Israeli and Egyptian forces patrolled by UNEF II troops, and it prohibited an Egyptian military buildup. It is significant that Kissinger as a foremost practitioner of power found that the United Nations peacekeeping forces were essential to his diplomacy in the Middle East.

These agreements set the stage for Camp David. Following a visit by Sadat to Jerusalem in November 1977, President Jimmy Carter began negotiations that led to two agreements. The September 1978 agreements, which were based on principles of UN Resolution 242 (Appendix C), set a framework for a peace treaty in which Israel would return the Sinai. The second one set a framework for peace in the Middle East between Israel and the Palestinians by providing for self-government on the West Bank. These agreements were incorporated in treaties signed on March 26, 1979.[26] Israeli forces withdrew from the Sinai on April 25, 1982, with General Sharon's troops dragging out the last Israeli settlers. Originally, the agreements called for UNEF II to patrol the Sinai, but as a result of opposition by Arab states, the Soviet Union, and by the PLO, UNEF II was terminated on July 24, 1979.

President Carter then set up a new multinational observer force modeled after the UN units to monitor the provisions of the peace treaty. The multinational force also patrols the Strait of Tiran, which is internationalized by the treaty. During the first year, the force had 2,600 personnel from 10 countries, and it was commanded by a Norwegian. Its budget was $103.5 million with one-third each contributed by Egypt, Israel, and the United States.

The Camp David agreements stabilized the situation in the Middle East by making peace between Israel and Egypt, by far the largest and most powerful Arab neighbor. With its southern border protected, Israel was much less threatened by Syria, Jordan, and Lebanon. For this reason the agreements were attacked by other Arab states, which broke off normal diplomatic relations with Egypt.

War in Lebanon

There was no peace in the area, however, The tensions were reflected in terrorist attacks against Israel mostly from Lebanon followed by retaliatory strikes. On March 15, 1978 following a Palestinian commando raid in Israel that killed 37 Israeli civilians, Israel invaded southern Lebanon. Israel and Lebanon both requested a meeting of the Security Council. Four days later the Council passed a resolution calling on Israel immediately to cease its military action against Lebanon and setting up a United Nations Interim Force in Lebanon (UNIFIL). The Israeli forces completed their withdrawal on June 13, 1978. The Security Council continued to extend UNIFIL every six months, and it has remained in southern Lebanon despite receiving heavy casualties and at times being circumvented by Israel.

The 6,000 soldiers of UNIFIL managed to help keep the lid on until June 1982, when Israeli forces mounted a major attack to destroy PLO bases in southern Lebanon. The Israeli leaders were alarmed at the continued build-up of PLO arms and strength in southern Lebanon, which it controlled. Israeli forces used the excuse of an attack on the Israeli ambassador in London by Palestinians to invade southern Lebanon again and destroy the PLO bases.[27] Some UNIFIL positions were bypassed or overrun; one Norwegian soldier was killed. The Israeli forces moved into Beirut where heavy fighting took place. Also, military clashes occurred with Syria during which Israel shot down 88 aircraft and destroyed Syrian surface-to-air missiles in Lebanon. The Security Council called for a cease-fire and endorsed the continued presence of UNIFIL. The Council's action was reinforced by efforts of U.S. Ambassador Philip Habib, who over a period of months negotiated an agreement on a withdrawal of about 10,000 PLO forces from Lebanon.

The United States, along with Britain, France, and Italy, sent a multilateral defense force into Lebanon to monitor the agreement negotiated by Ambassador Habib. These were not UN forces, but UN observers did monitor the situation in Beirut. The 10 UN observers were named the Observer Group Beirut (OGB). Later the Security Council increased the number to 50. At the beginning of 1983, however, 241 U.S. marines, who were part of the multilateral defense force, were killed in their Beirut headquarters by a terrorist bomb. Subsequently the United States withdrew its forces, eventually followed by those of Britain, France, and Italy. These troops were not under the United Nations, and their failure contrasts with the ability of the UN peacekeeping forces in the Middle East to maintain their positions.

After about two years of violent clashes between contending factions in Lebanon, a government backed by Syria was established that ended the open warfare but not periodic terrorist actions. Israel withdrew its forces finally at the end of 1985, but it periodically patrolled a "security zone" in a 25-mile strip within Lebanon's southern border. Violence and retaliation continued in the area, but UNIFIL forces provided an authority to which leaders could appeal who wished to end fighting in the region.

A new crisis broke out at the end of 1987 with the uprising of Palestinians against the Israeli occupation of the West Bank and Gaza. Israeli troops over the following years killed hundreds of demonstrators demanding a Palestine State and an end to the occupation. Over 1.2 million Palestinians live in the West Bank and Gaza. In November 1988 the PLO's Palestine National Council compromised by accepting UN Resolution 242, which indicated a willingness to recognize and negotiate with Israel. Arafat then applied for a U.S. visa to speak before the General Assembly, but it was refused by the United States on the grounds that he was associated with terrorist organizations. The General Assembly then voted to move its session temporarily to Geneva to hear Arafat speak. In ensuing negotiations Arafat drafted a statement acceptable to the United States denouncing terrorism and accepting UN resolutions. The United States then agreed to carry on conversations with him.

Secretary of State Baker in 1991 with repeated visits to the Middle East negotiated the breakthrough of face-to-face talks among Israel, the Arab States, and the PLO. The first sessision took place in Madrid followed by bilateral negotiations between Israel and its neighbors. Although at the insistence of Israel the United Nations was excluded, the conference was based on UN resolutions 242 and 338. The General Assembly in its 1991 session affirmed rights of the Palestinians, but also repealed the "zionism is racism" resolution, which had been offensive to Israel. After the moderate Labor Party won Israel's elections in 1992, there was hope the talks would help move the negotiations forward.

The United Nations has been at the center of Arab-Israeli wars and controversies since inheriting the Palestine problem from the League. It did not prevent these wars or solve the problems, but it did prevent the wars from escalating into conflicts involving forces of the major powers. The UN peacekeeping forces helped end the wars and monitor cease-fires. This qualified success for the United Nations was due in large part to support from the United States. Many other countries also helped by providing peacekeeping forces. Major failures in heading off the 1967 war and bringing an end to the conflict in Lebanon in the 1980s were associated with a failure of the United States to act within a UN framework.

The United Nations' peacekeeping units still patrol southern Lebanon, the Golan Heights, and the UNTSO observers patrol throughout the area. Thus, the United Nations and its peacekeeping forces are helping keep a lid on the continuing Mideast crises, despite the actions of terrorists and the clashes along the Israel-Lebanese border.[28]

The next chapter examines UN actions in conflicts where power politics dominated the scene.

Notes to Chapter 4

1. Y. Alexander and A. Nanes, *The United States and Iran: A Documentary History* (Frederick MD: University Press, 1980), pp. 145–189.

2. N. Khrushchev, *Khrushchev Remembers* (Boston: Little, Brown, 1979), pp. 367–373.

3. T. Lie, *In the Cause of Peace* (New York: Macmillan, 1954), p. 327.

4. S.D. Bailey, *Voting in the Security Council* (Bloomington: Indiana University Press, 1971) pp. 69–73.

5. *Lie, Peace*, pp. 334–336.

6. H. Truman, *Years of Decision* (New York: Doubleday, 1956), p. 280.

7. D. Acheson, *Present at the Creation* (New York: Norton, 1969), p. 405.

8. B. Smith, *Dean Acheson* (New York: Cooper Square, 1962), p. 417.

9. *New York Times*, September 29, 1950, p. 1; October 5, 1950, p. 1; October 8, 1950, p. 1.

10. U.S. Department of State, *Foreign Relations of the United States: East Asia and the Pacific, 1950* (Washington, DC: Government Printing Office, 1976), pp. 267–269, 291–298, 374–375.

11. Acheson, *Present*, 477–614.

12. D. Eisenhower, *Mandate for Change* (New York: Doubleday, 1963), p. 180–181.

13. D. Wainhouse, *International Peace Observation* (Baltimore: John Hopkins Press, 1966), p. 246.

14. Countries voting for the majority plan were Australia, Belgium, Bolivia, Brazil, Byelorussia, Canada, Costa Rica, Czechoslovakia, Denmark, the Dominican Republic, Ecuador, France, Guatamala, Haiti, Iceland, Liberia, Luxembourg, Netherlands, New Zealand, Nicaragua, Norway, Panama, Paraguay, Peru, Philippines, Poland, Sweden, Ukraine, Union of South Africa, The USSR, The United States, Uruguay, Venezuela, Lebanon, Pakistan, Saudi Arabia, Syria, Turkey, and Yemen. The countries abstaining were Argentina, Chile, China, Columbia, El Salvador, Ethiopia, Honduras, Mexico, the United Kingdom, and Yugoslavia.

15. L. Collins and D. Lapierre, *O Jerusalem* (New York: Pocket Books, 1976); G. Pasha, *A Soldier with the Arabs* (London: Hodder and Slaughton, 1957); M. Dayan, *The Story of My Life* (New York: Werner Books, 1966).

16. T. Hoopes, *The Devil and John Foster Dulles* (Boston: Little, Brown, 1973), p. 335.

17. B. Urquart, *Hammarskjold* (New York: Harper, 1981), pp. 132–162.

18. Ibid., p. 173.

19. Ibid., p. 193.

20. A. Lall, *The UN and the Middle East Crisis* (New York: Columbia University Press, 1970), pp. 29–30.

21. R. Siekman, Basic Documents on United Nations and Related Peace Keeping Forces (Boston: Martinus Nijhoff, 1985), pp. 4–7.

22. A. Lall, *The UN and the Middle East Crisis—1967* (New York: Columbia University Press, 1970), p. 20.

23. A. Sadat, *In Search of Identity* (New York: Harper & Row, 1977), pp. 215–231.

24. Lall, *UN*, pp. 34–35.

25. Sadat, *Search*, 213–233.

26. J. Carter. *Keeping Faith* (New York: Bantam, 1982), pp. 397–403.

27. J. Sisco, *Middle East: Progress or Lost Opportunity." America and the World—1982* (New York: Council on Foreign Relations, 1983).

28. H. Heiberg and J. Holst, "Peacekeeping in Lebanon—Comparing UNIFIL and the MNF," Survival (London: September/October, 1986).

Chapter V

THE UNITED NATIONS VERSUS POWER POLITICS

After the Eisenhower administration, U.S. support for the United Nations cooled. American secretaries of state and presidents regarded it more as an instrument that might be used in an emergency or as a last resort, rather than as a framework that could be strengthened to achieve a peaceful world order. Many countries held the United Nations in high regard, but the major powers relied on power politics. Secretary General Hammarskjold asserted the authority of the United Nations in settling the Congo crisis in the 1960s, but the effort cost him his life. Moreover, opposition of the Soviets and France to this initiative undermined the financial stability and weakened the organization for many years. At the end of the 1980s, with the end of the Cold War, the United Nations revived and took over many peacekeeping functions. Ironically, its financial stability again was threatened.

AGGRESSION RESTRAINED BY THE UNITED NATIONS

The Congo Operation

In the Congo crisis that began in 1960 the secretary general of the United Nations acted as commander-in-chief of a UN military force at times engaged in conventional military operations. Hammarskjold anticipated trouble as the Congo achieved independence and sent Ralph Bunche there by Independence Day to be available to advise the new government. The crisis started on July 5, 1960, five days after the Congo (now named Zaire) achieved independence from Belgium and its troops withdrew. Congolese soldiers mutinied against their officers, who were Belgian, and for the first time killed Europeans. Belgian government troops returned to restore order, despite opposition by the new head of state, Patrice Lumumba.

On July 14, the UN Security Council, in a resolution instigated by the secretary general, called upon Belgium to withdraw its troops from the Congo, and authorized the UN secretary general to provide military and technical assistance to the Congolese government until its security forces could "meet fully their tasks." The secretary general then formed the UN Operation in the Congo (ONUC), which rapidly built up to over 14,000 troops, most of them from African nations. No troops of the permanent members of the Security Council were included in the force. The Security Council resolutions authorized ONUC to use force to get Belgian troops to withdraw, to maintain law and order, and to prevent a civil war. The Security Council action reflected the common anti-colonial attitude of its members.[1]

Several years of confused actions occurred during which members of the Security Council were often at odds. The major political problem was that Katanga, the mineral-rich province, wished to secede with the help of Belgian forces. It took, therefore, Hammarskjold's personal intervention to introduce UN troops into the province and obtain the evacuation of Belgian forces.[2] The other major problem was the policy of the Soviet Union and the United States to support different factions in the Congo.

Hammarskjold's middle course and his blocking Soviet military support to the radical faction in the Congo enraged Khrushchev. He attacked Hammarskjold personally in a speech before the General Assembly and proposed replacing him with a troika, a three-person executive. Hammarskjold's moderate response defending the integrity of position of secretary general was greeted with a standing ovation. The following day Khrushchev warmly received him at a Soviet reception. The Soviets did not stop their attacks on Hammarskjold, however, or their support for the troika. Khrushchev's behavior reflected frustration over the power the secretary general was exercising that was not subject to the Soviet veto.[3]

The secretary general was able to take initiatives with his original authority, which was backed by the General Assembly's continued support to the central government of the Congo even when the Security Council could not reach agreement. At one point the mineral-rich province of Katanga resisted the entrance of UN troops until Hammarskjold personally persuaded President Tshombe, head of the Katanga province, to accept them. In September 1961, Secretary General Hammarskjold was killed in a plane crash on his way to confer with Tshombe.

The new acting secretary general, U Thant, received a strong mandate from the Security Council. Katanga, at first, did not cooperate and even fired on ONUC positions. By 1963, however, a new federal government of the Congo including Katanga was established. General Mobutu took over as president and was able to end the civil war. The United Nations provided major technical and economic assistance to the new government, which has maintained its integrity since that time.

The initiative of Secretary General Hammarskjold during the crisis cost him his life. The world lost a great public servant. Moreover, the heavy costs of the operation added to UN financial strains. The Soviet Union and France refused to regard costs of the Congo operations as regular expenses of the United Nations and refused to pay. After the Congo crisis secretary generals did not take major initiatives for peacekeeping operations without the approval of the Security Council, while the debts accumulated by the original Congo operations continued to threaten the UN's financial position.

The Cuban Missile Crisis

The crisis originated in the spring of 1960. At that time President Kennedy approved a plan started by President Eisenhower for the CIA to support the landing of Cuban exiles in Cuba with the aim of overthrowing Fidel Castro's Communist-style government. When the landing occurred, the poorly trained force of about 1,400 exiles, which was only indirectly supported by the U.S. military, failed miserably, and over 1,100 Cuban invaders were taken prisoner. Subsequently, U.S. covert support for attacks against Cuban targets and attempts to assassinate Castro continued.[4] This intervention violated international law, which is based on respect for sovereignty. The attacks and belligerent statements of the U.S. Congress created concern in Cuba and the USSR about future attacks against Cuba.[5]

Khrushchev stated that while visiting Romania he learned of U.S. missiles in Turkey. This plus concern about the U.S. threat to Cuba led to his decision to place Soviet missiles in Turkey. "In addition to protecting Cuba, our missiles would have equalized what the West likes to call 'the balance of power.' " It was high time, he wrote, that Americans knew what it felt like to have their own land and people threatened. Since the American long-range missiles outnumbered the Soviet long-range missiles by a factor of 10 to 1, Russia's placing 80 intermediate range missiles plus medium-range missiles in Cuba would have helped redress the balance. The major reason for the Soviet move is still disputed, but the threat of the U.S. missiles in Turkey was an important consideration.[6]

On October 16, 1962, Kennedy saw the first CIA pictures of the missile sites. During the next six days the high-level executive committee advising him debated what response to make. On Monday, October 23 Kennedy announced the United States would impose a "quarantine" on the shipment of offensive weapons to Cuba. The concept of a quarantine, or very limited blockade, was proposed by the committee to avoid imposing a "blockade," which is an act of war. Abram Chayes, the State Department's legal adviser during the crisis, points out in his book, *The Cuban Missile Crisis,* that over half of the executive committee were lawyers, which helps to explain the committee's concern about international law. For this reason, and in order to get support for the U.S. position, the United States took the matter to the United Nations and to the Organization of American States (OAS), which has regional responsibility for security matters under the UN Charter. The Executive Committee was relieved that the OAS gave the United States unanimous support on the quarantine. Also, the State Department produced a legal justification of U.S. action, that was so popular with the media it had to be reissued.

This is not to say that legal arguments persuaded the Soviets to withdraw the missiles in return for a pledge not to invade Cuba. It seems clear from their statements that they believed Robert Kennedy, speaking for the president, had given them an ultimatum to remove the missiles within 48 hours or the United States would act to remove them. Nevertheless, the unanimous support by the OAS for the quarantine and the widespread belief in NATO and by other nations that the U.S. action was justified legally and politically probably helped persuade the Soviets to remove the missiles.

On October 29 Khrushchev announced that the Soviets would withdraw the missiles since the United States had pledged not to invade Cuba. Some years later it was revealed that Robert Kennedy during the crisis had committed the United States to remove its missiles from Turkey within a few months, if the Russians kept this commitment secret. Then, in March 1987 Secretary of State Dean Rusk revealed at the Hawk's Cay conference in Florida that during the crisis President Kennedy had asked Rusk to request the former deputy secretary general of the United Nations, Andrew Cordier, to approach Secretary General U Thant suggesting U Thant propose that the United States withdraw missiles from Turkey and the Soviets withdraw their missiles from Cuba. If this appeared to be U Thant's idea, it would give the United States an excuse to remove the missiles without seeming to break a commitment to NATO on the Turkish missiles in the face of a Soviet threat. Khrushchev yielded before this ploy was put into effect. This would have been a last-ditch option to use the United Nations as an impartial umpire to propose a solution that both sides could accept without losing face. Although the crisis was resolved without this effort to solve the issue, the incident demonstrates how important a role the United Nations could have played in one of the most serious crises that the United States ever faced.

The India/Pakistan Conflicts

The United Nations was involved in the agonizing conflicts between India and Pakistan after 1948, when these two countries were formed from the British colony of India. The differences were rooted in religion—the Hindus worship many gods, whereas the Muslims believe in one god. When the Muslims entered India about 1000 A.D., they destroyed Hindu temples and sculptures as idolatrous. Their food laws were different. To Hindus, the cow is sacred and they would not eat beef. Muslims eat beef and consider pork unclean. There was virtually no intermarriage between Muslims and Hindus.

As Britain ended its colonial rule in India, a terrible civil conflict broke out, the most serious religious conflict of our era. Over 800,000 civilians were killed as Moslem refugees moved into Pakistan and Hindu refugees moved into areas of India. Lord Mountbatten stayed on as viceroy to referee the division of India. After a British geographer drew lines between the new states, there were two Pakistans—East Pakistan and West Pakistan— separated by 1,000 miles of India.

The United Nations was not involved in the original civil war, but after the lines between the two countries were determined, the United Nations was drawn into the disputes. The state of Jammu Kashmir, a beautiful resort area in northern India, was controlled by a Hindu prince, but its population was mostly Moslem. The Hindu prince decided to join India, which antagonized the new Pakistan, a Moslem state.

The Indians were furious when Pakistani tribesmen, obviously supported by the new Pakistan government, attacked the cities of Kashmir. India wanted to retaliate with its army, which could have caused a major war. The matter was brought before the Security Council by India on January 1, 1948. Pakistan entered a counter-complaint, charging that Indian forces had unlawfully occupied part of Kashmir and that the genocide of Moslems was being carried out in a pre-arranged plan.

On January 20, 1948, the UN Security Council established a three-member UN Commission for India/Pakistan (UNCIP), that included a U.S. member, to investigate and mediate. The commission arrived in July 1948 and on August 13 proposed a cease-fire with the disputed area being administered under the commission. There was a withdrawal of troops, and both governments finally accepted the cease-fire line in July 1949. Following this, the parties could not agree on the details of a plebiscite for a permanent settlement of the problem. Probably, India was afraid that it would lose control if the issue came to a vote of the largely Moslem population. In March 1950 the Security Council terminated UNCIP and established a UN representative to mediate. In March 1951 Frank Graham, an American, became the UN representative for these issues.

In 1949 the United Nations had also established the UN Military Observer Group in India and Pakistan (UNMOGIP) to supervise the cease-fire. That unit, under the secretary general, continued to operate, reporting violations and trying to prevent violation of the cease-fire line.

In 1965 Indian and Pakistan troops clashed on a border issue involving the Rann of Kutch, a small marshy area on the ocean along India's northwest border. The British government arranged a quick cease-fire and a hearing by a tribunal, which awarded about 90 percent of the area to India.

That same year, as tensions continued, a major war broke out again in Kashmir. In August 1965 Pakistan crossed the UN cease-fire line in an invasion of Kashmir. Indian forces retaliated successfully in an invasion of West Pakistan. The secretary general received reliable reports from UNMOGIP and appealed to the Indian and Pakistan representatives, and personally to the prime ministers of India and the President of Pakistan, for a cease-fire. India and Pakistan accepted his pleas on September 22.

The above conflicts were a spin-off of the original civil war, that were contained with the help of UN mediation, particularly by the secretary general. The 1971 war involved a new international dimension, one that threatened to bring about a confrontation between the superpowers (Map 3). East Pakistan was a very poor area, and the Bengalis of East Pakistan believed that they were neglected by West Pakistan, where the capital was. In 1970 there was a violent cyclone from the Bay of Bengal, which killed over 200,000 persons. The West Pakistan government was slow to aid devastated areas. This accerbated relations between the two parts of Pakistan, which have different languages and cultures, although both populations are Moslem.

Meanwhile President Yahya Khan was preparing to establish a democratic government for Pakistan. In March 1971 the elections were held. In East Pakistan, the Awami League won 167 out of 169 seats. This party strongly supported autonomy, and the 167 seats would have given it a majority in the new Pakistan parliament that could have forced a division of the two countries. Yahya Khan did not want to preside over the splitting up of Pakistan, so he postponed the convening of the new parliament. The Awami League responded with a campaign of civil disorder and a general strike. West Pakistan moved in its troops to suppress the rebellion, but 70,000 West Pakistan soldiers could not pacify 30 million East Pakistanis. In this civil conflict several hundred thousand Bengalis were killed, along with extensive rape and pillage. About 10 million Bengalis fled in terror from this conflict to the Bengali area of eastern India. Here the Bengalis were Hindu and not Moslem. The UN secretary general with the consent of the two

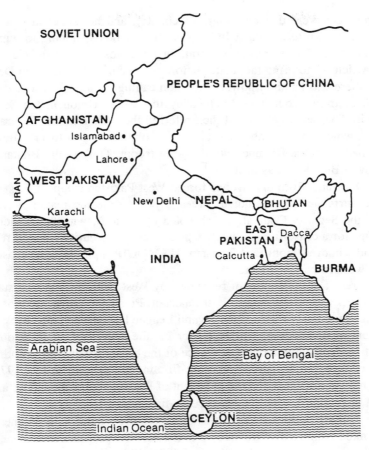

Map 3. India and Pakistan—1971

governments set up two large scale humanitarian programs—one for East Pakistan and the other for India—to assist the Bengali refugees.

During 1971 Prime Minister Indira Gandhi informed the United Nations and its members that India could not tolerate continuing to support 10 million Bengali refugees in the poorest part of India. Tensions rose when a study of an Indian research organization pointed out it would be cheaper to wage war than for India to continue to support these refugees.[7] One of the most serious sources of tension was that the leader of the Awami League had been arrested and imprisoned in West Pakistan. On July 20, 1971, the secretary general informed the president of the Security Council the situation was a threat to the peace. He continued to offer his good offices, but there was no move by Pakistan to pacify the situation and accept the refugees.

On November 26, 1971, Indian troops were reported to be participating in probes against East Pakistan. On December 3 Yahya Khan claimed that

Indian forces were dismembering his country, and he launched a surprise attack in the western part of India on Indian airfields, hoping to wipe out their air arm. The secretary general, in an almost unprecedented move, used Article 99 to bring the matter before the Security Council. On December 6, there was an eight-power resolution calling for a cease-fire and withdrawal of troops, but it was vetoed by the Soviet Union in the Security Council. The Security Council then referred the matter to the General Assembly, which on December 7 adopted a resolution by 104 to 11 calling for an immediate cease-fire and withdrawal of troops. Only India, Bhutan, and the Soviet Bloc voted against.

By December 16 Indian troops forced West Pakistan troops in East Pakistan to surrender to the Indian forces. By this time the matter was back before the Security Council, which voted by 13 to 0, with the Soviets abstaining, for a cease-fire. Indian troops obeyed the Security Council resolution and withdrew from East Pakistan. UNMOGIP supervised the cease-fire in the western part of India.

As a result of the ending of resistance by West Pakistan, the new state of Bangladesh was established in East Pakistan. President Yahya Khan of West Pakistan generously released the Awami League leader who came back to be president of Bangladesh. On December 21, the Security Council adopted a resolution demanding strict observance of the cease-fire and the withdrawal of armed forces to the agreed-on cease-fire line in Kashmir. In July 1972 the prime minister of India and the president of Pakistan confirmed these agreements, again confirming the basic cease-fire line of 1949.

The United Nations had successfully pressured India to limit the war. The United Nations also mounted a massive relief program to help resettle 10 million refugees created by the war. This efficient and rapid resettlement of refugees contrasts with the decades of strife that resulted from the displacement of one million Palestinian refugees.[8]

AGGRESSION NOT RESTRAINED BY THE UNITED NATIONS

In the above cases, the United Nations restrained the aggressor and helped contain the crises. In assessing the success of the United Nations in maintaining international peace, it is useful, also, to examine cases where the United Nations played a minor role and initially was not effective. However by the 1990s it was back on center stage in international crises.

Eastern Europe

After World War II the nations of the world recognized as a fact of international life the Soviet domination of a group of East European states. When the war ended, Soviet troops were occupying these countries, some of which had allied with Hitler. In summit meetings before the end of the war and before the United Nations was founded, a line was drawn through Europe dividing the areas occupied by the Soviets and those by the armies of the Western Allies. The Soviets did not keep their commitment in the Yalta agreement to form governments representative of their democratic elements through free elections. As the Western armies rapidly demobilized, the Western allies realized that they could not enforce the Yalta agreement or force the Soviet armies out of Eastern Europe without resuming the war.

When Hungary in 1956 and Czechoslovakia in 1968 tried to break out from Soviet control, Soviet armies invaded to restore order. In the case of Hungary, the new revolutionary government requested assistance of the Security Council to negotiate withdrawal of Soviet troops. The Soviet Union vetoed a Security Council resolution demanding this, and action was transferred to the General Assembly. During its meeting, a new Hungarian government installed by the Soviets informed the secretary general that all communications from the previous government were invalid. The General Assembly, on November 4, called on the USSR to withdraw, affirming the right of the Hungarian people to form their own government, and requesting the secretary general to investigate. The Soviets ignored this and subsequent resolutions. Finally, in 1962, after numerous UN resolutions, the matter was dropped. Meanwhile, about $20 million was provided through the United Nations for about 200,000 refugees fleeing from Hungary.

In Czechoslovakia in 1968 Dubcek, a new leader of the Communist Party, started to implement a series of liberal economic and political reforms including holding elections, reestablishing a parliament, and giving workers a stronger voice in management. The Soviets, alarmed by this challenge to the Communist systems of Europe, persuaded other Eastern European countries to join them in invading Czechoslovakia. The Czech government protested to the United Nations but ordered the Czech forces not to resist. The invasion was so quick and effective that the matter died in the Security Council after three days of consideration. At the end of that time, the new Czech government requested that the item be withdrawn from the agenda. A resolution condemning the intervention was vetoed by the Soviets.

These two cases demonstrated the basic weakness of the UN Charter—it is not designed to enforce a decision against one of the great powers. Theoretically, the General Assembly could have mobilized the world community to oppose the invasions or impose sanctions, but none of the countries were willing to confront the Soviets to that extent or to go to war with the Soviets, who were a nuclear power. Moreover, there was no indication that

Hungary or Czechoslovakia wanted to be liberated at the cost of being destroyed in such a war. These issues reflected the fact that the United Nations had inherited a situation in 1945 that could not have been corrected at that time without another world war. Moreover, it was believed necessary to keep both superpowers in the organization. The sequel was that East European countries were liberated peacefully after the 1989 anti-Communist revolutions.

The Vietnam War

The United Nations, not having the support of any of the great powers, played only a minimal role in the Vietnam War. After World War II a Communist insurgency led by Ho Chi Minh fought the French, trying to end their colonial rule. In 1954, after being defeated by Communist forces, the French negotiated the Geneva Agreements with North Vietnam. These provided for the establishment of the Democratic Republic of Vietnam in the north under Ho Chi Minh and a government in the south under Emperor Bao Dai and his prime minister, Ngo Dinh Diem. The United States, the Soviet Union, China, and Great Britain also participated in the negotiations. The agreements specified no role for the United Nations.

After 1954 South Vietnam was formally recognized as a government by over 90 nations, which were most of the countries of the world. These included the important nations outside the Communist Bloc. The Communist nations and a few others formally recognized North Vietnam. The Communist Bloc did not recognize South Vietnam, supporting North Vietnam's position that Vietnam should be unified under the Communist government of North Vietnam.

The United States supported the new government of South Vietnam with military and economic aid as the French withdrew. Under the 1954 agreement U.S. military advisers were limited to several hundred. In the late 1950s, as the Diem government arrested and fought the insurgents, North Vietnam sent tens of thousands of Communist cadres with military supplies to the South.[9] President Kennedy, aiming to stop the spread of Communism in Asia, increased aid and the number of U.S. military advisers to about 17,000.

After President Kennedy's assassination in 1963, President Johnson on August 4, 1964, requested an urgent meeting of the UN Security Council. He complained that U.S. naval vessels had been attacked by North Vietnam in international waters in the Gulf of Tonkin off the coast of North Vietnam. North Vietnam attended the Security Council meeting and responded that U.S. aircraft and warships had bombed and strafed North Vietnamese territory and supported raids by South Vietnam. Action was blocked by the possibility of a Soviet veto, and because other nations on the Council realized that the United States and North Vietnam were not willing to accept the judgment of the Security Council on the issues. The United States and North Vietnam continued escalating the conflict, with the United States eventually sending 535,000 of its own troops to South Vietnam.

After major escalation of the war, the United States on January 31, 1966, requested another meeting of the Security Council to consider the "question of Vietnam." The Council, after a debate, decided on February 2, 1966, to include Vietnam issues on the agenda by a vote of 9 to 2 with 4 abstentions. The President of the Council undertook private consultations and then reported that the members wanted to end the conflict but believed that negotiations should take place in another forum.

Secretary General U Thant, in an annual report to the General Assembly, explained why the United Nations would not take further steps to end the war. He noted the Geneva Agreements of 1954 prescribed no role for the United Nations and that neither North Vietnam or South Vietnam were UN members. He urged a revival of the Geneva Conference of 1954. He said he had, without success, devoted a great deal of effort to getting the parties (North Vietnam, South Vietnam, and the United States) to negotiate, but had failed because the struggle had been dominated by power politics.

North Vietnam was determined to unify the country under its control, and the United States was determined to support the South Vietnam government or a new government set up by free elections.[10] After a long and costly war involving extensive bombing of North Vietnam, a truce was negotiated in 1973 under President Nixon, and the United States withdrew its forces. In the spring of 1975 North Vietnam flagrantly violated the terms of the truce by a full-fledged invasion with its regular forces and within a few weeks had won the war and taken control of the South. By this time the United States was so tired of the war that it accepted the outcome.

The United Nations was virtually powerless in this war. Neither side wanted to yield, and did not want to turn over the issue to UN mediation or arbitration. In the early stages of the war, U.S. leaders believed the United States, as the most powerful nation in the world, could defeat the insurgency without complications of UN involvement. France, Britain, and other allies did not want to commit their forces since they had a realistic view of the political and military costs involved.

The United States lost the war because its political system would not have accepted the use of nuclear weapons in that conflict or the conventional escalation needed to "win." Moreover, a conventional escalation to attack North Vietnam might have again triggered participation of Chinese "volunteers," as happened in the Korean War. The result was a victory for North Vietnam and a stunning defeat for South Vietnam and the United States.[11]

Vietnam's Invasion of Kampuchea (Cambodia)

In the closing days of the Vietnam War, a radical Communist movement, the Khmer Rouge, overthrew the military government of Cambodia and imposed a repressive regime. In purging its country of "bourgeois elements," the Khmer Rouge caused the deaths of over 1 million Cambodians, as dramatized in the movie *The Killing Fields*. Its regime challenged the forces of the new Communist government of Vietnam in border clashes. At the end of 1978 about 120,000 Vietnamese troops invaded Kampuchea. Within a few days, Vietnam had established a puppet regime headed by Heng Samrin, a Communist defector from the Khmer Rouge. On February 19, 1979, Vietnam provided a *post facto* legal facade for the invasion by concluding a treaty providing for all necessary assistance by Vietnam when requested by the government of Kampuchea.

The world then watched in amazement as China and Vietnam, formerly allies in the Vietnam War, quarreled over Kampuchea. The Soviet Union lined up on the side of Vietnam, and China with Kampuchea. The Vietnamese propaganda claimed the Kampuchean people had faced extinction by the "monstrous neocolonialist regime imposed by Peking," and that the Vietnamese people could not refuse aid requested of them by the Kampuchean people. China, in the Security Council, denounced the "flagrant" military aggression of Vietnam, claiming its aim was to establish a colonial empire.

The bulk of the Khmer Rouge forces eluded the invading Vietnamese forces and began a campaign of opposition to the invaders. China continued to supply these forces through Thailand, while Vietnam strengthened its alliance with the Soviet Union, which provided large-scale aid.

The Vietnamese-Cambodian war escalated as Chinese forces invaded Vietnam's northern provinces on February 17, 1979. In the 17-day war, about 250,000 Chinese troops drove about 12 miles inside Vietnam causing extensive damage and tens of thousands of casualties. The Chinese announced their troops were sent to "teach a lesson" to the Vietnamese invaders of Kampuchea and to end its incursions into China. China was also retaliating against the Vietnamese government, which had forced over 170,000 ethnic Chinese to flee the country by nationalizing their shops and by other repressive actions.

After 17 days of bitter fighting and strong resistance by Vietnam, China announced that its mission was completed and withdrew from North Vietnam. During the conflict Moscow supported Vietnam by threatening China and airlifting supplies, and sent a naval task force to the South China Sea.[12]

Vietnam's aggression appeared aimed at achieving the historic aim of

Vietnam's Communist party of creating a federation out of the former area of French Indochina. China's reply was classic power politics aimed at forcing Vietnam to withdraw from Kampuchea and weakening the Vietnamese alliance with the Soviet Union, which threatened China. In the sense that it was helping defend Kampuchea and opposing aggression, it could be argued that China's action was supporting collective self-defense consistent with international law. The UN General Assembly accepted credentials of the old Khmer Rouge government and refused to seat the representatives of the new Kampuchean regime, regarding it as a puppet of the Vietnamese aggressors. As the former Communist allies quarreled, China supported Thailand to deter an attack from Vietnam and drew closer to the United States. China continued to supply the Kampuchean resistance forces through Thailand.

The Southeast Asian neighbors of Cambodia involved the United Nations, and encouraged peace talks in international meetings that included the United States, the Soviet Union, Britain, China, and other major powers along with a representative of the UN secretary general. In October 1991 the talks finally bridged the gap between Prince Sihanouk, former prime minister and a spokesman for the resistance, and Hung Sen, the prime minister of Kampuchea.

The final peace agreement provided for the most expensive UN peacekeeping operation in history, with about 16,000 participating. The annual cost was about $2 billion. The UN was tasked with disarming about 300,000 troops including the Khmer Rouge, helping resettle about 350,000 refugees from Thailand, overseeing government ministries, organizing free elections, and helping clear over one million mines. An advance UN mission arrived in November 1991 and large numbers of advisers and peacekeeping troops arrived the following spring. Observers described the task as "mission impossible." The political hatreds arising from the Cambodian holocaust would interfere with forming a representative government in the exhausted nation. The UN force, at least initially, brought an end to the war.

The Iran-Iraq War

Border skirmishes between Iran and Iraq escalated into a war in September 1980. The official reason for the war was Iraq's demand for control of the Shatt-al-Arab waterway, which divides the two countries and provides access to the Persian Gulf. Iraq asserted it wanted to extend its control to the entire waterway and not just half of it from a line drawn down the middle.

The real issues appeared to be historic hatreds, religious differences, and Iraq's desire to take over Arab leadership in the Gulf area. Iraq saw an opportunity to attack Iran, which was weakened by isolation of its government because of the call of its religious leader, Ayatollah Khomeini, for revolution throughout the Middle East (Map. 4). Iran was also weakened by the arms and economic embargo mounted by the United States in retaliation for Iran's seizure of over 50 diplomatic hostages, and by the overwhelming condemnation of Iran in the Security Council and General Assembly for this act.[13]

The Security Council repeatedly called for a cease-fire, and the secretary general, working with the Islamic League, tried to mediate in the war. However, Khomeini's insistence that the president of Iraq be replaced and that a huge indemnity be paid blocked progress in the negotiations.[14] The war continued in a bloody stalemate, despite the use of poison gas by Iraq, which was condemned by the Security Council. The superpowers and nations in the area realized that as long as one side did not break the stalemate and decisively defeat the other side, the balance of power in the area would not be disrupted. The UN members watched with apprehension, but they could see no lever to force a settlement. They had no stomach for forcefully confronting the fanatical religious and nationalistic emotions involved.

Finally, in the fall of 1988 after defeats of his troops and unrest in Iran, Khomeini announced he was ready to accept the "poison" of a peace settlement.[15] The UN secretary general helped negotiate a cease-fire in line with Security Council resolution 598. It also established a peacekeeping force, the United Nation Iran-Iraq Military Observer Group, to monitor the cease-

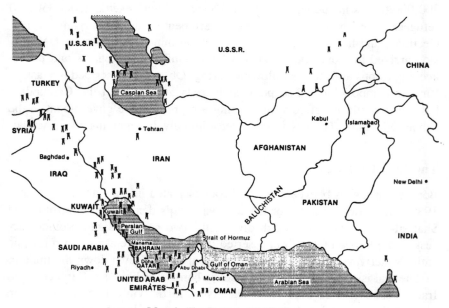

Map 4. The Strategic Middle East

fire. In 1992 the cease-fire was still holding, although no lasting peace had been achieved.

The Soviet Invasion of Afghanistan

The Soviet invasion of Afghanistan in 1979 challenged the United Nations with a new dimension of aggression. The UN in not repelling aggression by a permanent member of the Security Council reached a nadir, but within a few years it had not only recovered but attained a new level of respect. Underlying this change were the dramatic anti-Communist revolutions in Eastern Europe and the break-up of the Soviet empires.

A Communist coup in Afghanistan in 1978 was followed by a period of unrest and opposition by the Islamic mujahidin, nationalistic Muslims who had attacked and killed Russian military advisers trying to help the new Communist government establish order. After another coup in September 1979 a new president named Amin came to power, who, although he was a Communist, was not trusted by the Soviets. During the Christmas holidays of 1979 about 50,000 Soviet forces invaded, killing Amin and putting an old rival, Babrak Karmal, in his place. The Soviet invasion was so quick there was no opportunity for the Afghanistan government to appeal for help.[16]

The world was shocked by the brutal invasion, and 52 states called for a Security Council meeting. The United States sponsored a Security Council resolution of January 7, 1980, deploring the intervention and calling for immediate withdrawal of foreign troops from Afghanistan. The vote was 12 to 2 with five non-aligned nations joining in the affirmative vote, and with only East Germany, a Soviet satellite, voting with the Soviets. The Council under the uniting-for-peace procedure sent the issue to the General Assembly, which by a vote of 104 to 18 called for the withdrawal of foreign troops from Afghanistan. The new Afghani representative, appointed by the Karmal government, joined with the Soviets in opposing the resolutions. Cuba, by voting with the Soviet Union, lost respect and its chance for the Security Council seat it had been trying to obtain. Cuba realized at that point its candidacy was hopeless and withdrew, letting Mexico take the seat.

The United States, to show its disapproval, sharply cut back exports of grain to the minimum specified in its trade agreement with the Soviets, cut back further on exports of high-technology goods, and organized a boycott of 65 nations of the Olympic Games in Moscow the following summer. President Carter also withdrew consideration of the SALT II treaty from the Senate, and it was never again considered, although Presidents Carter and Reagan continued to observe the SALT II limits until 1986. The invasion destroyed détente, and the Cold War intensified.

During the fighting the U.S. Congress openly appropriated hundreds of millions of dollars for the resistance.[17] The Soviets and the Afghanistan government accused the United States of doing everything to intensify "subversive" activities and to prevent normalization of the situation with the aim of returning power to big landowners and local feudal chieftains. The United States replied that it was prepared to guarantee a comprehensive settlement consistent with General Assembly resolutions and predicated upon complete withdrawal of Soviet troops. The United States, moreover, insisted that its actions were in accord with international law since it was assisting legitimate opposition to aggressive action.[18]

Meanwhile, the United Nations, under the authority of the General Assembly, kept the matter on its agenda. It continued to pass with huge majorities resolutions calling for withdrawal of foreign forces from Afghanistan and expressing support for negotiations by the secretary general to find a solution. Mr. Perez de Cuellar, who began UN negotiations for peace, became UN secretary general on January 1, 1982, and appointed Diego Cordovez, under-secretary general for special political affairs, as his personal representative to continue the negotiations. Negotiations continued under the auspices of the United Nations between Afghanistan and Pakistan, which was burdened by over two million Afghani refugees. By 1986 four agreements were drafted that would require withdrawal of foreign troops, guarantees of non-intervention, and the voluntary return of refugees. Most issues were resolved, but the agreements stalled on when the Soviets would withdraw and arrange to implement the agreements.[19] On April 14, 1988, final agreement was reached and the accords were signed by Pakistan, Afghanistan, the Soviet Union, and the United States.

The agreements included provisions for the secretary general to appoint two headquarters units made up of existing UN operations and a small civilian staff that would be organized into inspection teams. The four countries signing the agreements pledged to give full cooperation to the secretary general and his personnel. The agreements also provided for Afghanistan and Pakistan to facilitate the voluntary return of all Afghani refugees staying in Pakistan. In a separate letter of April 15 Iran stated it supported those elements in Afghanistan who opposed the agreements, and that there should be an unconditional withdrawal of forces and a true representative government established by the Muslim people and the Afghani refugees. The Soviet withdrawal proceeded on schedule in 1988.[20]

The United States and the Soviet Union agreed to stop supplying arms to the opposing sides, but the civil war continued until the spring of 1992. At that time the rebel forces finally defeated the Communist government. The UN representatives assisted in forming a coalition government of the rebel political and military groups, which intermittently continued to fight among themselves.

Other Wars and Conflicts

There were other, minor conflicts that received much attention and also involved disregard for the norms of international law. In some the United Nations acted as a mediator. These other conflicts included the following:

In 1964 and again in 1974 a civil war erupted between Turkish and Greek communities on the highly strategic country of Cyprus. Forces of Turkey invaded in 1974 and took over control of part of the island for the Turkish minorities. The Security Council at the request of Cyprus and the British, who maintained a base on the island, met and agreed to send peacekeeping forces to separate the combatants. The Security Council established a peace-keeping force of 7,000 soldiers, which managed to contain the violence. Despite repeated efforts the United Nations had not brokered a settlement by the fall of 1992.[21]

On October 25, 1983, President Reagan surprised his nation and most of the world by ordering an invasion of Grenada, a small nation of less than 100,000 people, at the eastern entrance of the Caribbean. Previously, he had expressed concern about strong Communist influence in the government and about the construction of a large airport in the eastern Caribbean that could be used for military purposes. His justification was flimsy—that the United States was protecting American medical students and that neighboring nations had asked for the intervention. The invasion was condemned in an Organization of American States resolution. The UN Security Council, after a veto, passed the issue to the General Assembly, which deplored armed intervention, calling it a flagrant violation of international law. The vote was 108 for this resolution with 9 against and 27 abstentions. The U.S. forces withdrew a few weeks after the invasion, and a non-Communist government was set up with free elections. The people of Grenada appeared to welcome the U.S. action.[22]

In April 1986 the United States challenged Libya's claim to the Gulf of Sidra by sending U.S. naval units to the area. When Libya attacked U.S. planes with antiaircraft missiles, the United States responded by attacking military targets. The Security Council met four times without taking action. The Chinese delegate summarized the international law case against the United States by stating that the military maneuvers aggravated tensions. Both countries should solve problems, he said, in line with the Charter without the use of force. A month later the United States bombed what it called terrorist installations in Libya, in retaliation for a terrorist attack in Berlin in which a U.S. soldier had been killed. Nine of the Security Council members condemned the bombing, but the United States, France, and Britain vetoed the resolution. The General Assembly also condemned the bombing by a vote of 79 to 28 with 33 abstentions. The U.S. State Department's legal case that the U.S. action was justified in self-defense was not persuasive for the vote.[23]

In 1990 Pan Am Flight 103 was bombed with 270 killed. Investigators were able to trace the perpetrators to Libya. In March 1992 the United States obtained Security Council support (10 to 0 with five abstentions) for an air embargo against Libya, because of its refusal to cooperate in determining responsibility (turn over suspects for trial in the United States or Great Britain) for that terrorist bombing. The air embargo hurt Libya, but not nearly as much as an economic embargo would. By the summer of 1992 the UN Security Council action had brought forth proposed compromises by Libya for the trial, but the dispute was not settled.

At the end of 1989 U.S. forces invaded Panama to capture its military leader for trial on narcotics charges. The Security Council's resolution demanding withdrawal was defeated by a veto of the United States, Great Britain, and France. The General Assembly stayed in session over Christmas and voted 75 to 20 to demand a U.S. pull-out. The United States withdrew after installing a new president in Panama, who reportedly had been kept from the presidency by election fraud. The withdrawal did not prevent the additional blot on the U.S. record for violating international law.

THE UNITED NATIONS AND THE NEW ORDER

President Bush, former U.S. Ambassador to the United Nations, in mobilizing the coalition to repel Iraq's attack on Kuwait, stayed within the limits of UN Security Council resolutions. As the conflict began, he called for a new order in the world and respect for international law. Although questions remained about whether the overwhelming use of force in Kuwait was in the spirit of the Charter, the United States and its coalition waged war within limits of Security Council resolutions. Pundits said the United Nations was finally taking over the role envisaged by the Charter. Liberal internationalists, who support international law, were encouraged, although the same pundits underplayed UN accomplishments before the Kuwait War.

Repelling Iraq's Attack on Kuwait

Saddam Hussein, president of Iraq, at the beginning of August ordered his forces to invade Kuwait, one of the wealthiest oil nations of the Persian Gulf. The attack took the world by surprise since Iraq had suffered heavy casualties and had just been forced to make peace after its long and unsuccessful war against Iran. Kuwait was a small country with a population of about 2 million compared to Iraq's 18 million. The Kuwait military was able to make only token resistance. Saddam Hussein asserted Kuwait was rightfully part of Iraq and vowed he would never give it up.

The United States immediately called a meeting of the UN Security Council, which condemned the invasion and demanded withdrawal of the Iraqi troops. The invasion not only took over a major share of oil production of the Gulf area, but Iraq's huge buildup of troops threatened the Saudi Arabian oil fields concentrated 200 miles further down the coast (Map 4). The Saudi military did not immediately intervene and appeared to be no match for the Iraqi troops, who had been seasoned by about 10 years of war with Iraq. After a few days of consultation with Saudi Arabia the United States ordered a massive buildup of U.S. troops in Saudi Arabia in the areas facing Kuwait.

The Security Council acted quickly and after several hours of debate passed the first of a series of over a dozen resolutions condemning the Iraqi invasion and calling for assistance to Kuwait. The most controversial resolution was 678, which was passed with a great deal of pressure by the United States. The resolution referred to Chapter VII of the Charter with its provisions for enforcement and added the following: 1) Demands that Iraq comply fully with Resolution 660 and all subsequent relevant resolutions and decides, while maintaining all its decisions, to allow Iraq one final opportunity, as a pause of goodwill to do so. 2) Authorizes member states cooperating with the government of Kuwait, unless Iraq on or before January 15, 1991, fully implements the foregoing resolutions, to use all necessary means to uphold and implement the Security Council Resolution 660 and all subsequent relevant resolutions and to restore international peace and security in the area. 3) Requests all states to provide appropriate support. 4) Requests the states concerned to keep the Council informed of actions under the resolution.

It was not difficult for the United Nations to condemn aggression—the United Nations had done this many times—and to demand that Iraq withdraw. Amazingly, Secretary Baker and President Bush were able to convince the Security Council to set the January 15 deadline and to authorize "all necessary means" to enforce its resolutions. This allowed countries to use force without a UN command, as in Korea, although they were still bound by Security Council resolutions. President Bush did not want to place American soldiers in combat under UN control.

It was essential to get the approval of the Soviet Union for the UN vote, since it had a veto and since it had been a former ally of Iraq. Secretary Baker did this with hours of persuasion of Gorbachev and Foreign Minister Shevardnadze. Shortly after Soviet approval, the President authorized shipment of $1 billion worth of food to the Soviet Union. He persuaded China to abstain, and within a few days the President rewarded China by allowing the Chinese foreign minister to meet with the president, thus ending the U.S. ban on high-level meetings imposed after the Tiananmen Square tragedy. Reportedly a threat of suspension of aid was used to try to get approval of at least one other member of the Security Council.

The following consideration was important in approval of the deadline for Iraq's withdrawal. Why should other countries object to the United States' desire to fight their war against aggression and to maintain their supply of oil? Only Britain and Canada of the other 14 Security Council members supplied sizeable forces to the Gulf, and those were far below their share in proportion to population. The French contingent was much smaller. The other eleven countries of the Security Council supplied no military manpower and only token contingents. Thus, the United States with a major diplomatic effort twisted arms to get the UN resolution passed to let the United States carry the major burden of the war against Iraq.

After several weeks of bombing, the coalition of forces led by the United States defeated the Iraqi forces in a 5-day blitzkrieg. The UN coalition did not occupy Iraqi territory, but withdrew to Kuwait. Iraq suffered at least 20,000 deaths of military and civilians, while the U.S. coalition lost about 150. Iraq suffered heavy bombing damage, but Saddam Hussein remained defiant. During the following year of threats and pressures by the Security Council he admitted UN inspectors and allowed destruction of long-range rockets and facilities that could be used to make nuclear and chemical weapons.[24] Kuwait with its huge financial resources stopped the oil well fires and rebuilt from destruction of the war and vandalism of the Iraqi forces.

It was a dramatic victory for U.S. forces and the UN coalition. Saddam Hussein's military forces were decimated. The United Nations authorized forces to occupy northern Iraq to protect the Kurdish minority, which wanted to break off from Iraq. Egypt and other Arab troops under the UN umbrella played a major role in fighting Iraqi forces, which prevented Hussein from exploiting considerable support from Arab masses who resented Western intervention. After the war IAEA inspectors destroyed large quantities of Iraq's weapons and facilities for making weapons of mass destruction (see page 102). Although Hussein remained defiant, his fangs were pulled and he no longer was a military threat to his neighbors.

Central American Conflicts

When President Reagan took office, Nicaragua was dominated by a pro-Communist government. He authorized the CIA to support insurgents (Contras) against the government, and threatened it with U.S. maneuvers in neighboring Honduras. Beginning in 1982 Nicaragua succeeded in getting votes against the United States by the Security Council and the General Assembly and a ruling by the World Court against U.S. support for the Contras. The United States originally claimed it was trying to block shipments of arms by Nicaragua to insurgents trying to overthrow the El Salvador government, but the United States obviously aimed at overthrowing the pro-Communist Nicaraguan government. The Security Council and General Assembly condemned U.S. intervention and urged support of attempts of the Contadora group (Costa Rica, Mexico, Panama, Guatemala, and Honduras) to negotiate a solution. It did reach an agreement that involved the UN Mission for the Verification of Elections to monitor February 1990 elections. Violetto Charmarro won those elections and took office. The Sandinistas stepped down and became the parliamentary opposition, although they still controlled the armed forces.

Meanwhile, in El Salvador the government and the insurgents had agreed to the UN secretary general's mediation. The United States grudgingly supported the above mediation efforts of the Contadora group and the United Nations, while expressing pessimism about their effectiveness. Nevertheless, Secretary General Perez de Cuellar (from Venezuela) persisted, and on January 2, 1992, he mediated an end to the civil wars and arranged for the United Nations to monitor government reforms. The above successes reflected not only efforts of the United Nations, but the fading of the Cold War and ending of Soviet support to Cuba and the insurgents in Central America.

Yugoslavia's Civil War

In 1991 the Security Council in a major change of policy intervened with peacekeeping forces to end a civil war in Yugoslavia. The success of democratic revolutions in Eastern Europe had encouraged Yugoslavia's republics, which were dominated by non-Serbs, to break away from the Serbian-dominated, Communist-oriented central government. Anti-Communist slogans against the central government were added to their ethnic motives in the civil war that followed. At first the Security Council followed Article 1 (7) of the Charter, which prohibits intervention in matters within the domestic jurisdiction of a state, which includes civil wars. However, under international law if a civil war threatens international peace, the United Nations would have a right to intervene. The Yugoslav war met that test. Europeans remembered World War I started with an assassination involving Serbia. Moreover, Yugoslavia had ethnic groups with ties to other countries including Hungarians, Germans, Albanians, and Moslems.

Serious fighting broke out in the summer of 1991 as the northern republics of Slovenia and Croatia declared their independence, and the federal army fought to take over Serbian communities in Slovenia and Croatia. European Community representatives tried and failed to mediate a cease-fire. After European Community representatives tried and failed with 13 truces, the matter was turned over to the Security Council. Yugoslavia in a letter welcomed the Security Council meeting, stating the crisis threatened peace on a large scale. Cyrus Vance, former U.S. Secretary of State, was named as mediator and negotiated a successful cease-fire. The Security Council placed peacekeeping units, 14,000 strong in the area. The initial estimate of the cost was $634 million per year. The war by then had taken about 4,000 lives and made more than 500,000 people homeless. UN forces began establishing order in disputed areas of Croatia and Slovenia.[25]

Bosnia-Herzegovina then claimed independence. It consisted of three major communities—Moslem 40 percent, Serbs 33 percent, and Croats 18 percent. In a referendum boycotted by Serbs, an overwhelming majority voted for independence, but Serbian military units attacked, aiming to absorb the Serbian communities in Bosnia-Herzegovina. At least initially Serbian units were supported by the truncated Yugoslav government, although it disclaimed responsibility. The Serbian units attacked Serbian communities of Bosnia-Herzegovina to force evacuation of Moslems. The term "ethnic cleansing" was used to describe Serbian policy, and accounts of Serbian killings of the Moslem minorities had overtones of Hitler's racism.

The world was shocked as Serbian units attacked civilian targets and laid siege to Sarajevo, the capital of Bosnia-Herzegovina. It fought back and called on the United Nations for assistance. In May 1992 the Security Council imposed strict economic sanctions, including stopping oil shipments, and demanded that the fighting stop. However, the Serbian military units controlling Sarajevo's airport prevented planes from bringing relief supplies to Sarajevo, and attacked UN and Red Cross convoys of food for the civilian population. The new Secretary General Boutros-Ghali on Friday, June 26, reported that the Serbs were breaking a cease-fire by tank and artillery attacks against civilians. The Security Council publicly supported his public warning that the Security Council would meet on Monday, July 1, "to determine what other means would be necessary to bring relief to the suffering people of Sarajevo." That weekend President Mitterand broke the siege by personally flying to Sarajevo with relief supplies. The United States and the European countries sent air and naval units and infantry to protect convoys of relief supplies.

The United Nations began sending convoys of relief supplies to other parts of Bosnia-Herzegovina, but fighting continued. The United Nations was faced with the dilemma that fighting was carried out by local units that the Serbian government said it did not control. The Security Council demanded inspection of prison camps because of atrocity stories, and a number of camps were opened to inspection. On August 10 it authorized using any means necessary to deliver relief supplies. The United States called for setting up a war-crimes commission, modelled after the 1943 commission on Nazi war crimes, to collect evidence for trials. The Security Council approved it on October 7, 1992, but id did not set up a tribunal.

The UN High Commissioner for Refugees called an international conference in Geneva on July 29, 1992, for what was described as the largest flow of refugees in Europe since World War II. Germany had absorbed most of the refugees and Britain and France hardly any. The unfinished tragedy that the UN had to address was that the Serbs were gaining their goal of expelling Moslems from their homes in order to create a greater Serbia of Serbs.

POWER BROKERS VERSUS LIBERAL INTERNATIONALISTS

The Security Council and the General Assembly routinely condemn intervention outside limits of international law, including support of insurgencies. Nevertheless, before 1989 world leaders of great powers resorted to power politics to protect what they believed were their important interests. The Soviet Union, Eastern Europe, and Cuba gave material and ideological support to revolutionary movements in the Middle East, Africa, Latin America, and Asia. Arab countries provided support to Palestinian and other groups attacking Israeli targets. The United States gave military support in the Bay of Pigs attack against Cuba in 1961, and during the Reagan administration invaded Grenada and gave support to the Contras' battle against the Nicaraguan government. The U.S. actions were freely admitted and featured in the world's news media.

The Security Council and the General Assembly condemned the above types of intervention. The General Assembly's Declaration on Friendly Relations of 1970 and its Definition of Aggression of 1974 state that every state should refuse to assist terrorist acts against another state or help insurgent movements against another state. This is an elaboration of Article 2, Paragraph 4 of the Charter, which prohibits the use of force against the territorial integrity or political independence of any state. General Assembly and Security Council majorities supported many resolutions condemning such acts. However, the brutal fact of international relations was that neither the superpowers nor many of their allies were willing to give up the use of force in international politics and support the norms of international law.

Although the United Nations did not prevent all international violence, it played a major role in containing wars and bringing them to an end. It helped prevent troops of the superpowers and their close allies from confrontations and battling each other. Where the United States gave strong support to the UN peace process, the United Nations was successful in almost every case in helping bring an end to major wars. This included the Korean War, the Arab-Israeli Wars, the Congo War, the Iraq-Iran War, and the India-Pakistan War of 1971. In these and other cases of aggression the third-world countries voted against the aggressor, including cases where the United States intervened, such as Nicaragua and Grenada.

As the Cold War ended, the United Nations was supporting the following peacekeeping operations and personnel under Secretary General Perez de Cuellar: Angola, El Salvador, Western Sahara, and Iraq-Kuwait in addition to ongoing ones in Lebanon, the Golan Heights, Cyprus, India-Pakistan, and areas along the borders of Israel with Arab states (UNTSO). In 1992 the new secretary general, Boutros-Ghali, added units for Somalia, Cambodia, and Yugoslavia (Table 1).

Successes of the above UN operations in containing conflicts contrasted with failures of power politics. North Korea and North Vietnam were devastated by wars they started. the Soviets were forced to withdraw after their invasion of Afghanistan. They used force to control Eastern Europe but resentment exploded and broke up their empire in 1989. Vietnam also was forced to withdraw after a costly war in Cambodia. Iraq was devastated by its wars against Iran and Kuwait.

The United States failed to defend South Vietnam outside the UN framework, and it was forced to withdraw from Vietnam after failing to turn back attacks of North Vietnam. It was also forced out of Lebanon after it tried to set up international patrols there outside the framework of the United Nations. The U.S. support of the Contras against Nicaragua was closed out by the Contadora agreement to set up a democratic government. Terrorism against U.S. targets did not decrease after its bombing of Libya in 1986.[26]

Why did nations' leaders insist on the use of force? One reason is the United Nations is a political instrument, and successful settlement of wars often take much time and palaver. This helps explain former U.S. presidents' impatience with the UN system, and their inclination to take action outside the United Nations. However, it is significant that in the Cuban missile crisis, one of the most serious crises of our era, President Kennedy took steps to ask the UN secretary general to play a mediating role.

After 1989 a number of developments converged to bring the United Nations again to the center of action on matters of war and peace. The huge increases in public debt made U.S. leaders realize they could no longer afford to be the world's policeman.[27] Secretary of State Baker was forced to solicit tens of billions of dollars to help finance the cost of the U.S. military action to defend Kuwait. The anti-Communist revolutions beginning in 1989 destroyed the Soviet external and internal empires and ended the Cold War. The Russians were anxious to support the UN and international law because their power base was decimated. President Bush, a former UN ambassador, realized the potential of the United Nations for mobilizing countries to action and removing the stigma of U.S. superpower domination of diplomatic moves. He was aided by a very competent secretary of state. The above trends came together with the dramatic defeat of Iraq's aggression.

Within 3 years the United States changed from flouting international law in attacks on Libya, Grenada, and Panama, to one of the strongest supporters of international law. In the conflicts in Yugoslavia the United States led the world in calling on the United Nations to intervene. The United States was committing itself to its own slogan of a new world order of reliance on the United Nations and international law. It would be regarded as a hypocrite if it resumed its old power politics.

The next chapter examines the network of nuclear arms control agreements.

Notes to Chapter 5

1. B. Urquart, *Hammarskjold* (New York: Harper, 1972), Chapters 15, 16, 18, 21.

2. Ibid., pp. 54–55.

3. Ibid., pp. 462–470.

4. U.S. Congress, Senate Select Committee, *Alleged Assassination Plots Involving Foreign Leaders* (Washington, DC: Government Printing Office, 1975); A. Schlesinger, *A Thousand Days* (New York: Fawcett, 1965), pp. 223–243; D. Phillips, *The Night Watch* (New York: Ballantine, 1977), Chap. iv; R. Garthoff, *Reflections on the Cuban Missile Crisis* (Washington, DC: Brookings, 1987).

5. Garthoff, *Reflections,* pp. 54–55.

6. Ibid., pp. 6–7.

7. J. Stoessinger, *Why Nations Go to War* (New York: St. Martins, 1974), p. 163.

8. *Everyone's United Nations* (New York: U.S. Office of Public Information) and the *U.N. Chronicle* are excellent sources giving the factual framework of UN actions. The annual *U.S. Participation in the U.N.,* published by the U.S. Department of State, also gives a factual account of the U.S. position on UN issues. See also H. Kissinger, *White House Years* (Boston: Little, Brown, 1979), Chapter XXI, and A. Yoder, *World Politics and the Causes of War Since 1914* (Lanham, MD: University Press of America, 1986).

9. M. Gravel, *The Pentagon Papers* (Boston: Beacon Press, 1971).

10. L. Johnson, *The Vantage Point* (New York: Popular Library, 1971), p. 127.

11. G. Herring, *America's Longest War* (New York: John Wiley, 1979); L. Gelb and R. Betts, *The Irony of Vietnam* (Washington, DC: Brookings, 1979); and P. Poole, *The United States and Indochina from FDR to Nixon* (Hinsdale, IL: Dryden, 1973).

12. G. Porter, "The Sino-Soviet Conflict in Southeast Asia," *Current History,* December 1978; S. Simon, "Kampuchea: Vietnam's Vietnam," *Current History,* December 1979.

13. A. Dawisha, "Iraq, The West's Opportunity," *Foreign Policy,* Winter 1981, pp.

134–153; A. Khomeini, *Ayatollah Khomeini: On Issues Related to the Struggle of the Muslim People of Iran,* Embassy of the Islamic Republic of Iran, November 29, 1979.

14. *New York Times,* July 30, 1980.

15. Dawisha, *Iraq,* pp. 124–153. Khomeini, "Ayatollah."

16. Z. Khalilzad, "Afghanistan and the Crisis in American Foreign Policy," *Survival* (International Institute for Strategic Studies, July/August 1980), p. 152; U.S. Department of State, "Soviet Dilemmas in Afghanistan," June 1980.

17. *Washington Post,* January 12, 1985.

18. *U.N. Chronicle,* June 1988, pp. 4–17.

19. *Foreign Affairs,* American and the World 1985.

20. *U.N. Chronicle,* June 1988, pp. 4–17.

21. J. M. Murphy, *The United Nations and the Control of International Violence* (Totowa, NJ: Towman and Allenheld, 1982), p. 46.

22. P. Seabury and W. McDougall, *The Grenada Papers* (San Francisco: Institute of Contemporary Studies, 1984).

23. A. Sofaer, "Terrorism and the Law," *Foreign Affairs,* Spring 1986.

24. *U.N. Chronicle,* June 1992, pp. 24–28.

25. *U.N. Chronicle,* December 1991, pp. 35–36; *U.N. Chronicle,* March 1992, pp. 72–73; J. Tessitore and S. Woolfson (ed.), *A Global Agenda* (Lanham: University Press of America, 1992), pp. 4–16.

26. *The Economist,* July 26, 1986, p. 32.

27. Secretary of State Baker's testimony before the Senate Foreign Relations Committee, June 23, 1992.

Chapter VI

THE NETWORK OF NUCLEAR ARMS CONTROL AGREEMENTS

After World War II international politics centered on the Cold War and the ultimate threat of a nuclear holocaust. World leaders looked into the abyss several times during the Cuban missile crisis and other crises. In the era of the nuclear threat there was a running debate on how to avoid nuclear war. Strategists of the nuclear powers believed in deterrence, which meant frightening potential enemies. During the ensuing arms race the Soviets and the United States made about 50,000 nuclear warheads, each one capable of destroying a city. Other leaders, reflecting the force of public opinion, including pressures by UN bodies, believed the way to peace was to negotiate limits on nuclear weapons, and some said they hoped eventually to abolish all nuclear weapons. Perceptive observers bridged the two strategies by stating that the process of negotiating nuclear arms agreements was more important than the agreements themselves. They said that leaders who are negotiating arrangements to abolish weapons and to avoid a nuclear holocaust are not likely to initiate such a war. After the democratic revolutions of 1989, the process permitted drastic reductions in nuclear arsenals and helped end the Cold War. After the Cold War ended, negotiators then shifted their attention to chemical weapons of mass destruction, which are much easier and cheaper to make and much more difficult to control.

The Russians initiated the arms reduction process at the beginning of this century. There was no progress until after World War I, and those efforts ended with the outbreak of World War II. Beginning with the 1960s a network of over a dozen important nuclear arms control agreements were negotiated and put into effect. Many of these agreements were linked with UN agreements. In the 1980s the Reagan administration accepted the agreements but did not extend the network until toward the end of its term. In the summer of 1986 President Reagan was so concerned that U.S. security was undermined by proposed limits of the second strategic arms limitation treaty (SALT II), he announced the United States would no longer honor those ceilings on strategic nuclear missiles. In October 1986, however, at a meeting in Iceland, President Reagan and General Secretary Gorbachev revived the nuclear arms negotiating process, and a historic agreement abolishing all intermediate-range missiles was ratified in Moscow in June 1988. After the 1989 democratic revolutions, negotiations accelerated to the point it was difficult to keep track of nuclear arms reductions.

EARLY EFFORTS AT LIMITING ARMS

The Russian Tsar took the initiative at the beginning of the century to call the two Hague Conferences of 1899 and 1907. These conferences are not taken seriously today because of the cataclysm of World War I that followed, but events precipitating that war showed the potential of the conference process for preventing war. (See also chapter 2.) The Russian Tsar probably was inspired to call the Hague Conferences by his great-grandfather who had concluded the Holy Alliance. That alliance, which had been proposed in 1815, called for the great powers to base their relations upon the "sublime truths" of the Christian religion. The Holy Alliance is often confused with the Quadruple Alliance of that time, which was used to suppress radical movements that could threaten the principal monarchs of Europe.

The 1899 invitation was accepted by all 26 major governments to whom it was addressed, including the United States. Three major conventions were adopted relating to the pacific settlement of international conflicts, the laws of war, and maritime warfare. Three additional declarations were adopted that prohibited launching projectiles and explosives from balloons, using poison gas, and using dumdum bullets. The Convention on the Pacific Settlement of Disputes obligated powers to solve disputes by legal methods including a commission of inquiry and arbitration. It established a Permanent Court of Arbitration with a panel of arbitrators for this purpose. During the next 15 years three major disputes were settled by the court.

The Tsar called a follow-up conference in 1907, which was attended by 54 nations including those from Latin America. Important conventions were adopted again on the pacific settlement of international disputes and restriction of force for recovering contract debts as well as on laws of warfare. This conference agreed that the contracting powers should have recourse as far as possible to good offices or mediation of disputes by other powers. Unfortunately, the great powers did not observe these agreements, and they blundered into World War I as a result. Many historians and diplomats of that time believed that if the great powers could only have met together and discussed the relatively minor problem of the assassination of the Austrian archduke by Serbian terrorists who triggered the war, World War I could have been avoided. Periodic peace conferences obviously were not enough.

As indicated in Chapter II, the surviving leaders designed the League of Nations to remedy this gap by providing for a permanent organization of nations to prevent war. The Versailles Treaty, which established the League, also provided for strict limits on German rearmament including demilitarizing the Rhineland. The League Covenant called for measures of disarmament, and in the 1920s and particularly in the 1930s, there were major meetings to try to reach agreement on limiting arms. The Versailles Treaty and the negotiations sponsored by the League of Nations were shattered by the Axis powers in their drive for world domination.

The United States, whose failure to join the League seriously weakened it, demonstrated to the world that it did not need the League for measures of disarmament by calling the Washington Naval Conference of 1921 and 1922. Secretary of State Hughes, chairman of the conference, startled the delegates and the world by an audacious proposal to scrap major naval vessels of the three great powers so that their strength and tonnage would be left at a ratio of 5-5-3 (United States, United Kingdom, and Japan). This proposal involved the destruction of 30 American ships and a total of 66 ships with a total tonnage of almost 2 million tons. One British reporter stated that this was more than all the admirals of the world had sunk in a cycle of centuries.[1] After further negotiations, France and Italy joined with smaller limits on their ships. The agreement stayed in effect almost 15 years. It may be noted that the number and tonnage of naval ships was relatively easy to verify by counting, so that there was little suspicion that the limits would be exceeded. (Today, limits on strategic delivery systems like submarines and bombers are checked by counting by satellites.) In 1930 a subsequent treaty was signed in London that limited other classes of warships and provided for a third naval conference in 1935. The above naval treaties expired in 1936 following the Japanese refusal to continue the arrangements.

There was one other major arms limitation agreement of that era, the Geneva Protocol prohibiting the use of poison gas and bacteriological weapons in war. This was concluded in 1925, and it was generally observed during

World War II, although Italy used poison gas during the 1936 war against Ethiopia. The United States, however, did not ratify the agreement until 1975. One of the major issues in 1975 was whether riot control agents and herbicides were included, and the U.S. government when ratifying indicated that it did not consider these weapons covered by the protocol.[2]

The experience of the 1930s made a deep impression on that generation. Some were convinced that nations should rely on military strength including nuclear deterrence. Others were convinced that a strong international organization and persistent efforts to limit arms were the ways to peace. The initial efforts on arms control focused on controlling nuclear weapons.

FAILURES AFTER WORLD WAR II

The nuclear destruction of Hiroshima and Nagasaki at the close of World War II gave a new emphasis to arms control efforts. World War II was the first major war of our era in which civilians suffered many more deaths than the military, and it was evident with the nuclear weapons of destruction that world civilization was threatened if there should be another war. Most writers emphasize the terrible dimensions of the nuclear threat, and it is true that Hiroshima and Nagasaki demonstrated the awesome power of nuclear weapons. However, during the 1920s and 1930s there was a comparable fear of the threat of poison gas as demonstrated in World War I, but the threat of that terrible weapon did not deter war.

At the end of World War II there was hope that the two powerful victors could cooperate to establish a system of peace, but as indicated in previous chapters, the Cold War dominated international politics. It hindered but did not prevent slow progress toward nuclear arms control.

Article 26 of the UN Charter gives the Security Council the responsibility for formulating plans for disarmament, whereas Article II provides that the General Assembly may also consider this issue. The General Assembly in its first resolution, on January 24, 1946, established the International Atomic Energy Commission with instructions to submit proposals for the elimination of atomic weapons and other weapons of mass destruction. At its first meeting in June the United States submitted the Baruch Plan calling for an international authority to own all uranium mines and plants capable of producing atomic weapons. Inspection teams under the United Nations would not be subject to the great power veto of the Security Council. Many Americans took the plan seriously, not realizing that the proposal was a nonstarter from the beginning. Not only were suspicious hardliners in charge of negotiations, but in retrospect it is clear that the Soviets at that state in history would not have allowed inspectors free reign within their borders. The Soviets criticized the plan as a capitalist plot to interfere with Soviet industrial production. In fact, the U.S. president and his advisors anticipated that the Russians would not accept the control plan.[3] The verification and control issues have continued to be the most difficult to negotiate.

The Soviets countered with their own proposal and propagandistic peace campaign. They called for prohibiting the manufacture of nuclear weapons and destroying present stocks of weapons with no provisions for verification. Meanwhile, they pressed on with developing their own weapons and exploded their first atomic bomb in 1949, earlier than had been anticipated by the West. Their propaganda campaign continued with the World Peace Congress out in front supported by Communists and many well-meaning people anxious to eliminate the threat of nuclear war. Millions of signatures were mobilized under the Soviet campaign.

The victorious Western allies were anxious to include German armies in a defensive NATO alliance but at the same time to insure that Germany never again would be able to threaten aggression in Central Europe. They solved this dilemma by persuading the German authorities to accept the ABC Agreement, which is still in effect and which prohibits certain powers of the Brussels Pact (Netherlands, Belgium, Luxemburg, and Germany) from making or obtaining atomic, bacteriological, or chemical weapons. The Western European Union of 1948 succeeded the Brussels Pact. In 1955, with French fears alleviated, the Germans joined NATO and provided the major forces of that alliance. The Soviets countered with the Warsaw Pact.

Meanwhile, the Soviets, alarmed at German rearmament, proposed reducing conventional forces and destroying nuclear stockpiles. Their proposal provided for control posts at the big ports, railway junctions, motor roads, and airfields to see that no dangerous concentration of land, air, or naval forces was effected. Their proposals were not accepted by the NATO powers, which believed both German arms and nuclear arms were necessary for their defense.

The Soviets also advocated a nuclear test ban at this time. It had first been proposed by Prime Minister Nehru in 1954. The problem of verification prevented negotiations making headway since the United States was convinced with the technology of that era that it would require hundreds of inspectors to check on such an agreement.

In 1957 the Polish foreign minister, Adam Rapacke, called for a denuclearized zone in Central Europe. His proposal was to prohibit manufacturing or stockpiling of nuclear weapons or materials in East and West Germany, Poland, or Czechoslovakia. The West attacked the plan because it believed that it needed nuclear weapons based in Germany for the defense of Western Europe.

In 1958 the United States and the Soviet Union observed a voluntary nuclear test ban. In 1961 as a result of tensions over Berlin and other issues, the United States announced that it would no longer be bound by the informal agreement, and the Soviets then broke it by testing nuclear weapons. In 1963, however, as a result of the Soviet initiative, the Kennedy administration negotiated the partial nuclear test ban treaty, as indicated in the next section.

NUCLEAR ARMS AGREEMENTS SINCE TRUMAN

In its first meetings the General Assembly established a commission for negotiating disarmament of nuclear and conventional weapons. This and subsequent UN conferences with varying membership, usually meeting in Geneva, have pressured the major and minor powers to conclude agreements on disarmament. The most ambitious plans have failed to win approval of the major powers, but the General Assembly and its commissions have initiated action and mobilized support for the International Atomic Energy Agency (IAEA), the nonproliferation treaty, the Latin American nuclear weapon-free zone and seabeds treaty, the outer space treaty, and test ban treaties. These are described below. As yet the General Assembly has not succeeded in getting a comprehensive test ban treaty accepted, although the Soviet Union stopped its tests in 1986 in an attempt to persuade the United States also to stop.

The United Nations has also initiated and approved authoritative reports on the economic and social consequences of the arms race (1971 and 1977); a report on the ways of implementing an agreement on reducing military budgets (1974 and 1977); the effects of atomic radiation (1958, 1966, and 1969); and a comprehensive study on nuclear weapons (1980).

In 1961 the General Assembly declared that the use of nuclear weapons would violate the UN Charter. In 1964 when China exploded its first nuclear device, it announced that it would never be the first to use nuclear weapons. In 1982 at the second special General Assembly session on disarament (the first was in 1976), the foreign minister of the Soviet Union announced that his country would not be the first to use nuclear weapons, and he called for similar commitments from other nuclear states. The United States refused to make such a pledge, believing it was necessary to reserve the use of nuclear weapons for defending against possible Soviet aggression in Western Europe.

The UN commissions, the UN conferences on disarament, and the General Assembly have also called for a freeze in the production of nuclear weapons, and the General Assembly in 1982 called especially for the two major nuclear weapons states to proclaim an immediate freeze on the production and testing of nuclear weapons. The United States refused, pointing out that American and Western defensive strategy viewed nuclear weapons as a means of deterring war. In 1983 and 1984 the General Assembly adopted additional resolutions calling for a freeze.

The millions of words in meetings and reports of UN bodies proposing nuclear disarmament and freezes have had direct and indirect impacts on the negotiation of nuclear arms agreements. Set forth below are the highlights of the important agreements that were finally concluded after the ambitious Baruch Plan under President Truman failed to get support. The agreements are also listed and described in Table 2.

The first nuclear agreement established the important International Atomic Energy Agency (IAEA). President Eisenhower proposed it in a 1953 speech before the United Nations General Assembly as a means of promoting the peaceful use of nuclear energy by nonnuclear powers and discouraging the proliferation of nuclear weapons. By 1956 the draft of the agreement was unanimously approved by a conference at UN headquarters, and within three months it had been signed by 80 nations. In 1990 the IAEA had 112 members and a staff of 1,892. The IAEA's staff of inspectors monitors the use of nuclear materials for peaceful uses to see that they are not diverted for weapons, establishes safety standards, and provides technical advice. After the Chernobyl nuclear disaster in Russia in 1986, the IAEA inspected the site and offered advice on how to avoid future disasters of this nature. The IAEA was given the additional task of providing inspectors for the nonproliferation treaty, which was concluded 13 years after the IAEA treaty came into force.

For years the General Assembly discussed banning nuclear weapons from certain areas of the world. The first agreement of this nature was initiated under Eisenhower in 1958. The Antarctic Treaty, which prohibits nuclear weapons in that area, came out of the cooperation of 12 nations in the UN International Geophysical Year. The treaty calls for cooperation in Antarctic research with Specialized Agencies of the United Nations. Eisenhower, in an address to the General Assembly in 1960, also initiated the negotiation

Table 2
The Network of Nuclear Arms Agreements

Agreement and Date in Force	Comments
1. International Atomic Energy Agency. July 1957. Eisenhower	Promotes peaceful use of nuclear energy. Checks of NPT (see below). Reports to Security Council.
2. The Antarctic Treaty. June 1961. Eisenhower	Prohibits nuclear weapons in Antarctic. All buildings open for inspections.
3. The Hot Line Agreement. June 1963. Kennedy	Establishes communications between White House and Kremlin.
4. Limited Test Ban Treaty. October 1963. Kennedy	Prohibits tests causing fallout in neighboring countries.
5. The Outer-Space Treaty. October 1967. Johnson	Prohibits placing weapons of mass destruction in outer space.
6. The Latin American Nuclear Free Zone. April 1968. Johnson	Prohibits the stationing of weapons in Latin America.
7. The Non-Proliferation Treaty (NPT). March 1970. Nixon	Commits countries not to build or help countries build nuclear weapons.
8. The Sea-Beds Treaty. May 1972. Nixon	Prohibits nuclear weapons on seabeds, but not on submarines or ships.
9. Agreement to Reduce Risk of Nuclear War. September 1971. Nixon	Safeguards against accidental launch and prohibits nuclear threats.
10. SALT I. October 1972. Nixon	Provides ceilings on ICBMs and SLBMs.
11. Anti-Ballistic Missile Treaty. October 1972. Nixon	Prohibits ABM tests and more than one ABM site.
12. Agreement on Prevention of Nuclear War. June 1973. Nixon	Parties agree to consult, to not use force, and to keep UN informed.
13. Threshold Test Ban Treaty. Signed July 1974. Nixon	Prohibits tests of nuclear weapons of over 150 kilotons.
14. The Vladivostok Agreement. November 1974. Ford	Joint U.S.–Soviet statement setting framework for SALT II.
15. SALT II. Signed 1979. Carter	Not ratified but its ceilings were observed on strategic weapons.
16. The Intermediate Nuclear Force Agreement. June 1988. Reagan	Abolishes all intermediate and "shorter range" nuclear missiles.
17. Peaceful Nuclear Explosions Treaty	Provides verification of nuclear explosions for peaceful purposes.
18. START I Treaty. July 1991. Bush	Cuts strategic weapons 25–35%.
19. Unilateral Cut. September 1991. Bush	Would cut tactical nuclear weapons in Europe, except for that on aircraft.
20. START II Agreement. Initialled June 1992. Bush	Would cut strategic weapons 50–66%.

of the outer space treaty, which prohibits weapons of mass destruction being deployed in outer space including celestial bodies. Both treaties allow open inspection to verify their provisions.[4]

The next major treaty was the Limited Test Ban Treaty, which grew out of a UN initiative of 1954. At that time the United States tested a fusion bomb in the Pacific on the Bikini Atoll. The explosion spread radioactive fallout for hundreds of miles, some of which fell on the Japanese ship *Lucky Dragon*. The sailors did not know what had hit them until after they had returned to Japan and sold some of the contaminated fish in the local market. By that time some of them were ill, and one of the men actually died. As a result of the outcry and other objections to fallout from nuclear tests, about a dozen resolutions were passed in the General Assembly calling for an end to atmospheric tests. The subject of test bans received more attention in UN bodies than any other subject of nuclear disarmament.

Negotiations between the Soviet Union and the United States made little progress until 1963, when Chairman Khrushchev proposed a compromise of prohibiting nuclear tests of a kind where the fallout would be detected in a neighboring state. This solved the verification problem and was acceptable to President Kennedy. An agreement was negotiated in about a week in Moscow between the Soviets, the United States, and Britain to prohibit such tests. These nations subsequently conducted their nuclear tests underground. President Nixon negotiated a follow-up treaty prohibiting all tests over 150 kilotons, which is about 10 times the strength of the Hiroshima bomb. In 1990 the United States and the Soviet Union finally reached agreement on verification procedures and ratified protocols on the Threshold Test Ban treaty as well as the Peaceful Nuclear Explosions Treaty.

The Hot Line Agreement came out of the Cuban missile crisis. Kennedy's and Khrushchev's personal communications were key factors in solving that crisis. They saw the need to speed up communications since each side was only one-half hour away from destruction by ICBMs. Direct communication lines serviced by interpreters have been established between the White House and the Kremlin under this agreement to permit direct talks between both locations during a serious world crisis. The agreement was signed in 1963 by the U.S. and Russian representatives to the UN Eighteen Nation Conference on Disarmament in Geneva.

President Nixon also concluded the important Non-Proliferation Treaty (NPT); negotiations had been started by President Johnson. This agreement arose from pressure by the General Assembly, which over 10 years earlier by a vote of 69 to 0 had called for such a treaty. The major issue preventing early agreement was that the Soviets did not want the United States to deploy nuclear weapons in other countries of Western Europe. The United States, on the other hand, insisted that NATO must have these weapons. After about 10 years of negotiations, the Russians accepted the fact that U.S. nuclear weapons would be deployed in Europe. The United States explained that these were placed under U.S. control by requiring a U.S. officer to insert a key for launching such a nuclear missile. The treaty pledges countries not to produce or help another country to produce nuclear weapons, and commits them to extensive verification from IAEA inspectors mentioned above. Article 6 requires the nuclear powers to pursue negotiations to cease the nuclear arms race and complete disarmament under strict and effective international control. The major INF and ABM agreements discussed below between Russia and the United States acknowledge their commitment under the NPT Treaty. The countries signing the NPT pledge not to develop nuclear weapons hoped to avoid any reason for a nuclear power to involve them in a nuclear war, to prevent a possible enemy from developing nuclear weapons, and put pressure on the nuclear powers to end the arms race. A UN Security Council resolution of 1959 pledges assistance by its permanent members to a nation threatened by a nuclear power if the threatened nation is nonnuclear and a party to the NPT. By 1992 151 states were parties including nuclear states and most of those states which might be on the threshold of producing such weapons.

After the 1991 Gulf War IAEA inspectors discovered Iraq was engaged in an extensive program to develop weapons of mass destruction including chemical weapons and nuclear facilities that had escaped the eye of previous IAEA inspectors and the U.S. bombing. These included facilities to enrich uranium and to carry out research for nuclear weapons. The inspectors supervised destruction of these installations and thousands of weapons. As a result of this experience, the IAEA strengthened its inspection procedures including those for surprise inspections.[5] The aftermath of the Gulf War demonstrated that IAEA on-the-ground operations were much more effective than bombing in destroying weapons of mass destruction.

The Seabeds Treaty of 1972, which prevents emplacement of nuclear weapons on the seabed, was also begun by a resolution in the General Assembly of 1967. In December 1970 the General Assembly called for such a treaty by a vote of 102 to 2. The treaty was negotiated by the UN Eighteen-Nation Disarmament Committee that later became known as the Conference of the Committee on Disarmament. It went into effect in 1972.

In 1969 President Nixon became concerned the Soviets could surge ahead in numbers of strategic nuclear weapons. In 1971 the U.S. negotiated the SALT I agreement that provided for more Soviets ICBMs to be balanced by the U.S. lead in heavy bombers, which were not covered by the agreement. The preamble of the agreement noted the obligation of the two superpowers to take such effective measures to cease the nuclear arms race under article VI of the Nuclear Non-proliferation Treaty, which as noted above was sponsored by the United Nations.[6]

SALT I was an "interim" agreement, not a treaty, and both sides began negotiating a new agreement that would include bombers and also put a limit on MIRVs (multiple independently targeted reentry vehicles) and on the Soviet heavy missiles. President Ford and General Secretary Brezhnev set the framework with the joint Vladivostok statement. President Carter then negotiated the SALT II agreement with such limits. Although it was not formally ratified, its ceilings were observed by both sides until late in the Reagan administration.

An antiballistic missile (ABM) "treaty" was closely associated with SALT I. This treaty and a later protocol limited deployment of antiballistic missile systems to one each, and it strictly limited ABM radar and tests. The net effect was that in case of a nuclear war only one small area of each of the superpowers would be protected or partially protected from nuclear attack. The purpose of this "mutual assured destruction" (MAD) policy was to prevent, by the threat of mutual suicide, nuclear war between the superpowers. This treaty also recognized the obligation to take effective measures to cease the nuclear arms race under article VI of the Nuclear Non-Proliferation Treaty. The treaty was ratified by an overwhelming vote in the Senate.[7]

Nixon and General Secretary Brezhnev in 1973 also signed the Agreement on the Prevention of War. This agreement pledged to refrain from the threat or use of force and urgently to consult together in the event of a risk of nuclear war. Each party in such a case is free to inform the UN Security Council and the secretary general of the progress of such consultation. They also agreed that nothing in the agreement should impair the provisions of the Charter of the United Nations. This agreement is often overlooked by commentators, but since the time it was negotiated, the United States and Russia have not threatened to attack each other as in the days of Khrushchev, or in the days of Dulles and the "massive retaliation" doctrine. As in the case of the other agreements, this agreement reflects the common interest of the two superpowers.

Table 1 summarizes the above agreements. They restrained the arms race for 14 years, but by 1986 the network of agreements had begun to tear apart. The basic problem appeared to be that President Reagan believed that the Soviets had superior strength in nuclear weapons, particularly in the heavy missiles, and that theoretically in a first strike they could wipe out the U.S.

Minuteman ICBM force, leaving the United States at the mercy of a further strike that could annihilate its cities. Reagan's initial negotiating proposals to limit strategic arms were nonstarters. They would have cancelled the SALT II agreement, which had been agreed on by the Carter administration, and would have reduced Soviet heavy missiles, where they have an advantage, without comparable reductions by the United States. The Soviets, on the other hand, called for a freeze in further installation of nuclear weapons and also a ban on testing of nuclear weapons.

In 1986 the Soviets voluntarily halted their tests, calling for a freeze on testing. In April 1986 the Reagan administration continued its series of nuclear tests, rejecting the chance for a freeze on the tests. The U.S. rationale for continuing the tests was to ensure that the nuclear warheads that it possessed would work and thus preserve a "deterrent" against a Soviet attack and to develop new weapons. Press reports indicating that the United States was also interested in testing nuclear devices that could create laser beams for the Star Wars program, discussed below. In the summer of 1986 Reagan announced that the United States would no longer be bound by the SALT II ceilings. This threatened a serious tear in the network of nuclear arms control agreements and little prospect for future agreements.

On March 22, 1983 President Reagan had proposed creating a total defense against ballistic missiles, thus implying a radical change in nuclear doctrine. The speech called for futuristic weapons in space and was called the Strategic Defense Initiative (SDI). Before that U.S. doctrine had been based on mutual assured destruction (MAD) to deter war. Under this doctrine if either side is attacked, it would have enough nuclear weapons left to destroy the aggressor, because neither side would have an effective defense. As noted above, the ABM Treaty is associated with this MAD doctrine of deterrence. The Russians had chosen Moscow for its one ABM site, whereas the United States chose Grand Forks, North Dakota, to protect its Minuteman missile field there. The United States subsequently decided that it was so expensive and impracticable to develop such weapons that it did not even activate the one defensive site. Meanwhile, the Russians placed nuclear-capable defensive missiles in a ring around Moscow to defend it. The ABM Treaty also severely limited radars capable of tracking incoming missiles. Research and limited ABM systems, however, are permitted if located at present test sites. Reagan's Star Wars, or SDI, proposals would violate the ABM Treaty by expanding ABM systems into outer space. (State Department officials tried to persuade Congress without success that the treaty approved by the Senate did permit such space systems.)

Opponents of the Star Wars program argued that the side creating an effective defense could threaten the other side with the possibility of a first strike and encourage the other side to create more offensive missiles to offset the possible defensive potential of an ABM system. The other argument against Star Wars accepted by many scientists is that an ABM system is impracticable. The technical problems of shooting down with a high degree of certainty thousands of missiles fired from space as well as from submarines and cruise missiles are impossible to solve. Even if a system were put in place, scientists argue, it would be easy to disrupt it by decoys and an attack on key elements of the system. If only a few missiles got through, they continued, this would still be adequate to devastate the defenders.

The Soviets violently attacked the Star Wars program as designed to give the United States nuclear superiority that could threaten the Soviets with a first strike. They opposed an arms race in space since it would be costly for them to try to keep up with the new defense techniques. They initially linked any negotiated limits on nuclear weapons with ending the Star Wars program, because they did not wish to have their offensive capability offset by a U.S. lead in defensive technology.

In a related series of negotiations the United States and Soviets had discussed the possibility of limiting or eliminating intermediate range missiles in Europe. In the late 1970s, as a result of a decision under Carter, the United States decided to deploy cruise and Pershing missiles in Europe to offset the intermediate-range Soviet SS 20s that were being installed there. As the United States started to deploy these Pershing and cruise missiles under the Reagan administration, the Soviets made various offers to try to stop this threat to their command centers. The Soviets reasoned that the Pershing missiles could reach their command centers and major cities in seven minutes and, therefore, represented a more serious threat than the long-range intercontinental missiles from the United States that take about a half-hour in flight.

As policymakers faced rising political pressures and the no-win situation of a nuclear arms race, there was a dramatic development in nuclear arms negotiations. President Reagan and General Secretary Gorbachev met for two days in October 1986 in Iceland and agreed on a general framework of concessions on the following major issues:

Intercontinental Missiles

1. The two leaders agreed to a 50 percent reduction in strategic missiles and warheads over a period of five years. (Later their spokesman disagreed whether they had agreed to go on from that point and eliminate all "nuclear strategic weapons" or all "ballistic missiles," which would not include bombers and cruise missiles.)

2. The Russians agreed to major cuts in their biggest missiles, which the United States considers the most threatening.

Intermediate-Range and Short-Range Missiles

1. The Russians agreed to remove all their SS 20s, and the United States agreed to remove all Pershings and cruise missiles from Europe.
2. The Soviets would keep only 100 SS 20s in Asia; the United States would keep only 100 intermediate-range weapons in the United States.

Nuclear Tests

1. The two sides agreed on improved verification.
2. The United States did not agree to stop tests, but it agreed to negotiate a reduction in tests with the aim of ultimately eliminating all tests.

The major issue not settled was the Soviet demand to limit strictly SDI testing, and the Russians conditioned the above proposals on settling the SDI issue. First reports indicated that the Soviets took a more restrictive position on SDI than that of the ABM Treaty, although this was not clear because both sides had a different interpretation of the treaty. Both sides agreed, however, to continue negotiations in Vienna to try to clarify and settle the above issues.

The breakthrough came in the following year when the Soviets yielded on the Star Wars issue in the context of the intermediate-range missiles. At a Washington summit they signed an agreement for completely eliminating *all* medium-range and "shorter range" nuclear missiles with a range of 300 to 3,400 miles. There were detailed provisions to monitor the destruction of the missiles and to make detailed on-site inspections in over 100 places in Russia and 30 places in Europe and the United States in order to verify that the missiles were actually destroyed. The Star Wars issues was left unresolved with both sides agreeing to conduct research, development, and testing of ABM systems as permitted by the ABM Treaty.

The implications of the INF Treaty were breathtaking, although some commentators tended to downplay its importance. For the first time entire classes of nuclear missiles totalling about 2,000 were to be destroyed. For the first time the Soviets and the United States would permit extensive inspections of military facilities. The agreements took place in the framework of friendly and businesslike meetings including extensive media coverage in Russia. Both leaders appeared determined to press forward with an agreement to cut strategic missiles by 50 percent, and agreement was reached on many issues involved. The experience from inspections and verification under the INF Treaty would help in negotiating the strategic arms reduction treaty (START).

After 1989 with the breaking up of the Soviet's East European and internal empires under Mikhail Gorbachev, negotiations on nuclear arms control accelerated. They were aided by the termination of the Warsaw Pact military alliance in 1991 and agreements on major reductions of Soviet and American troops and conventional weapons in Europe.

In July 1991 after about 9 years of negotiations, Presidents Bush and Gorbachev signed the START treaty cutting U.S. strategic nuclear warheads by 25 percent and the comparable Soviet weapons about 35 percent. Verification procedures included on-the-spot inspections.

Then, as Gorbachev made a last-ditch struggle to keep his position and to hold the Soviet Union together in the fall of 1991, President Bush announced the United States would unilaterally withdraw and destroy its nuclear weapons in Europe and cut back on strategic weapons. This included withdrawing and destroying all nuclear artillery shells and warheads for short-range missiles, removing all tactical nuclear weapons including nuclear cruise missiles from surface ships and nuclear submarines, removing tactical nuclear missiles from naval aircraft, and dropping plans to deploy the strategic mobile MX missiles and smaller Midgetman missiles. He completed the above reductions by July 2, 1992. However, the United States retained tactical nuclear weapons for aircraft. Bush invited the Soviets to make similar concessions.

On February 17, 1992, Yeltsin, the new president of Russia, and Secretary of State Baker announced agreement on U.S. technical assistance in dismantling Russia's nuclear arsenal, including providing special boxcars and containers to transport nuclear warheads. The highly enriched uranium and plutonium would be entombed in underground bunkers to be monitored by the International Atomic Energy Agency (IAEA) or converted to use for power or research. Meanwhile, former Soviet republics that had achieved independence agreed to a joint nuclear command with Russia and to accept the arms limitation treaties of the former Soviet Union. They also accepted U.S. technical assistance in removing their nuclear weapons.

In June 1992, during a red-carpet visit to the United States, President Yeltsin joined President Bush in initially an agreement for further drastic cuts in nuclear weapons. Each side would reduce its long-range weapons from the START ceiling of 6,900–8,600 to 3,000–3,500. Destroying those weapons is so time consuming it was estimated it would take until the year 2,000 or 2,003 to complete the task. In October 1992 the Senate approved this 1991 START treaty, which would provide machinery to help implement the later cuts. Presidents Bush and Yeltsin signed the final draft on January 3, 1993.

The changed outlook of Soviet and Russian leaders that helped bring about the agreements was a natural result of their democratic and market-oriented reforms. Their major concessions included allowing foreign inspectors access to Soviet military bases and showing flexibility on the Star Wars issue. The desire to attract foreign investment and aid and to limit the costly arms race, as well as an end of their paranoia about the German threat, influenced Gorbachev's and Yeltsin's decisions.

With these nuclear agreements the psychology of the Cold War evaporated. Leaders destroying nuclear weapons are not likely to be preparing for war. Popular opinion, that is the determination "of the people of the United Nations" (including those of the Soviet Union) to save "succeeding generations from the scourge of war" and a faith in "fundamental human rights" not only helped form the UN Charter but eventually influenced Communist leaders to establish democracies and reduce nuclear arsenals.

The next challenge would be to complete the treaty on chemical weapons. Negotiations on it began in 1986. In 1992 the UN Conference on Disarmament was close to agreement on a text. However, the frustrations of the IAEA in inspecting Iraq's weapons facilities threatened to complicate what had been seen as the final stages of negotiations of the chemical weapons treaty.

Another challenge would be to implement the 1991 General Assembly resolution providing for a register for transfers of weapons and holdings of weapons. Its aim is to discourage large sales and stockpiling of arms. The League of Nations had administered such a registry from 1925 to 1928.

Notes to Chapter 6

1. T. Bailey, *A Diplomatic History of the American People* (New York: F. S. Crofts, 1945), p. 691.

2. U.S. Arms Control and Disarmament Agency (ACDA), *Arms Control and Disarmament Agreements* (Washington, DC: GPO, 1980), p. 4.

3. H. Truman, *Years of Decision,* vol. 2. (New York: Doubleday, 1956), p. 11.

4. ACDA, *Arms Control,* 1980.

5. J. Tessitore and S. Woolfson (eds.), *A Global Agenda* (Lanham MD: University Press of America, 1992), pp. 124–130.

6. H. Kissinger, *Whitehouse Years*, pp. 130–138.

7. ACDA, *Arms Control,* p. 80.

Chapter VII

THE UNITED NATIONS AND INTERNATIONAL LAW

There are two major types of international law. The first is called public international law. It is practiced mostly by diplomats and lawmakers who draft and negotiate treaties and other international agreements such as the INF Treaty, the Canadian free trade agreement, the Panama Canal Treaty, and many other international agreements. Their international agreements for the most part cover problems of relations between states, and they are a major source of international law.

The other type is concerned with "conflict of laws" and is called private international law. It is practiced by lawyers who are largely concerned with international business arrangements and problems arising from different provisions of laws in different countries, particularly for foreigners and foreign business concerns. Its practioners are mostly lawyers who deal with the laws of various nations and use the court systems when necessary. These lawyers help individuals and firms, since one of the principles of international law is that the individual should first try the local courts and local officials for assistance before diplomats of his or her government take the case. This is called exhausting the local remedies.

American and other courts practice the principle of comity, or recognizing and enforcing legal actions of foreign courts and governments, unless there is reason to believe they were not fair. This means that jurisdictional conflicts are seldom submitted to dispute-settlement procedures.

This chapter deals mostly with public law, and particularly how international law relates to the major issues of war and peace. It also examines several important examples of the use of international law, including how nations have cooperated to reduce international terrorism, to promote human rights, and to establish a body of law for issues relating to the sea.

109

World leaders and academics have severely criticized as idealists the leaders and diplomats who have tried to use international law as a guide for diplomacy and build a system of collective security based on it. President Wilson, a liberal internationalist, was severely criticized by some writers for supporting a framework of international law of the League of Nations. Presidents Truman and Eisenhower to a large extent escaped such criticism when their policies supported the United Nations and international law, since they also used a blend of power politics with international law to reinforce their positions, and the United Nations supported them in their efforts. President Carter was severely criticized for being weak in the Iranian hostage crisis because he resorted to diplomacy and the United Nations rather than force. President Reagan attacked Carter for this and became one of the most popular presidents largely because of his macho stance against the Communists. In 1986 he rejected the World Court's and UN's condemnation of the United States for supporting the Contras' attacks against Nicaragua, which Reagan accused of being Communist. He later confounded critics of his hard line by making one of the most far-reaching treaties on nuclear arms control, which was linked to the extensive network of nuclear arms control agreements originating in the UN System.

President Reagan demonstrated a lack of respect for international law and the United Nations by the attacks against Nicaragua and Grenada. His lawyers' assertions were not convincing that the intervention was for self-defense and in support of insurgents fighting for the UN Charter's principles of self-determination.[1] Reagan's officials distrusted trying peaceful means through the United Nations because they believed it was dominated by third-world nations opposed to U.S. policies. However, after Secretary of State Shultz negotiated a carefully drafted INF treaty on nuclear arms, respect for international law naturally followed. He requested Congress to stop slashing the UN budget, and it did so.

There was hope when President Bush took office that U.S. support for the UN would be strengthened. He formerly had served as U.S. ambassador to the UN and knew how to work within its framework. That hope was undermined when the United States unilaterally invaded Panama at the end of 1989 to capture its military leader and bring him to trial on narcotics charges. That violation of Panama's sovereignty and international law was condemned by the General Assembly.

However, at the end of 1990 when Kuwait was overrun by Iraq, and Middle East oil was threatened, President Bush and Secretary of State Baker mobilized UN Security Council support with the slogan of supporting the "rule of law." This helped mobilize international support including that of

Arab nations. Their support was a buffer against resentment of Arab masses. With success of the war against Iraq, the United States became committed to the UN Security Council and international law. The United States found itself in a position where it would be regarded as a hypocrite if it ignored international law in the use of force.

THE SOURCES OF INTERNATIONAL LAW

International law is a body of principles, customs, and rules that are recognized as binding obligations by sovereign states and international organizations in their mutual relations. The father of international law is often said to be Hugo Grotius, whose *Concerning the Law of War and Peace* was written after the terrible Thirty Year's War, which devastated Europe at the beginning of the seventeenth century. There is a parallel today. The revival of international law under the United Nations also came after a terrible war— World War II, the worst war in history. Grotius was concerned about the disintegration of society and the need for a system of law to replace spiritual unity of Christendom, which had been broken by war. He proposed a system derived from natural law and the Christian conscience to preserve the sovereignty of states.[2] He compiled the international customs and precedents of that day for his seminal work.

International law governs relations between states, and only states can take up cases before international tribunals. One important exception is the optional protocol of the Covenant of Economic and Cultural Rights of 1976, discussed below. This broke new ground by allowing individuals and groups to appeal to the UN Commission on Human Rights.

Individuals as a rule apply international law in domestic courts. Such cases include issues involving foreign corporations, jurisdiction over foreigners, extradition to other countries, crimes committed aboard ships, and many other cases involving suits between foreigners and citizens of a country.

The sources of international law are listed in Article 38 of the Statute of the International Court of Justice, which is part of the United Nations Charter, as follows: (1) Treaties. This covers international agreements, or treaties, such as treaties, conventions, pacts, and executive agreements, although in the United States treaties in a narrow sense mean only those international agreements approved by two-thirds of the Senate. Unilateral statements by presidents can be recognized as international agreements and commitments under international law. Article 102 of the UN Charter requires all treaties and other international agreements to be registered with the United Nations, and states may not invoke such an agreement unless it is registered. (2) Custom. This includes the rules that are generally accepted by states and observed in their relations with each other. The classic court case is that of the *Scotia*. The U.S. Supreme Court in 1872 ruled that the ship *Birkshire* could not collect damages from the ship *Scotia* because the *Birkshire* had not been following the custom of using different colored lights and was only displaying white lights. At that time, most ships were observing British regulations that required colored lights to show fore and aft, and white lights starboard and port. Since that time the many customs for shipping, trade, and many other international transactions have been formalized in international agreements, so that they, rather than custom, are a much more important source of international law today. (3) General principles of law. This covers principally Roman law, and ordinary law principles covering property and territorial rights. (4) Judicial and arbitral decisions of previous cases involving international law. There is, of course, a growing body of this law. (5) Writings by scholars in journals and reviews of international law. This has become much less important as norms have been formalized in international agreements.

The United Nations has been a major source for international law. Under Article 13 the General Assembly shall make recommendations for encouraging progressive development of international law and its codification. The major instruments for this are the International Law Commission and the General Assembly's sixth committee, which debates the commission's reports. The International Law Commission was established by the General Assembly in 1947 to promote the development and codification of international law. Its 34 members, who meet annually in Geneva, are experts, serving as individuals and not as representatives of governments. The commission prepares drafts of conventions for consideration of ECOSOC and the General Assembly. Generally, the commission approves and calls an international conference of plenipotentiaries to approve and "sign" the agreements. Alternatively, agreements may be approved by the General Assembly. The agreements do not come into effect, however, until the specific ratifications are obtained through the countries' legal processes. In the United States this normally involves a two-thirds approval by the Senate. Other parts of the UN System also initiate international conventions and agreements in their areas of specialty, which go through a similar signature and ratification process. Resolutions and agreements approved by the General Assembly can become evidence of international law even if they are not formally ratified.

WAR AND INTERVENTION UNDER INTERNATIONAL LAW

There is a considerable body of international agreements developed since the beginning of the century that forbids offensive war.

Article 1 of the UN Charter states the major purpose of the United Nations as maintaining peace within a framework of international law:

> 1. To maintain international peace and security and to that end: to take effective measures for the prevention and removal of threats to the peace, and for the suppression of acts of aggression or other breaches of the peace, and to bring about by peaceful means and in conformity with the principles of justice and international law, adjustment or settlement of international disputes or situations which might lead to a breach of the peace.

Paragraph 3 of Article 2 states that "All members shall settle their international disputes by peaceful means in such a manner that international peace and security, and justice, are not endangered." Article 33 requires parties to a dispute to seek to settle it by peaceful means and if that does not succeed to bring it to the Security Council, which then has the power to settle it.

As noted in the introduction, the United Nations grew out of the League of Nations experience and a body of international law that opposed aggression. The League itself was designed to prevent war. Article 1 obligated League members not to resort to war, and Article 10 called on members to respect the territorial integrity of other members. Articles 15 and 16 stated that if any nation went to war in disregard of the actions of the League, it was deemed to have gone to war against all the members. Some authors have stressed that there was a loophole in these articles implying that a state could go to war if unanimous agreement in the League council did not oppose such action. However, that loophole was only a loophole, and it does not invalidate the plain language of the rest of the Covenant.

The Hague conventions of 1907 and 1899 also had committed nations to use their best efforts to settle disputes peacefully, and they set up the Permanent Court of Arbitration for this purpose. It was able to arbitrate several important disputes before World War I.

In 1928 the world nations formally renounced war and agreed to settle all disputes by peaceful means. The Kellog-Briand Pact, or Pact of Paris, which grew out of an American initiative, was ratified by the important nations of the world. It renounced recourse to war and committed the signatories not to seek settlement of disputes except by peaceful means. This "outlawry of war" proved to be ineffective, however, against the World War II aggression of the Axis powers.

At the close of the war, Britain, France, and United States, and the Soviet Union set up the Nuremburg tribunal, which tried Nazi war criminals. The jurisdiction of the court included "crimes against peace: namely, planning, preparation, initiation or waging of a war of aggression or a war in violation of international treaties." The UN General Assembly endorsed the principles of the Nuremburg trials unanimously in a resolution on December 11, 1946.

The General Assembly in 1987 adopted without a vote resolutions calling on nations to refrain from the threat or use of force, suggesting negotiation of disputes and encouraging the secretary general to exercise his functions fully in the cause of peace and to make use of the International Court.

The point is that there is a solid body of precedent and international agreements for prohibiting war and requiring nations to settle disputes peacefully. This precedent is routinely supported in UN resolutions by the Security Council and General Assembly in dealing with aggression. This precedent, as noted in previous chapters, has played an important part over the long run in containing and discouraging aggression. "A habit of reliance on an international institution to deal with large political questions even if only in debate will increase the pressure for recourse to that institution at the crisis point.[3] However, the appeasement of aggression of the 1930s and 1940s created cynicism about the effectiveness of international law and a belief in the need to rely on military power. After World War II the philosophers of power politics were more popular among the diplomats and academics than the international lawyers, who had dominated the university courses on international affairs in the 1930s.

As indicated, the major international law issue of recent years for the United States has involved intervention. International law was founded on Grotius' aim of promoting a respect for sovereignty. Intervention is an attack on that sovereignty through "dictatorial interference by one state in the affairs of another state for the purpose of either maintaining or changing the existing order of things."[4] In December 1974, about 24 years after the General Assembly had first considered the matter, it approved by consensus a draft definition of aggression, which is the most flagrant kind of intervention. The sponsors of the resolution included the United States and the Soviet Union. The definitions of aggression, in addition to obvious aggression by military attacks, included a state allowing its territory for perpetrating an act of an aggression against another state, and also the sending of armed bands of mercenaries against another state. Article 5 added that no consideration whatever may serve as a justification for aggression.[5]

International law like domestic law is frequently broken, and there have been numerous wars since the United Nations was established. The previous chapter noted that the Soviet Union and the United States, although sponsors of the UN definition of aggression, had themselves committed aggression. The previous two chapters also described the procedures used in the United Nations to oppose aggression. These chapters stressed that the UN Charter is a flexible instrument and showed the many ways it was used to contain and settle wars. It is even designed to take care of the problem of the "rogue cop" in which one of the permanent members supports aggression. In that case the issue can be transferred to the General Assembly by a procedural vote of the Security Council not subject to the veto. In a number of cases beginning with the Korean War, the General Assembly took charge of protecting the victim of aggression.

There are cases in which the right of intervention is recognized under international law. The right of intervention may be by right when it takes place at the explicit invitation of the lawful government of a state. Examples are the landing of American troops in Lebanon in 1958 at the invitation of that government. They were withdrawn within a few months. French forces have intervened in Chad to protect against a rebellion sponsored by Libya. Often aggressors make a false claim that they have been invited to intervene—Germany in invading Austria in 1938 and the Soviet Union in invading Afghanistan in 1979. Such intervention, of course, is a flagrant violation of international law.

There is considerable debate among international lawyers about the allowable intervention in a civil war. Article 2, paragraph 7 states that "Nothing contained in the present Charter shall authorize the United Nations to intervene in matters which are essentially within the domestic jurisdiction of any state . . ." This is generally interpreted to prohibit intervention in a civil war. On the other hand, when foreign assistance is given to the rebels, it is generally assumed that providing aid to the government threatened is legal.[6] However, there usually is much room for debate whether a government is legitimate, how much a rebel force is being aided from the outside, and how much the government that intervenes takes over control of the local government and thereby intervenes excessively.

The major difference between international and domestic law is that there is no governmental police or military force to enforce the former. International law still depends largely upon the willingness of world leaders to work within the United Nations to settle disputes, and that in turn depends in large part upon the public support for the United Nations. Colonel House, President Wilson's foreign policy advisor, in exploring ideas for the League of Nations in a letter to Lord Robert Cecil of Great Britain, said:

I believe the most vital element in bringing about a worldwide reign of peace is to have the same stigma rest upon the acts of nations as upon the acts of individuals. When the people of a country are held up to the scorn and condemnation of the world because of the dishonorable acts of their representatives, they will no longer tolerate such acts.

President Wilson repeated this theme in his inaugural address. John F. Kennedy in reporting on the founding of the United Nations made a similar statement. He was disappointed that the leaders did not create a stronger organization to keep the peace but added that they were not at fault—the people must insist on giving up sovereignty to the organization. He was one of the war heroes, but he added: "War will exist until the conscientious objector enjoys the same prestige as the warrior has today."

The supporters of international law call upon their governments to respect international law in dealings with other nations. They are planning for the long run and hope to create public acceptance of a system where nations respect sovereignty of other nations and not use force or else face punishment by the world community. It is easy for a powerful president to become impatient with the slowness of diplomacy and difficulties of working through the UN Security Council or General Assembly and to take unilateral action without regard for United Nations procedures and international law. The previous chapter showed, however, that there were serious failures in the United States using power politics and some important successes in using the United Nations to settle and contain wars.

THE WORLD COURT

The International Court of Justice is the supreme court of international law, but it is outside the mainstream of settling disputes that could lead to war. None of the major disputes that led to war described in the previous chapters were submitted to the International Court. The Court is situated at the Hague and its statute is a part of the UN Charter. It inherited the records and the precedents of the Permanent Court of International Justice, which functioned under the League of Nations.

Under Article 36 of the statute of the International Court, states may accept compulsory jurisdiction in all legal disputes concerning (1) interpretation of a treaty, (2) a question of international law, (3) existence of any fact that might constitute breach of international law, and (4) reparation for breach of an international obligation. This sounds much like the charge of domestic courts interpreting contracts and agreements and judging cases of breaking the law. The United Nations can also seek an advisory opinion from the International Court on issues in dispute. The United States, in approving the statute of the International Court of Justice, adopted the famous Connally amendment. Under it, the United States does not have to submit cases it considers to be within its domestic jurisdiction, and it can decide whether such cases are within its jurisdiction or not. About 100 of the 160 countries that have ratified the UN Charter and the Statute of the Court have made similar reservations.

The court consists of 15 independent judges elected by the Security Council and the General Assembly. They are elected for nine years, and the terms of five expire every three years, permitting a rotation of the membership. If there is no judge of the nationality of a party before the court, that party can choose one to take part. In the 1980s the International Court had a budget of about $6 million, with about 31 on its payroll.

Major issues of war and peace between great powers are seldom submitted to the court. A typical case is that of the United Kingdom v. Norway (Norwegian Fisheries Case) of 1951. This dispute originated when British fishing vessels operated in waters claimed by Norway. The court ruled in favor of Norway, approving the Norwegian practice of drawing the boundary for its territorial sea from straight baselines following the general directions of the coast but not the indentations of that coast. This case set a precedent used by the International Law Commission in drafting provisions on the limits of the territorial sea in the subsequent Law of the Sea conventions.

The cases involving the international status of Southwest Africa in 1950, 1962, and 1966 illustrate the limitations of the court but also the potential of the United Nations for enforcing international law. A basic issue addressed in these cases was the status of Southwest Africa (now called Namibia), which had been a mandate under the League of Nations and was controlled by South Africa. Ethiopia and Liberia brought the case before the International Court objecting to South Africa's suspension of human rights there and requesting it to enforce conditions of the League mandate for Southwest Africa. In 1962 the court ruled that South Africa's obligations under the mandate continued, but in 1966 by another split decision it ruled that United Nations members could not invoke compulsory jurisdiction of the court on these issues. However, political pressures of the African countries in the United Nations resulted in the Security Council condemning South Africa for not giving Namibia independence and for continuing the practice of apartheid. The Council imposed sanctions against South Africa prohibiting the export to it of military goods. Similar resolutions supporting Namibia and condemning apartheid were also passed by the General Assembly, which then refused to recognize the credentials of South Africa and in effect suspended its membership in the United Nations. The United States at first voted against such actions as interference in internal affairs not authorized by the Charter, but public opposition to the South African apartheid continued to mount. By 1985 as a result of congressional acts the United States government joined other UN nations in invoking economic sanctions against that country. Thus, although the World Court could not directly enforce its ruling on South Africa, other organs of the UN System took strong action in line with the court's decisions to condemn South Africa for its policies of apartheid. These political organs of the United Nations System made South Africa feel the weight of international condemnation. By the end of 1988 South Africa had negotiated an agreement for Namibian independence, including elections supervised by the United Nations.

In April 1984 Nicaragua lodged a complaint that the United States had supported military and paramilitary action against the Sandinista government. On May 10 the court gave an initial ruling that the United States should respect Nicaragua's sovereignty. In November in a series of rulings it ruled that the court had jurisdiction over the dispute. On January 18, 1985 the United States unilaterally withdrew from the hearing and denounced the court. As indicated above, however, the U.S. Congress ended military aid to the Contras, and the international condemnation including the court's action was reflected in the congressional action.

The court also ruled against the United States in an advisory opinion of April 26, 1988 that the United States was obligated to arbitrate its demand that the PLO close its office in New York. The Manhatten Federal Court ruled against the Department of Justice's position on this case. This was a victory of sorts for the Department of State, which had openly opposed the Department of Justice on this issue on the grounds that the Justice position violated the U.S. host-country agreement with the United Nations.

On the other hand, the court gave support to the United States during the Iranian hostage crisis beginning in November 1979 by condemning Iran's action in holding as hostages about 50 American diplomatic personnel. This was a small part of the pressures exerted on Iran, which included unanimous resolutions in the Security Council and U.S. government action to freeze about $13 billion of Iranian assets in the United States. The crisis was resolved in complicated negotiations headed by Algeria after the Iranian prime minister visited the United Nations hoping to get support against Iraq in the Iraq-Iran war and finding the UN diplomats overwhelmingly condemning Iran on the hostage issue. Although the court action in itself was not at the center of the action, it, as well as UN resolutions, helped demonstrate international support for the basic principle of international law, which requires the host country to protect diplomats. Support of this principle by the diplomatic community exerted a great deal of pressure on Iran to release the hostages.

Although the International Court has not been used to settle the major issues of war and peace, it has been used to reinforce respect for international law on several major controversies affecting the United States. These include the Iran-hostage issue and U.S. use of the CIA to attack Nicaragua. In both these cases the general support of the international community for the position enunciated by the court helped bring about an eventual solution.

Over the years the World Court supported granting independence of Namibia, which helped eventually in bringing about a solution of that issue in 1988 after many years of negotiation in other forums. This demonstrates how the court can be used in major disputes. In 1988 as political solutions were negotiated for the Afghanistan war, the Iran-Iraq conflict, the Vietnam-Kampuchea war, and others, there was hope that the World Court could play a larger role in adjudicating issues, giving opinions, and reinforcing moves toward peace. It is more than a truism that international peace depends on countries developing a respect for international law.

THE LAW OF THE SEA AND OTHER INTERNATIONAL AGREEMENTS

The Law of the Sea conferences illustrate an important area where the United Nations has codified international law. On September 17, 1976 Secretary of State Kissinger stated that these negotiations were among the most important, complex, and difficult of any of this century. He explained that they were aimed at establishing a legal regime for about three-fourths of the surface of the globe. However, this effort as of 1992 has not been completely successful, because the treaty that was negotiated has not received the endorsement of the United States.

At its first session the International Law Commission included the law of the sea as a topic for codification. This has continued to be one of the most ambitious attempts to codify international law on an important subject. The commission appointed a special rapporteur who prepared reports for consideration of the topics involved, and articles were prepared and submitted to governments for comments. This prepared the way for the General Assembly to call the First United Nations Conference on the Law of the Sea in 1958, which prepared four conventions: the high seas, the continental shelf, the territorial sea and contiguous zone, and fishing. These were duly ratified by 1966 and became part of international law. The Second UN Conference on the Law of the Sea in 1958 did not accomplish any important substantive business.

In 1967 Ambassador Arvid Pardo from Malta proposed that resources of the seabed "beyond the limits of present national jurisdiction" be declared "the common heritage of mankind" to be held in trust by a new international authority. This resolution was approved in 1970 by the General Assembly by a vote of 108 to 0 with only 14 abstentions, mostly from the Soviet Bloc. (The United States voted in favor, but as indicated below, the Reagan administration later reversed the U.S. position.) The General Assembly then called, in 1973, the Third United Nations Conference on the Law of the Sea. It was charged to try again to set an agreed breadth for the territorial sea, involving jurisdiction over navigation, and to define the rights and duties of all states in the oceans.

Major divisions of opinion centered around the industrial states with advanced ocean technology versus the Third World states without such technology, and those states with coastlines versus those without. After extended negotiations, agreement was reached on these issues, including establishment of a regime that would administer the resources of the high seas for the benefit of all. The third conference produced a UN convention addressing this and other issues including:

—breadth of the territorial sea
—freedom of transit through straits
—jurisdiction over adjacent marine resources
—control of mining
—pollution
—scientific research
—settlement of disputes

The convention is designed to enter into force one year from the date of the 60th ratification. As of the beginning of 1992, 159 states had signed and 51 had ratified the convention. The United States refused to sign the treaty because it insisted that beyond the narrow belt of territorial waters the seas are open to all nations including mining its resources. The United States has signed another agreement with the United Kingdom, Germany, France, Japan, Belgium, Italy, and the Netherlands for settling disputes on deep seabed mining matters, but the United States refused to recognize the regime set up by the Third Law of the Sea Conference to administer those resources. The United States, on March 10, 1983, announced, however, that it recognizes the provisions of that convention on the territorial sea and on transit rights, which the United States said confirmed existing maritime law and practice.

A UN commission has been established that is preparing to put the UN convention in effect, and it has already helped settle competing claims for mining the resources of the sea. In 1992, however, it was marking time waiting to see if the United States would change its policies after the presidential elections. The part of the agreement that sets up "The Enterprise" to manage such claims depends on the cooperation of the United States, the most powerful maritime nation in the world.

The International Maritime Organization, a Specialized Agency, carries on activities related to the law of the sea. IMO has worked on technical matters, including pollution issues. Its convention on pollution as amended in 1962 and 1969 requires states not to discharge their ballast tanks or leave visible traces on the water within 50 miles of coastal zones. Photographs from aircraft are admissible as evidence of violation of this convention. A 1973 convention requires separate ballast tanks on tankers over 70,000 deadweight tons so they do not pollute the sea with ballast tanks that held petroleum.

The sixth committee of the General Assembly has drafted conventions on privileges and immunities of the United Nations and a convention providing punishment for genocide. The genocide convention was approved unanimously by the UN General Assembly in 1948, but it was not approved by the U.S. Senate until 1986. The implementing legislation was not passed until 1988, 40 years after the initial approval by the United Nations. Opponents of the treaty were afraid that it would supersede the U.S. Constitution and be used in ways detrimental to the United States. The U.S. Senate approved the convention with reservations in 1986.

Other bodies created by the General Assembly for drafting international law include the Commission on International Trade Law, which was established in 1966. It has completed many conventions on international trade including one on the sale of goods and one on international bills of exchange.

The Specialized Agencies also are in the act. The International Labor Organization has drafted numerous conventions on labor welfare. The International Bank for Reconstruction and Development has drafted an important convention on settling investment disputes. The United States is a party to well over a hundred multilateral agreements negotiated within the UN System.[7]

UN ATTEMPTS TO CONTAIN INTERNATIONAL TERRORISM

The United Nations has addressed international terrorism, but like its other international law activities, its actions have not been so dramatic or newsworthy as more direct action. The widespread outrage against acts of international terrorists in 1986 generated a surge of opinion demanding that the United States strike back and punish those responsible for violent crimes. The voices calling for reasoned and legal action against such crimes were lost in the public call for retribution. This section examines what has been accomplished in the United Nations through cooperation under international law and evaluates chances for success in comparison to the forceful actions that have been taken outside that framework.[8]

We first look at the general UN resolution calling for cooperation against international terrorism and then evaluate the specific conventions that cover hijacking of aircraft, taking of hostages, attacking diplomatic targets, and supporting nuclear terrorism. The United Nations System is not in a position to act like an international police force to arrest terrorists and punish countries that support them. The United Nations is more like a forum to promote cooperation and develop a body of international law to help countries act together. Such an international process can precipitate positive action and fix positions near a high level of cooperation.

UN Resolutions

The May 1972 massacre of 28 civilian passengers at Israel's Lod Airport by Japanese terrorists working with a Palestine group, and the September 1972 Munich massacre of 11 Israeli athletes by the Palestinian Black September group stimulated worldwide horror and determination to take action. Secretary General Waldheim asked that terrorism be placed on the agenda of the General Assembly. The Arab nations agreed, but they insisted that the agenda item also include a study of the underlying causes of terrorist acts. The Arab nations supported the Palestine Liberation Organization, whereas the Africans did not want to hamper the "freedom fighters" fighting the colonial powers in Portugal and South Africa.

The United States tabled a convention to punish acts of terrorism. The initial General Assembly action was to approve a resolution creating a 35 member *ad hoc* committee in 1972 to study the matter. The United States opposed the wording of the resolution because it appeared to limit condemnation of terrorism to acts committed by colonial, racial, and alien (Israeli) regimes and implied encouragement of violence by "freedom fighters."

During years of negotiation that followed, the West continued to condemn all acts of international terrorism, whereas Communists and Arab-Africans did not want to condemn "national liberation" struggles. Certain delegates pointed out that the way to go was to conclude specific conventions, such as those against hijacking and the protection of diplomats. Finally, by December 1979 the first major antiterrorist resolution was adopted by 118 countries with 22 abstentions including the United States and Western Europe. The United States and certain Western European countries abstained because changes were made in the final resolution from what had been agreed on in the working group. However, by 1981 as the subject received its annual consideration by the General Assembly, the United States and Western Europe approved a resolution that condemned all acts of international terrorism but did not propose to give a free reign when colonial, racist, and alien regimes were involved. By December 9, 1985 in another resolution, the UN General Assembly adopted a general resolution against terrorism without a role-call vote with no objections. The compromise wording of the resolution reaffirmed the inalienable right to self-determination and independence of all peoples under colonial and racist regimes, thus meeting the problem of the Arab-African delegations.

The resolution unequivocally condemned as criminal all acts of terrorism and deplored the loss of innocent lives from such acts. It appealed to all states to become party to the existing international conventions such as those on hijacking and hostages. It called on states to fulfill their obligations under international law not to assist terrorist acts and urged them to cooperate in exchanging information and to enforce the law against persons committing acts of international terrorism.

This was a major step forward, but there is little prospect that the United Nations will agree on a comprehensive convention on international terrorism. On the one hand, the Arab-African group and the Communists do not want to provide legal instruments that could be used to oppose national liberation struggles; moreover, the European countries are concerned about legal safeguards to protect individuals for asylum against prosecution for political crimes. Nevertheless, the above resolution and the following agreements show that there is a growing body of international law and increasing international cooperation against terrorist crimes.[9]

ICAO Conventions

The actions of the International Civil Aviation Organization (ICAO) against terrorism demonstrate what can be accomplished by international cooperation and respect for international law. In the late 1960s hijacking of aircraft peaked, stimulating action by national governments and the ICAO. The first important agreement was the Tokyo Convention of 1963, which defined jurisdiction for hijacking crimes and gave power to the aircraft commanders to act against hijackers. This was followed by the Hague Convention of 1970, which obligated states to punish the guilty severely or to extradite them expeditiously. Although nations under this convention could refuse to extradite prisoners if the crime were politically motivated, this loophole has not been used to a significant extent to permit hijackers to escape trial and punishment. This was followed by the Montreal Convention of 1971, which covers unlawful acts on the ground and obligates states to take measures to prevent such crimes. The above conventions were reinforced by ICAO technical manuals to strengthen precautions against skyjacking. In 1987 ICAO adopted another protocol on acts of violence at airports. In 1991 its protocol controlling plastic explosives was signed by 41 countries.

Over 110 countries cooperated under these conventions to stop skyjacking. As a result, the number of terrorist skyjackings or attempted skyjackings fell from a high of about 18 in 1969 to an average of 1.5 in 1986–87.[10]

The United States in the 1960s was particularly affected by skyjackers who forced planes to go to Cuba. Although Cuba is not a member of ICAO and did not subscribe to the above conventions, it negotiated a special agreement with the United States that provided for extradition or punishment of hijackers. It has punished them severely with sentences ranging from 2 to 50 years. Following the negotiation of this agreement, hijacking to Cuba fell drastically. It is interesting to note that the special agreement included something for Cuba, namely that the parties to the agreement would not support armed probes against the other. This reflected Cuba's concern about the CIA probes after the Bay of Pigs incident that were mounted from Florida during the Kennedy administration against Cuban targets.

Crimes Against Diplomats

The United States was the primary sponsor of measures to protect diplomats. On November 28, 1972 a General Assembly resolution formed a committee to draft articles, and a convention was approved by Resolution 3166 of December 14, 1973. In 1985 65 nations were parties, including the United

States. The aim of the convention is to prosecute or extradite persons alleged to have committed serious crimes against diplomats and "internationally protected persons." This requires states to conform their legislation to the international conventions. This presented a problem for the United States, which has a tradition of leaving to local officials rather than to the national government the responsibility for protecting consuls and diplomats. This is expensive, and local governments have problems covering the cost. Under subsequent U.S. legislation, limited authority is provided for the national government to extend financial assistance to any of the 50 American states burdened with this problem.[11]

Convention on the Taking of Hostages

The Federal Republic of Germany instigated discussions in 1976 on a convention against the taking of hostages. Germany had been shocked by a siege of its embassy in Sweden by terrorists. The General Assembly passed the German proposal to the General Assembly's Sixth Committee in 1976.

The 1979 convention adopted by the General Assembly obligates states to punish offenders or to extradite them. The major problem was that Algeria and Libya wanted to exclude populations attacking racist and colonial regimes; others wanted to exclude national liberation movements from penalties for hostage taking. The Western nations, on the other hand, insisted on no exceptions for hostage-takers. The national liberation movement issue was settled by letting the Geneva Convention of 1949 on the laws of war apply to national liberation conflicts.[12] This convention does prohibit hostage taking. Another issue arose out of the Israeli attack at the Entebbe Airport of Uganda, when terrorists held a plane hostage and the Ugandan government took no effective action. Israeli commandos attacked the airport, destroyed the plane, and rescued the hostages with a few casualties among the passengers and terrorists. The convention on the taking of hostages states that nothing in this convention should be construed as justifying the violation of territorial integrity of the state. Finally, the asylum issue was settled by a similar provision that nothing in the convention would impair the right of asylum. The General Assembly adopted the hostage convention in December 1979 opening it for signature. In June 1985 it was in effect for 27 countries and was being observed by many more.[13]

In 1992 there was dramatic success by behind-the-scenes UN diplomacy in getting hostages released. Years of U.S. efforts, including trading arms for hostages in the Iran-Contra scandal, had failed. Lebanon had been the source of most hostage problems. The UN Secretary General and his aide, Giandomenico Picco, took over behind-the-scenes negotiations, which

were aided by the decision of the Arab countries to begin face-to-face negotiations with Israel. Between August and December 1991 nine Western hostages and remains of another were released in Lebanon, and 91 Lebanese
detainees were released in South Lebanon and Israel. The secretary general
kept details of negotiations secret, but he thanked groups in Lebanon and
the assistance of Israel, Iran, Libya, and Syria.

In February 1992 the Security Council in a resolution urged Libya to
meet U.S. and British demands to try suspects accused of bombing Pan Am
flight 103 in which 270 people were killed. The International Court rejected
an appeal from Libya to stop the United States from using a threat of force
to coerce Libya to turn over the suspects. Libya did not meet the deadline,
so on March 31, 1992, the Security Council passed a resolution imposing
sanctions. There were no negative votes, although there were abstentions.
The sanctions included an air embargo and an end to arms sales. The same
day the International Court rejected a Libyan appeal to declare the sanctions
invalid. Libya was forced to offer compromises such as offering to have the
accused tried in Malta, but they were rejected by the Security Council. The
Security Council's resolution was a landmark, the first time a country had
been punitively isolated by that body. After the sanctions, press reports
indicated 1,700 Soviet military and technical advisers left Libya, severely
weakening its air defense system.

International Cooperation to Recover
Nuclear Materials

In the last 20 years, there were moves to control nuclear materials to prevent terrorist groups from using them. The major agreement was a treaty
ratified in 1982 that had been negotiated at meetings of the International
Atomic Energy Agency in its headquarters in Vienna. It sets standards for
shipment and storage of sensitive nuclear materials used for peaceful purposes and includes provisions for guards. States must punish or extradite
offenders and assist each other in prosecution.

In the years before the agreement there had been many incidents. In
1974, police had arrested men plotting to steal uranium in India. In 1977,
undercover U.S. agents arrested persons offering two tons of nuclear material for sale. In 1979, federal officials arrested two other persons who stole
thousands of pounds of semi-refined uranium ore from a New Mexico uranium mill. From 1977 to 1982, eight nuclear reactors in Germany were

sabotaged. Similar incidents occurred in France. From 1970 to 1982, there were 60 threats against American cities claiming nuclear devices were involved, but all were hoaxes.[14]

A major effort was made during the breakup of the Soviet Union for Moscow to keep control of its nuclear weapons. Also, the June 1992 agreement of the U.S. and Russia to cut nuclear arms included provisions for a senior group to protect against limited nuclear launches. Its primary goal would be anti-ballistic missile defense. Such a group would also want to coordinate action on terrorist use of nuclear weapons.

The above provisions of international law against various types of terrorism leave a gap for acts not involving aircraft, diplomatic persons, nuclear terrorism, or hostages. For example, no international agreement covered the bombing of a nightclub in Berlin in which innocent people were killed. However, local law would punish criminals involved in such crimes, and many states routinely cooperate in extraditing criminals for crimes. The most dangerous gap is nuclear terrorism, a crisis in which terrorists would steal nuclear weapons, but the major nuclear powers are trying to close that gap. Moroever, when hijackings and terrorist incidents occur, there is international cooperation, including that of third-world governments to punish the culprits. This includes refusing to let hijacked planes land, and refusing demands to release terrorists already imprisoned. The UN resolutions of 1979 to 1985 provide a general obligation for such cooperation.

There was a great increase in international terrorism after 1980. However, cooperation under the ICAO dramatically lessened terrorist skyjackings and attempted skyjackings from an average of about 18 in 1970 to less than 2 at the end of the 1980s.

In contrast the overall number of terrorist incidents increased about 50 percent from 1980 to 1985.[15] The main targets of Palestinian and Lebanese terrorists were Israel and, as the principal supporter of Israel, the United States. The United States provides billions of dollars of assistance to Israel annually and is a source of most of its military equipment. (The United States provides a similar amount of aid to Egypt.) The Palestinians regard Israel as having stolen their territory because of Israel's occupation of the West Bank after the 1967 war.

The United States took a prominent role through Ambassador Habib in negotiating the withdrawal of the PLO from Lebanon in 1983. When the United States attempted to support the Lebanese government by stationing U.S. armed forces there, terrorists attacked and killed 241 Marines by blowing up the Marine headquarters in Beirut; subsequently, the United States retaliated with bombing targets in Lebanon and shelling from U.S. battleships offshore. This use of power politics failed to stabilize the situation, and the United States in frustration withdrew its forces from Lebanon.

Iranian hatred of the United States had been stimulated by the CIA intervention under President Eisenhower in 1952 to support the Shah against a popular movement to unseat him. Subsequently, the United States provided major military and economic aid, including assistance to the hated Savak police. In Latin America, CIA support for the Contras' attacks against Nicaragua helped stimulate terrorist incidents against Americans in Latin America. Also, many of the incidents were related to trying to suppress the drug trade.

In the 1980s there was an increasing cycle of violence and retaliation by the United States against international terrorists. The action against terrorists accelerated in the spring of 1986 after a bombing of a nightclub in Berlin in which an American sergeant and a Turkish seaman were killed and about 100 people were injured. President Reagan, who had evidence Libya was involved, ordered an attack by F-111s based in Britain and carrier aircraft based in the Mediterranian against targets in Libya. As a result of these raids against a sovereign Arab state, which violated international law, Arab nations unanimously condemned the raid against Libya, and the UN Security Council voted 10-5 to condemn the bombing of Libya, but the resolution was vetoed by the United States, Britain, and France with nay votes from Denmark and Australia. The General Assembly in November, 1986, condemned the U.S. attack by a vote of 79 to 28, with 33 abstentions.

This does not mean the U.S. policies were the original cause of terrorism, but U.S. retaliation exaccerbated the problem. Its violent response in Libya and Lebanon contrasted with the moderate, cooperative efforts of nations under the International Civil Aviation Organization and the secretary general that conformed to international law and effectively reduced terrorist skyjacking. International terrorism will probably exist as long as war does. However, the success of the United Nations under ICAO agreements against skyjacking, in negotiation for the release of hostages from Lebanon, and the Security Council's sanctions against Libyan terrorism show what can be done under international law and the United Nations, in contrast to the failure of U.S. attacks in Lebanon.

HUMAN RIGHTS

The UN Charter differs from the League Covenant in affirming as a principal objective the encouraging of respect for human rights. The United Nations has not only been used to oppose international terrorism by private groups, but it is also used to promote freedom and oppose oppression and terrorism by the states against their own citizens. The Charter is not clear on this point, because Article 2, paragraph 7 states that nothing in the Charter shall authorize the United Nations to intervene in matters essentially within the domestic jurisdiction of a state. This provision can be broadly interpreted to mean that when violations of human rights are flagrant, they have international repercussions, and then are subject to UN action.

A number of conventions relating to basic human rights have been approved in the UN System in addition to the two comprehensive conventions on political and economic and social rights. These other conventions include additional conventions against slavery (1953, 1957), the ILO convention on the abolition of forced labor and the conventions relating to refugees and stateless persons (1954 and 1960). The United States finally ratified the 1951 convention on genocide in 1986, but the Senate included reservations requiring the United States to agree in each case before a case could go to the World Court, and an "understanding" stating acts during armed conflicts without specific intent, as required by the convention, would not constitute genocide.

In a practical sense, various bodies of the United Nations have vigorously promoted political and social rights, even though there has been little enforcement because of practical and legalistic problems. The Commission on Human Rights established by the General Assembly began its work in January 1947 under the chairmanship of Eleanor Roosevelt. (President Franklin D. Roosevelt was her husband.) It held hearings and prepared a Universal Declaration of Human Rights, which was adopted by the General Assembly on December 10, 1948 by a vote of 48 in favor, 8 abstentions, and 2 absent, with no nation voting against. The commission then began incorporating these principles into a covenant on civil and political rights and a covenant on economic and cultural rights. After many years of painstaking efforts, the two covenants were approved by the General Assembly on December 16, 1966. They came into effect in 1976 after 35 ratifications each. In addition there is an optional protocol by which nations agree to act on individual complaints of human rights violations submitted to the UN Human Rights Committee.

The covenants include in great detail provisions for civil and political rights such as those included in the U.S. Bill of Rights. The covenant on economic and cultural rights is more far-reaching. The first covenant includes the right to life, liberty, and security of person, freedom from slavery, freedom from arbitrary arrest and detention, the right to a fair trial and to be presumed innocent until proved guilty, inviolability of the home, freedom of movement, freedom of opinion and peaceful assembly, and the right to vote and participate in government. The second includes the right to social security, the right to work, the right to education, and the right to an adequate standard of living.

The UN Human Rights Commission has established working groups and rapporteurs for the following types of human rights violations: torture, disappearances, arbitrary execution, religious intolerance, and arbitrary detention. They take action and report to the commission after investigating and asking governments to explain thousands of alleged human rights violations. Only a small percentage of the violations are clarified, and perhaps the most effective actions are taken by the private groups such as Amnesty International. Nevertheless, the UN action reinforces actions of private groups and establishes international standards against which the actions of states can be measured. Condemnation by the international community of human rights violations can have an effect on even the most hardened regimes and rulers, and help correct at least the most blatant violations.

Obviously human rights will not be honored throughout the world until the millenium, and for this reason some writers take a cynical view toward the conventions. This causes problems of ratification by legislators who take laws seriously, particularly in the United States, although the United States is one of the leading supporters of such rights. Another problem is a fear by some U.S. politicians that the United Nations would use the UN Covenants to threaten the sovereignty of the United States. Also, critics say that the covenants are not taken seriously by some states, and they, therefore, are not important. Moreover, the provision guaranteeing a job and social security causes problems for those advocating a free enterprise philosophy and opposing excessive state intervention.

Supporters of the covenants reply that these are goals that nations should seek to achieve and that the covenants give leverage to those supporting human rights as an international policy objective. As an argument they note that many domestic laws are not enforced strictly—as many as 90 percent of incidents of theft in the United States are not punished, but this does not mean it should not bother with laws against theft.

Support by the United States for the covenants on human rights reached a high point under President Carter, who supported them by speeches and actions. Reports on human rights were used in decisions on aid programs.[16]

His ambassador to the United Nations, Andrew Young, a black, carried the flag on this issue including a visit to South Africa.

As new African members were admitted to the United Nations, it took increasingly strong action against racism, particularly apartheid policies of South Africa. The Security Council approved a voluntary arms embargo in 1963 and a mandatory one in 1977. The United States tended to lag behind in such actions asserting that racism was a matter of domestic jurisdiction. Congress with President Carter's encouragement supported the embargo in 1977. In 1986 Congress increased sanctions against South Africa.

From December 12 to 14, 1989, the General Assembly held a special session on apartheid and proposed specific guidelines for dismantling the system. Events accelerated in the following year under the new South African president F. W. de Klerk. He lifted the ban on political action by the African National Congress, which represented black opposition to the government, and released its leader, Nelson Mandela, from prison. The UN pressures and Mandela's moderation encouraged the South African government to repeal major pieces of discriminatory legislation, including laws that restricted movement and areas where blacks could live. The government entered into negotiations with black political groups on amendments to the constitution that would give blacks the vote and equal political rights.

There was more success on the Namibian issue. In 1945 the United Nations had inherited the South African mandate of South-West Africa, now recognized as Namibia. For over 40 years the United Nations in resolutions and action by the International Court tried to get South Africa to agree to Namibian independence. South Africa finally tied the issue to the presence of Cuban troops in Angola, which had intervened in South-West Africa. On December 22, 1988, two agreements, reflecting a U.S. initiative, were signed at UN headquarters providing for withdrawing Cuban troops from Angola, and for holding elections monitored by the United Nations. The elections were held with 97 percent participation, and on March 21, 1990, Namibia achieved its independence. The UN force of 7,900 military and civilian personnel was withdrawn at the end of March.

The basis of international law is for nations to respect other's sovereignty and to settle disputes peacefully. It differs from domestic law in that there is no powerful supergovernment to enforce its norms and rulings of the International Court. Enforcement of international law to maintain the peace is left to individual governments and political processes of the Security Council, which is composed of sovereign governments. The great powers in the past have used the court and international law only when convenient to reinforce their positions.

Leaders of the great powers have tended to rely on power politics to achieve their goals, and on many occasions have not kept their actions within international law. Other leaders, particularly of smaller nations and officials who worked in the UN System, often had a longer-range view of strengthening international law to achieve world peace. However, when Iraq attacked Kuwait in 1990, the United States was so successful in mobilizing UN support to repel the invasion, the United Nations and international law had a major revival of prestige, particularly in the United States.

Meanwhile, the United States negotiated treaties, the major instruments of international law, with drastic reductions in nuclear weapons. In the spring of 1992 the United States, Great Britain, and France were able to work through the Security Council to put sanctions on Libya, pressuring it to turn over for trial men accused of international terrorism. With growing interdependence of states the UN System continued to extend the rule of international law in the fields of trade and commerce, labor standards, protection of diplomats and other fields of international relations. The United States recognized many provisions of the new law of the sea convention even though it did not ratify it.

In previous years the peaceful processes of the UN System had other major successes, not so well publicized. The pressure of Security Council sanctions supported by the International Court and the General Assembly helped persuade South Africa to give Namibia independence and repeal apartheid legislation. In 1992 it was negotiating changes in its constitution to give the blacks the vote.

The process of negotiation and international cooperation to control terrorism showed marked success in drastically reducing skyjacking as a form of international terrorism. This contrasted with the lack of success of the United States as it tried to stop terrorism by retaliation, such as bombing Libya and Lebanon, which could not be justified under international law.

UN support for human rights faces the hurdle of the international law principle of not interfering in matters of domestic jurisdiction. In the past, human rights and civil war have been considered matters of domestic jurisdiction, unless violations were so flagrant they caused international problems, such as in the case of the Yugoslav civil war. However, in recent years the United Nations has become more assertive for human rights. The "ethnic cleansing" by Servian forces caused public outrage, and the United Nations responded by imposing sanctions and sending UN forces to Yugoslavia. The caucus of black nations in the United Nations led the way in approving sanctions on South Africa to end apartheid policies. The United States was a leader in getting the Human Rights Commission to investigate Yugoslav atrocities and in objecting to human rights violations in Cuba.

China and Cuba have not succeeded in stopping extension of UN human rights activities. The end of the Cold War and the new cooperation of Russia, including candor about the Soviets' former violations of human rights, accelerated the process of extending the rule of law.

The above are only examples of how the United Nations acts in the field of international law. The entire UN System works within that framework, and the final chapter evaluates its effectiveness.

Notes to Chapter 7

1. Louis Henkin et al., *Right v. Might: International Law and the Use of Force* (New York: Council of Foreign Relations Press, 1989).

2. R. Falk, F. Kratochivil, and S. Medelovitz (eds.), *Intenrational Law* (Boulder, CO: Westview Press, 1985); H. Lauterpaucht, in H. Falk et al., *The Grotian Tradition in International Law* (Boulder, CO: Westview Press, 1985).

3. A. Chayes, *The Cuban Missile Crises* (New York: Oxford University Press, 1974), p. 106.

4. G. von Glahn, *Law Among Nations* (New York: Macmillan, 1981), p. 160.

5. *UN Monthly Chronicle*, January, 1975, p. 104; and May, 1974, p. 96.

6. B. Weston et al., *International Law and World Order* (St. Paul: West, 1980), pp. 302–310.

7. U.S. Department of State, *Treaties in Force* (Washington, DC: GPO, 1981).

8. *Terrorism, An International Journal*, Vol. 6, Number 4, 1983.

9. A. Yoder, "United Nation's Resolutions Against International Terrorism," *Terrorism*, Vol. 6, No. 4, 503–512.

10. U.S. Department of State, Office of the Ambassador at Large for Counterterrorism, "International Terrorist Incidents, 1968–1987."

11. K. Shamwell, "Implementing the Convention on the Prevention and Punishment of Crimes Against Internationally Protected Persons, Including Diplomatic Agents," *Terrorism, An International Journal*, Vol. 6, No. 4, 1983.

12. In the view of Abraham Sofaer, legal adviser to the Department of State, this did not create a gap in the hostage convention. He goes on to say that it did permit some states to have a rhetorical and political victory, which I translate as saving face. "Terrorism and the Law," *Foreign Affairs* (Summer 1986), pp. 901–922.

13. J. McDonald, "The UN Convention Against Hostage-Taking," *Terrorism, An International Journal*, Vol. 4, No. 4, 1983.

14. B. Jenkins, "International Cooperation in Locating and Recovering Stolen Nuclear Materials," *Terrorism, An International Journal*, Vol. 6, No. 4, 1983.

15. U.S. Department of State, 1987.

16. J. Carter, *Keeping Faith* (New York: Bantam, 1982), pp. 143–163.

Chapter VIII

ECONOMIC AND SOCIAL RESPONSIBILITIES OF THE UNITED NATIONS

The General Assembly and its Economic and Social Council (ECOSOC) are the central UN organs for promoting international cooperation for economic and social problems. This is one of the principal aims of the Charter, and about 80 percent of the budget of the UN System is spent for this purpose. The General Assembly determines policies for the economic and social activities of the United Nations. With 175 members and only a limited meeting time each fall, the General Assembly has come to depend on the ECOSOC to do the spade work and make recommendations for approval by the Assembly.

THE ECONOMIC AND SOCIAL COUNCIL

The functions of the Economic and Social Council, which are covered in Chapter 10 of the Charter, reflect recommendations made by a League of Nations committee to establish a special organ for such work. As laid out in the Charter, ECOSOC carries out studies and reports, calls international conferences, prepares draft conventions, and sets up commissions to accomplish its aims.

ECOSOC has 54 members that rotate every three years. By custom the United States and other large powers stay on ECOSOC and do not take turns because ECOSOC resolutions would have little meaning if they were not approved by these larger nations. The Charter was amended twice to increase its size at the demand of the smaller states, which wanted an opportunity to be represented more often on this body.

ECOSOC works efficiently as a committee, considering its size. It has two major meetings a year, one in Geneva and one in New York. With a limited time to work through an ambitious agenda, it avoids long debates in its plenary sessions by passing on to the next item and letting concerned nations settle issues outside the plenary. When these issues are settled, they are brought back to the plenary.

The section on the UN Conference on Trade and Development (UNCTAD), below, describes the complicated compromises on multinational corporations, the international monetary reform, and trade negotiations. The negotiations for the compromises were begun first in the UNCTAD context, but they were concluded in a July 1972 ECOSOC resolution.[1] It is revealing to review other major issues considered by ECOSOC in the 1970s, and then examine major issues taken up in the 1980s and 1990s.

In the 1970s the developing countries were pressing for support for international commodity agreements. They were led and supported by the newly rich oil countries that pointed to the Organization of Petroleum Exporting Countries (OPEC) as the model for making commodity agreements and getting bargaining power vis-a-vis the developed countries. They hoped to create a "new international economic order" with such agreements and with other major reforms to the international trading system. The developing countries found, however, that this was not a panacea, because some were buyers as well as sellers of commodities, and high prices would hurt some of them and help others. OPEC was not a valid model, because the developed countries bought the great bulk of the petroleum from the OPEC cartel, but here, too, many developing countries suffered from high oil prices.

In the 1980s ECOSOC and the International Monetary Fund, particularly, were concerned with the debt burden of the developing countries. The debts were caused in part by high oil prices and inflation, which helped increase interest rates on the debts. By the 1990s the slogan of "sustainable development" was popular. This bridged a gap between developed countries, which emphasized progress on environmental issues, and developing countries, which needed foreign investments to employ their people, introduce new technology, thus relieving poverty. The developing countries hoped that the end of the Cold War would allow some of the tremendous sums used for armaments to be transferred to development.

Critics have asserted that a lot of the resolutions on such general issues are wasted effort because ECOSOC does not control the funds and organizations that carry out broad economic programs. However, this overlooks the fact that for the most part the same nations that are represented on ECOSOC are also members of governing boards of Specialized Agencies, including the powerful International Monetary Fund. Governments try to be consistent, so that compromises in general resolutions hammered out by countries in ECOSOC will normally be honored by these countries in other organizations of the UN System. Moreover, representatives of these other organizations attend ECOSOC meetings and are consulted on controversial issues.

The General Assembly and ECOSOC also give policy guidelines for the work of the various bodies of the UN proper, whereas the secretary general appoints their heads and is responsible for administering them. Most of these organs have their own governing bodies and sources of funds, and the major donor nations tend to have the most influence in their activity. In this chapter we focus on the work of the social and economic organs of the UN proper that are most active, including the UN Development Program (UNDP), the UN Children's Emergency Fund (UNICEF), the UN High Commissioner for Refugees (UNHCR), the UN Environment Program (UNEP), the population organs, the UN Conference on Trade and Development (UNCTAD), and those dealing with the transnational corporations. It is not a comprehensive survey, but it illustrates interactions that take place among the many UN agencies. In the previous chapter we covered social and economic activities of the United Nations in the field of international law, including civil aviation, law of the sea, and human rights.

The next chapter examines the work of the Specialized Agencies, many of which have been around longer than the United Nations and are closely associated with it. Representatives of these agencies report to ECOSOC and the General Assembly, although they take policy direction only from their governing bodies. As in the case of the bodies in the UN System, the fact that the Specialized Agencies report to the General Assembly and ECOSOC and the fact that the same governments give directions both to the United Nations and to the Specialized Agencies allows the United Nations to coordinate activities of the Specialized Agencies at the top. UNDP representatives coordinate them at the local level. Appendix E lists the Specialized Agencies and other units of the UN System with their budgets.

THE REGIONAL ECONOMIC COMMISSIONS

The regional economic commissions act like regional coordinating bodies for UN activities. The first one established by the Economic and Social Council was the Economic Commission for Europe (ECE), designed to help in the economic reconstruction of Europe after World War II. The Marshall

Plan and the Organization for European Economic Cooperation (OEEC) took over this function in Western Europe.[2] Since then ECE has become an important center for promoting East-West trade, particularly through standardization of administrative procedures. It leaves the major initiatives to promoting trade among Western European counties to the European Economic Community. The regular membership of ECE consists of European nations plus Canada and the United States.

The ECE's work is carried out by 10 subsidiary bodies and 4 working parties. Important work of the Inland Transport Committee includes reducing paperwork and restrictions. Its Senior Advisor on Environmental Problems represent countries causing about 90 percent of the world's industrial pollution, so that ECE promotes international cooperation in this area. In recent years it has called on governments to use water resources more effectively, since irrational use of water is a major factor limiting development and causing pollution.

The Economic and Social Commission for Asia and the Pacific (ESCAP), formerly the Economic Commission for Asia and the Far East (ECAFE), points with pride to establishing the Asian Bank and promoting regional projects such as in the Mekong Valley, the Asian Telecommunications Network, and links in the Asian Highway. Four of its five nonregional members (the United States, France, the Netherlands, and the United Kingdom) have provided considerable economic and technical assistance in promoting the above projects. Contributions of the other member, the Soviet Union, have been minor. The success in helping promote the region's industrial development was reflected by the need for a 1985 ministerial meeting to deal with environment problems caused by industrial pollution.

The Economic Commission for Latin America and the Caribean (ECLAC) has four nonregional members—France, the Netherlands, Spain, and the United Kingdom. It has concentrated on promoting economic integration and has attempted to reactivate the Central American Common Market, but this has been blocked by the political conflicts in the area. ECLAC has called for support of the Contadora peace process for Nicaragua and an end to foreign intervention against peace and economic development in the region. Its major concern has shifted from trade restrictions to the foreign debt problem in recent years.

The Economic Commission for Africa, established in 1958, initially concentrated on developing a statistical and factual base for development activities. Its substantive work concentrates on agriculture, and a joint ECA/ Food and Agriculture Organization Division assists livestock and food production of small farmers. ECA also tried to help meet the almost unlimited need to promote and coordinate transport and communications in Africa. As indicated above, the severe drought problem has been managed by UNDP, but ECA has carried out long-term studies of the problem.

The headquarters of the Economic and Social Commission for Western Asia was moved from Baghdad to Amman, Jordan after the outbreak of the Gulf War in 1991. Its meetings have been highly politicized by admitting the PLO but not admitting Israel as a member.

THE UN DEVELOPMENT PROGRAM

The UNDP is one of the most important of the regular UN bodies, although it is not featured in the organization charts. It was formed originally as the Expanded Program of Technical Assistance by General Assembly Resolution 304 of November 16, 1949. This grew out of the inspiration of President Truman's Point 4 Program, which proposed that the United States and other nations provide technical assistance to the developing world.

The UNDP is under the UN secretary general, but it has its own governing council of 48 members. It gets virtually all of its money from voluntary contributions. In fact, its budget is somewhat larger than the regular budget of the United Nations. In recognition of the fact that the United States has contributed a large share of its total budget, its directors have been U.S. citizens.

The UNDP is under the UN secretary general. It obtains virtually all its money from voluntary contributions. Its budget includes that of the UN Fund for Population Activities and other funds. It also helps administer the $1 billion budget of the UN Environment Program. The U.S. contributions fell from about 30 percent of the UNDP budget to about 10 percent under the Reagan and Bush administrations.[3] Recipients of UNDP aid also contribute substantially projects in their own countries (Table 3).

The UNDP assists about 5,000 projects annually in over 170 countries and territories. Every year it is supporting about 11,000 experts in developing countries and awarding about 14,000 fellowships for study abroad. After 1991 most of its resources will go to the 45 poorest countries of the world, most of which are in Africa. It provides technical assistance to better-off third world countries but expects payment in those cases. New programs include those for the Commonwealth of Independent States.

Most of UNDP technical assistance is oriented toward problem solving. This consists of relatively short-range projects requested by a country to solve production and other problems in agriculture, industry, and other areas. Another major category of UNDP activity covers preinvestment surveys in mineral exploration, hydraulic development, power, and similar areas. In 1991 UNDP estimated that it generated $9 billion in private investment from its preinvestment and other studies, including investment from external sources.[4]

The Senegal River project is an example of such follow-up investments. Mali, Mauritania, and Senegal in Africa's Sahel region have a combined population of 14 million. They have in common the 1,000-mile Senegal River with its flow rate varying as much as 200 percent in any three-to-four-year period, and with its flow dropping drastically downstream where rainfall is least. Salinization prevented food production on some 12,000 square miles of farmland. The major irrigation dam of the system is being built with the aid of the World Bank. The UNDP worked with a trigovernmental coordinating committee (OMVS), and assisted in studies and training for rural development, in surveys of natural resources, control of crop pests, animal husbandry, fish production, and relocation of people displaced by the dam. By the end of 1981 UNDP had helped mobilize $900 million in investment for the projects. About $360 million of this was from Arab resources with the remainder by Western Europe, the United States, the African Development Bank, and the European Development Fund. Work is underway on the irrigation and hydropower dam at Mannantali, Mali, for an antisalt barrier at the river's mouth, and a harbor 500 miles upstream.[5] UNDP played a major role in assisting the trigovernmental committee coordinate the development efforts assisted with the project.

Following (Table 3) is a breakdown by sector of UNDP's activities in 1991, including both the investment surveys and the problem-solving activities.

Table 3
Types of UNDP Activities—1991

	Percent
Agriculture, forestry, and fisheries	17.6
Industry	10.6
Natural resources	9.8
Transport and communications	7.4
Health	5.2
Employment	4.7
Other	40.

Source: 1991 UNDP Annual Report (United Nations: New York, 1992), p. 21.

One of the innovations of UNDP in the field of technical assistance is the TOKTEN program to reverse the brain drain. The program of *transfer of know-how through expatriate nationals* involves sending experts who have settled in other countries back to their home nations for volunteer consultation for three to five weeks. They welcome a chance to visit friends and family. With their knowledge of the language and culture, they often can make quick and meaningful contributions on technical problems. By 1982 about 350 consultancies had been completed. The consultants normally waive consulting fees and settle for per diem and economy-class fares. More often than not, the TOKTEN experts carry more weight in advising than the foreign expert, although sometimes their advice is discounted.[6]

The UNDP administrator also manages the UN Volunteer Program, established by the General Assembly in 1970 along the lines of the U.S. Peace Corps program. By 1990 about 1,900 UN volunteers were in over 100 countries with 83 percent coming from developing countries and the rest from the industrialized nations. About 58 or 3 percent were from the United States. The U.S. Peace Corps worked closely helping to recruit and sponsor volunteers. In the early 1980s the United States through the Peace Corps budget provided the largest contribution to this UN program and in addition spent over $200,000 on the U.S. volunteer expenses. Often the UN volunteers were assigned to UNDP projects. By 1987, however, with pressure to cut the U.S. budget, U.S. contributions were cut drastically.

The fellowship programs are another important part of technical assistance. The UNDP in 1991 financed about 12,000 students and trainees. Generally, the selection of students and trainees grows out of a specific project. Training is usually for three months to a year and does not involve working for a higher degree (see Table 4).

The UNDP Resident Representatives (Resreps) for over 25 years have coordinated and evaluated aid programs of the United Nations and the Specialized Agencies. In 1983 the UN Joint Inspection Unit (JIU), which evaluates the management of UN organizations, recommended that the UNDP should continue evaluations of other agencies because of its special relationship with host governments and with the UN agencies which provide the technical experts. In line with JIU recommendations UNDP established a small, independent evaluation unit in UNDP to oversee that function of the UNDP field offices. While the office was being established, UNDP published evaluations on the technical assistance activities of UNIDO, WHO, UNESCO, and the International Trade Center.

In 1989 UNDP and the World Bank published a study of development strategies and concluded that African countries carrying out the conserva-

Table 4

Location of Principal Expenditures for UNDP Projects–1991
(Millions of U.S. Dollars)

China	48.9
Vietnam	33.9*
Sudan	25.1
Bangladesh	23.6
Pakistan	23.5
Mozambique	22.0
Brazil	21.7*
India	21.6
Nepal	18.9
Myanmar	17.9
Indonesia	17.1
Afghanistan	16.3
Tanzania	16.1
Uganda	15.5
Malawi	15.0
Angola	14.5
Niger	14.4
Kenya	14.3
Madagascar	14.3
Ethiopia	13.6
Burundi	13.1
Malawi	11.5
Zaire	11.5
Chad	11.3
Rwanda	11.2
Ghana	11.1
Burkina Faso	11.1
Regional	155.
Interregional	46.
Other (127 Countries)	532.
Total	1,123

Source: UNDP, "Annual Report of the Administrator for 1991" Add. 2, pp. 13–18.

*The Brazilian and Vietnamese governments covered about 80 percent of their program's cost. On the average local governments covered about 20 percent of the cost.

tive adjustment programs of the World Bank were showing the most success in development. These policies included balancing government budgets, privatizing enterprises, and freeing trade and exchange rates. African countries, the Economic Commission for Africa, other UN bodies, and the Organization for African Unity took exception and pointed at devastating social consequences of the above adjustments. They blamed factors such as low levels of aid and low commodity prices for development problems.

For many years the UNDP Resreps have prepared annual reports on donor aid activities in their countries, which are useful for country planning. They have had varying degrees of success in getting other bodies of the UN System to provide information for these reports because of a natural inclination of some of the Specialized Agencies to protect their turf.

In a follow-up to the UN conference on least-developed countries held in Paris in 1981, the UNDP organized round tables in certain countries to help the many aid agencies coordinate their aid efforts. The *1983 OECD Review* noted that although it is too early to assess the effectiveness of the UNDP round tables for coordinating assistance, they had contributed to improved planning and setting of priorities.[7]

The UNDP is sensitive to the need for the developing countries themselves to provide the leadership in its round tables. The annual report of the administrator for 1983 noted that government administrative structures could be overwhelmed by what could often be a hundred or more bilateral, multilateral, and nongovernmental aid organizations knocking at the door.[8] Even with the help of the UNDP Resrep, governments coordinating the assistance of dozens of donors is an immense task.

For a number of countries the roundtables gave them their first opportunity to present their requirements to donors as a group. Isabell V. Gruhn, in her article "The U.N. Maze Confounds Development," throws up her hands as if such coordination is a hopeless task, even for an experienced and effective UNDP representative.[9] OECD and the UN reports agree that such coordination is difficult, but they are more optimistic about the potential for the UNDP round tables as a useful instrument. The chairman of OECD/DAC notified member governments to request their local representatives to extend full cooperation in these consultations at the country level. UNDP noted that the approach of the resident coordinator is to let the host government make the ultimate decision, while UNDP assists it in the process.

The leading role of the Resrep at the local level has made the Resrep a natural coordinator for the United Nations in emergency and disaster operations. The UN Disaster Relief Organization (UNDRO), rather than establishing a network of officials in various countries waiting for a disaster, relies on the local UNDP Resrep to represent it locally when a disaster occurs. In the summer of 1984 at the beginning of the severe famine in the Sahel, the UNDP administrator obtained a special allocation from the UNDP council for the volunteers to help deal with the tragic food emergency in Africa. On the average, UNDP helps provide emergency disaster assistance to about 20 countries a year, while continuing to follow up on similar assistance to numerous other countries in previous years. Meanwhile, UNDRO has prepared a draft convention to facilitate clearances for emergency deliveries of aid.[10]

The UNDP is in a unique position in the UN system to evaluate and coordinate the many UN and other multilateral and bilateral aid activities carried on in the developing world. The UNDP's control of technical assistance funds, which it contracts out to the various Specialized Agencies, gives it leverage to get their cooperation in evaluating aid activities. The fact that UNDP does not have to renew their contracts leads to more efficient aid projects and works against a tendency for them to become self-perpetuating. With UNDP's extensive operational and coordinating responsibilities, one would expect a large bureaucratic organization. However, its central headquarters staff is relatively small. The overhead cost of UNDP for its projects was only 17 percent in 1991.

Developing countries obviously have a stake in continuing UNDP technical assistance projects, and they support UNDP. They do not, however, control the U.S. government's appropriations, which have been reduced in recent years. UNDP in recent years has obtained relatively less support for technical assistance than that provided to the UN Specialized Agencies. The above brief survey of its activities indicates that it is doing an essential job of coordination and a useful job of providing a major share of the technical assistance to the developing world.

THE UN CHILDREN'S FUND (UNICEF)

The United Nations Children's Fund (UNICEF) is the best-known subsidiary organ of the United Nations. Children in the United States solicit contributions for it at Halloween, and many people send UNICEF Christmas cards. With its imaginative ways of obtaining contributions, it has a budget about 40 percent of the size of its parent, the United Nations.

UNICEF was created by a unanimous vote of the General Assembly, December 11, 1946, to provide emergency relief for children victimized by

World War II. It took over from the UN Relief and Rehabilitation Administration (UNRRA), which was the principal relief organization for Europe after World War II. UNICEF works closely with the World Health Organization on immunization of children, on AIDS and other health matters, on nutrition, and on education. (See page 170.) Donor and beneficiary governments have equal voices on its executive board. Recipient governments have assumed responsibility for delivering supplies provided by UNICEF. In December 1965 UNICEF was awarded the Nobel Peace Prize for its work.

The 1990 World Summit for Children sponsored by UNICEF announced that UNICEF and the World Health Organization in 1990 were close to their goal of immunizing from diphtheria, polio, tetanus, whooping cough, tuberculosis, and measles 80 percent of the children under 1 year of age. The conference report estimated that the effort already made had saved over 12 million young lives. The World Summit set ambitious and probably unrealistic goals for the year 2000 that included reducing under-five death rates by one-third, halving maternal mortality, developing safe water, and halving children's severe and moderate malnutrition. In the 1990s UNICEF was emphasizing AIDS prevention including saving children from prostitution. Its *UNICEF Quarterly* (April–June 1992) indicated as many as 1 million children are forced into prostitution every year, which may mean a death sentence from AIDS for many.

REFUGEE RELIEF

The League of Nations organized international assistance to refugees in 1921 under the High Commissioner for Refugees. In 1943 the United Nations Relief and Rehabilitation Commission was set up to help the millions of displaced persons of World War II. In 1946 the International Refugee Organization took over refugee relief from UNRRA, and in 1951 the UN High Commissioner for Refugees assumed the task. UNHCR has had its mandate renewed at five-year intervals by the General Assembly. The High Commissioner reports to that body and works under the guidance of a 41-member executive committee. The High Commissioner not only provides aid to refugees but attempts to help voluntary repatriation or permanent resettlement in an asylum country.

The legal status of refugees is defined in two international treaties, the 1951 Convention on Refugees and the 1967 Protocol on Refugees. This defines refugees as persons outside their country who have a well-founded fear of persecution on the basis of race, nationality, and political opinion.

It has promoted the principle of *nonrefoulement*, which prohibits the expulsion or forcible return of a person to a country where he or she has reason to fear persecution. Almost 100 countries have agreed to be bound by these international agreements.

For many years UNHCR has assisted over 5 million refugees affected by severe African droughts, and it helped coordinate the major world relief effort of 1985 and the following years to assist these people. Other large UNHCR programs included assistance to the millions of refugees created by the war in Afghanistan, the hundreds of thousands of "boat people" fleeing from Vietnam, and over 1 million refugees in Central America. In 1945 and 1981 it received the Nobel Prize for its operations.

The assistance to the 2.4 million Palestinian refugees has been carried out by the UN Relief and Works Agency for Palestine Refugees in the Near East (UNRWA). It not only has provided food for the refugees created by the wars, but also has established schools and provided other assistance for their camps. The General Assembly has continued to call in vain for a solution to this problem through permitting refugees to return to their original homes in Israel and the West Bank. As indicated earlier, little progress has been made on this issue since Camp David.

THE UN ENVIRONMENT PROGRAM (UNEP)

The growing concern in the late 1960s about the environment stimulated convening the UN Conference on the Human Environment in Stockholm in 1972. The delegates formulated 109 recommendations, including a proposal to establish the UN Environment Program (UNEP). This body has no operating functions, but it works through committees under a 58-member governing council. It provides an annual state-of-the-environment report and facilitates cooperation and the exchange of knowledge in this field. It actively promotes cooperation in the pollution problem of the Mediterranean and other regional seas, and works with the International Maritime Organization (IMO) to prevent polluting the oceans. It has established the Global Environmental Monitoring System (GEMS) and a computerized information bank. It has also set up a fund for financing environmental programs. It has received donations of about $40 million a year for this fund.

The 1981 session of the General Assembly requested UNEP to prepare a list of products that governments consider harmful to the health and environment. The resolution was adopted by a vote of 146 to 1, with the United States in opposition because it considered the resolution ambiguous and expensive. UNEP now maintains the "International Register of Potentially Toxic Chemicals."

In March 1985 a UNEP-sponsored conference produced the Convention for the Protection of the Ozone Layer, which promotes research and an exchange of information. An annex referred to the need to limit production of chlorofluorocarbons. In 1987 another conference in Montreal agreed on a protocol for restricting the uses of substances that damage the ozone layer. One of the consequences if this problem is not solved would be an increase in skin cancers. UNEP also continued work on guidelines for disposal of toxic wastes.

POPULATION ACTIVITIES

Population activities are carried out by the Population Commission of ECOSOC and by the UN Fund for Population Activities (UNFPA). The commission provides analyses of world population trends and technical help to countries planning population programs. The UNFPA was set up as a trust fund in 1967 by the UN secretary general to assist countries to obtain basic data on population and later to help them formulate programs for research and family planning. Since 1973 it has operated under the guidance of ECOSOC and the UNDP.

The Population Commission organized the World Population Conference of 1974 in Bucharest, which laid out a plan of action that has been used as guidelines for countries developing programs for population control. Since some countries attending the conference wanted to promote population growth, the World Plan of Action of the conference was not consistently against population growth. Nevertheless, for countries wanting to put such programs into effect, the UNFPA is the world's largest source of funds and technical help. A new world conference was schedule for 1994.

Countries are sensitive about aid in this field. Originally, the program in India, supported by the United States, ran into trouble in the 1960s because of criticisms about infections with the "loops" and medical problems with "the pill." The Indian government phased out the U.S. program, and the World Bank substituted a loan program for family planning centers without political criticism.

In 1985 the United States withheld $10 million of its $46 million contribution to the UNFPA, because the United States alleged that there were abuses in the Chinese family planning program. (The China program was about 8 percent of the total UNFPA program.) The executive director of

UNFPA said that these charges were in error and that they had been refuted by the U.S. Agency for International Development (USAID) itself. USAID then replied it might resume its support to the UNFPA program. The United States continued to have reservations about the Chinese program, and this has remained an irritant in their relations.

The above demonstrates the advantage of channeling aid for family planning through UNFPA, because of the increased potential for political criticism where countries with different philosophies of family planning are directly involved in a donor-recipient relationship.

DRUG ABUSE CONTROL

The League of Nations from the beginning took responsibility for drug abuse control. The Hague Convention of 1912 came into effect under Article 295 of the Treaty of Versailles. An energetic American delegation and a group of reformers by 1925 brought reforming zeal to the League's Opium Committee and by 1925 obtained approval of the Geneva Convention of 1925, which limited manufacture of narcotic drugs to medical and scientific needs. The League's Permanent Central Opium Board and supervisory body evaluated and worked to control the quantity of drugs produced in over 60 signatory states. Its powers were transferred to the United Nations, ECOSOC, and its International Narcotics Control Board.

There are three basic treaties negotiated under UN auspices against the drug traffic. The treaty of 1961 brought together the major provisions of previous treaties and provides for controlling licit drugs. The 1972 treaty covers artificial drugs. A 1988 treaty was negotiated by 107 countries and signed by 57. It provides for cooperation in arresting smugglers including police cooperation and access to bank records.

In 1990 UN drug control activities were integrated under the UN International Drug Control Program. This included activities of the UN Secretariat's Division of Narcotic Drugs, the UN Fund for Drug Abuse Control, and the International Narcotics Control Board of ECOSOC. The Board had begun operations in 1968. Its 13 experts serving in their personal capacities evaluate and supervise implementation of the above drug control treaties. It determines where illicit drug activities exist and then consults with the governments concerned.

In connection with the General Assembly's International Drug Control Strategy adopted in 1981 and a Latin American initiative at a 1987 conference in Vienna, a UN conference of 108 states on December 19, 1988 approved a new convention against illicit traffic in narcotic drugs and psychotropic substances. It provides for confiscating proceeds of drug-related offences and court orders for seizing financial records and freezing assets. A June 1987 International Conference on Drug Abuse and Illicit Trafficking (INCDAIT) had set forth practical measures for fighting drug traffic. As a result of increased emphasis on the problem there were pledges of $76 million in 1991 for drug control projects finaced by the UN Fund for Drug Abuse Control compared to $52 million in 1990. The U.S. pledged $4.5 million in 1991. The Fund financed projects in 67 countries.

An example of UN programs is in Bolivia, where about half of the world's cocaine originates. It is well into a multinational drug plan to eradicate illicit coca cultivation. The UN Fund for Drug Abuse Control has donated $26 million for a crop substitution program there, and the United States has pledged $115 million to the program.[11]

Although the legal and technical work of the United Nations does not get the headlines that dramatic drug busts do, these efforts have provided a framework for extensive cooperation of the police and experts to eradicate the trade and illicit production.

THE UN CONFERENCE ON TRADE AND DEVELOPMENT (UNCTAD)

UNCTAD grew out of an idea of Raul Prebish, a prominent Latin American economist and statesman. He believed that the major problems of the developing world centered on foreign trade and that if developing countries could be given adequate access to the markets of the industrial countries and if they obtained a fair price for their commodity exports, they would not need huge amounts of aid. As a result of his influence, the General Assembly in December 1962 authorized a world conference, which was held in 1964 to establish UNCTAD. The UNCTAD conference, which is the governing body, meets every four years to consider problems of trade and development. In the interim the issues are considered by its Trade and Development Board and subsidiary committees, which meet mostly in Geneva. These bodies are supported by a large UNCTAD secretariat under a secretary general appointed by the UN secretary general.

UNCTAD and its subsidiary committees set broad policy guidelines on development and trade issues and propose action on these problems. It is dominated by the developing countries. As in the General Assembly and ECOSOC, the developed countries seriously consider the positions of the developing nations and often respond to their pressures. Considering the controversial issues involved, the spirit of the meetings is businesslike. For example, in the 1972 meeting in Santiago, Chile, during the Vietnam War, Cuba, the Peoples' Republic of China, and certain other countries made speeches criticizing the United States and proposed a critical resolution on Vietnam, but by a vote of 50 to 26 with 67 abstentions, the conference supported a U.S. motion declaring the Vietnam issue not within UNCTAD's competence. The conference returned to trade and development issues. In recent years it has been distracted by the Palestinian issue, but the most recent conference described below did not let that controversial issue interfere with the negotiation of trade and development issues.

UNCTAD VII took place in Geneva from July 9 to August 3, 1987, with increased concern about the debt problems of developing countries, inadequate capital flows, weak commodity prices, and stagnating world trade. The final statement was adopted by consensus among the developed and developing countries. It agreed that any solution to the debt problem must be sought within a growth-oriented strategy that takes account of the particular circumstances of each country. It was suggested that the debt service burden be eased through lower interest and longer repayment periods, especially through arrangements with the Paris Club (described in the next chapter). This statement was consistent with the current policies of the International Monetary Fund and the World Bank (also discussed in the next chapter). The statement as usual called for additional aid, particularly to the 40 Least Developed Countries (LDCs) whose per capita GNP in the last eight years had declined from about $220 to $200. (Twenty-seven of the LDC countries are in Africa).

UNCTAD VIII, which met from February 8 to 25, 1991, in Cartagena, Colombia added little to the above. It proposed that the secretary general should hold consultations about a world conference on commodities.

Little mention was made of the Common Fund established by UNCTAD to stabilize prices of major world commodities through financial intervention in the markets. The United States generally opposed such intervention in world markets. The fund faced the insoluble problem of establishing high market prices for producers and low market prices for consumers. The fund was directed to concentrate on 18 commodities—coffee, cocoa, bananas, hard fibers, cotton and cotton yarn, copper, bauxite, sugar, tea, beef, jute and jute products, rubber, tropical timber, vegetable oil and oil seeds, iron ore, manganese, phosphates, and tin. The fund's initial capital was only $250 million. Even OPEC's oil cartel has not been able to deal effectively with this problem in the case of petroleum in recent years. Observers who had watched organizations struggle with this concern for decades gave the new organization little chance of success.

The final UNCTAD statement also noted with approval the current Ecuador round of tariff negotiations. It offered technical assistance from the UNCTAD staff to developing countries participating in the negotiations.

The programs initiated in UNCTAD in the past have been regarded as radical by developed country delegates, but many get accepted by developed countries in a watered-down and revised form within five or 10 years after they are first proposed. UNCTAD was used in pressing for trade preferences for developing countries, establishing arrangements to stabilize world commodity prices, and negotiating a code of conduct for multinational firms. UNCTAD has also played a leading role in demands for providing more aid to the least-developed countries and in giving developing countries more voice in the international monetary reform. The above issues are usually on the agenda of the UNCTAD conferences, and over the years progress has been made in other organs in implementing the above policies for trade and development. The latest UNCTAD conference demonstrated an encouraging convergence of views on the foreign debt problem and other basic issues of development.

UN MONITORING OF TRANSNATIONAL CORPORATIONS

Tracing actions on the transnational corporation issues demonstrates how the UN System works as a system and also how it can take years to produce results. Multinational corporation (MNC) issues have been at the center of North-South controversies among spokespeople for developed and developing countries. Socialists and Communists attribute many of the world's problems, including war and technological backwardness in the Third World, to MNCs and their influence on public policies. Spokespeople of the market economies, on the other hand, stress the contributions of MNCs to economic development. Some academic observers claim the MNCs are becoming so powerful that they are becoming independent of nation states and even limiting a state's sovereignity by creating webs of economic interdependence. Other scholars claim MNCs and U.S. leaders collaborate in their common aims of maintaining a strong U.S. position in foreign economies and access to raw materials.

Meanwhile, UN bodies are trying to bridge these gaps between North and South ideologues by studying the issues and drafting codes of conduct affecting MNCs. The aim is to harness the MNCs in the service of economic development by establishing guidelines affecting operations of these powerful firms. In assessing these efforts, it is useful to look at the background of the decisions and how they worked their way through the UN system. What were the motives of those initiating this process and what important deals were made during the negotiations? Did the powerful MNCs support these moves, or did they attempt to block attempts to set standards for their operations? What concrete effects would the codes and monitoring process, if approved, have on the MNC operations in developing countries?

The inital MNC resolution was tied to an important compromise for increasing the voice of developing countries in an international monetary reform and GATT trade negotiations. In this sense the resolution became a part of the developing countries' program for a "new international economic order" (NIEO).

The initial resolution calling for a "group of eminent" persons to study the impact of the MNCs on development and to submit recommendations for appropriate action was passed in the July 1972 meeting of the UN Economic and Social Council (ECOSOC) just two months after the end of the third major world UN Conference on Trade Development (UNCTAD III) held in Santiago, Chile.

A close examination of the record discloses the seed of these ideas. At UNCTAD III President Allende of Chile, the host and first speaker, did not float the idea in his lengthy opening address, but his ambassador, Hernandes Santa Cruz, who was the leader of the Group of 77 (the caucus of developing countries), in his address referred to UN Undersecretary Philip de Seynes' statement that it would be unreasonable to continue to ignore a serious gap in international institutions, the lack of arrangements for supervising the activities of MNCs. Obviously, these two leaders had consulted on this idea.

At UNCTAD III Ambassador Bernard Zagorin of the United States represented the country with the most powerful MNCs in the world, whereas Ambassador Santa Cruz represented Chile. Jack Anderson of the *Washington Post* had just published U.S. documents about the scheme of the International Telephone and Telegraph Company (ITT) to give $1 million to help the CIA oppose Allende's election and later help in his overthrow. These were published all through Latin America, and during the UNCTAD Conference there were frequent demonstrations by Chileans against CIA and ITT. (A subsequent Senate investigation of the CIA indicated that it did not accept the ITT money, although the CIA did support groups opposing Allende.) President Allende's police maintained good order during the conference, and its work was not disrupted. Despite the ITT controversy, Ambassador Zagorin, chairman of the U.S. delegation, established a good working relationship with Ambassador Santa Cruz of Chile that permitted agreement on a wide range of UNCTAD resolutions. This laid the basis for the agreement on the Economic and Social Council (ECOSOC) resolution two months later requesting the UN secretary general to establish a "group of eminent persons" to study the MNC impact on development and to recommend action. The two ambassadors rose above the ITT controversy and reached agreement on the great majority of resolutions passed by the UNCTAD conference.

Santa Cruz introduced the ECOSOC resolution on MNCs at the July 1972 ECOSOC meeting in Geneva with a customary flourish, making a hard-hitting attack on ITT for attempting to undermine the Allende government. His resolution, however, appeared designed for compromise. After negotiations with Zagorin and others, Santa Cruz agreed to drafting changes acceptable to all delegations. The plenary ECOSOC sessions gave delegates, including those from Communist countries, a chance to vent their ire on the multinationals. After procedural wrangles and beating off an amendment referring to previous controversial resolutions on the expropriation issue, the ECOSOC delegates adopted the resolution.

The deal made during the negotiation of the ECOSOC resolution is evident in its second part, which "stressed the need" for the "full, effective and continuous participation of developing countries in the forthcoming GATT multilateral trade negotiations, and in the decisionmaking process in the reform of the international monetary system." The deal also included the withdrawal by Ambassador Santa Cruz of an amendment that called for all interested states, including the Soviet Union, to participate in the above economic negotiations.

The international monetary reform part of this resolution was implemented in the same month by the establishment of the "Committee of Twenty" in the International Monetary Fund. About half of this committee were developing nations. During the next few years the committee designed a basic reform of the international monetary system that was put into effect on April 1, 1978. The GATT multilateral trade negotiations that continued during the decade accepted developing country demands for concessions of tariff preferences, and they were put into effect by the end of the decade. This demonstrates how coordination of policies can occur in the UN System since the same governments control the different international bodies.[14]

The underlying element in achieving agreement on the 1972 ECOSOC resolution and subsequent related UN resolutions on monetary and trade matters was the need for both developed and developing countries to cooperate on financial and trade negotiations to address fundamental problems in the world economic order. In the process of carrying out the compromise on the resolution, the moderates agreed to reforms in the world's monetary and trading system and thereby preempted the attempt of the radicals to develop support for converting the market system into one of controlled government planning. Both moderates and radicals used the slogan of a new international economic order. There were extensive consultations among the governments concerned on MNC issues, but there was no evidence of important MNC pressures on the U.S. government in the negotiation of the 1972 resolution.

The UN secretary general, in line with the 1972 ECOSOC resolution, appointed a "Group of Eminent Persons" numbering 20 to study the MNC issues. American representatives were J. Irwin Miller, chairman of the Cummins Engine Co. as vice chairman of the Group, and Senator Jacob Javits of New York. The Group also included Juan Somavia of Chile, a son-in-law of Ambassador Santa Cruz, and representatives from Russia and Yugoslavia. The two consultants were Raul Prebish, the father of UNCTAD, and Nat Weinberg, formerly an official of the United Automobile Workers. The Group, with wide variations in opinion, held sessions in New York, Geneva, Rome, and New Delhi in a total meeting time of two to three months. At these meetings, spokesmen of MNCs testified as did Communists, Socialists, labor representatives, and others. With the help of the UN secretariat, the Group prepared comments on major substantive issues.

The key input into the Group of Eminent Persons' hearings was the background study prepared by the UN Secretariat under the leadership of Philip de Seynes. This study was a detailed and objective assessment of the role of MNCs in world trade, and it contained three important recommendations on setting up machinery to monitor the activities of MNCs. These included forming a committee under ECOSOC for airing views and problems of MNCs and developing policies and programs for action, extablishing a center in the UN for information on MNCs, and negotiating a code of conduct for MNCs. It is not surprising that the Group included these recommendations in its final report, which was prepared with the aid of the UN Secretariat. The Group envisioned the code as an instrument of moral persuasion more than a binding agreement. The recommendations, in turn, helped persuade ECOSOC to establish these bodies.

ECOSOC subsequently established the Commission of Transnational Corporations with the major task of overseeing the work of the UN Center on Transnational Corporations and the work of an Intergovernmental Working Group drafting the Code of Conduct for MNCs. The Working Group for a Code of conduct recognized "that the code could become effective only if it were widely accepted or adopted." Its spirit of compromise and its reports helped tone down the rhetoric and controversies over MNC issues that colored debates in the early 1970s. In 1992 the Commission transferred the functions of the UN Center on Transnational Corporations to a division of the UN Department of Economic and Social Development of the UN Secretariat.

Major issues to be covered by a code of conduct included: whether public enterprises should be included in the definition of a MNC, whether MNCs should get preferential treatment in order to promote investment, how they should set prices, and how governments could provide for consumer and environmental protection. There appeared to be no insuperable obstacles to a code since MNCs would welcome rules of the game that they could depend on after they invest. On the other hand, developing countries and even socialist countries desire foreign investments. The United States is one of the largest sources of international investment and a principal home for MNCs, and U.S. representatives played a key role in the negotiations. However, negotiations slowed down under the Reagan and Bush administrations because of their adversion to government intervention.

If agreement on a code of conduct is reached, this could encourage increased investment by MNCs for development. This would help the third world cooperate with developed countries on other international problems.

UN WORLD CONFERENCES

The UN has used world conferences to stimulate and coordinate international action. These conferences are more than meetings, since they typically require years of preparation by governments and private specialists. Under Article 62 of the UN Charter, ECOSOC may call a conference, but in practice such conferences are approved by the General Assembly. The largest and most successful have been those dealing with environmental problems.

The Law of the Sea conventions originated in world conferences on the law of the sea. Also, the UN Environmental Program (UNEP) was created as a result of the 1972 UN Conference on the Environment held in Stockholm. A 27-nation preparatory committee held four sessions of two weeks each in preparing for the convention and producing initial texts of documents. They were the bases of agreements on preventing marine pollution, monitoring the environment, and other conservation issues. The UN Secretariat played a key role in drafting background documents for the convention.

In 1989 the General Assembly launched the United Nations Conference on Environment and Development that was held in June 1992 in Rio de Janiero. The ways such conferences mobilize public support were demonstrated in this conference. A total of about 35,000 officials, reporters, and others interested in environmental matters attended. The Conference of 172 nations received top-of-the news attention. Drama was provided by the initially cool attitude of the United States toward the conference. In May 1990 the head of the U.S. Environmental Protection Agency had been ordered by the White House not to attend a preparatory meeting for the Conference.[15] Public support for action on the environment built up to such an extent that President Bush attended the Rio conference. This support for action had been reflected in a Lou Harris poll of May 1989 that revealed at least 75 percent of the people in every country surveyed believed that stronger government action is needed to fight pollution.

The United States was able to water down the Global Warming Convention, thus preventing the setting of definite targets for cutting back on carbon dioxide and other warming gasses. The United States did not sign the biodiversity treaty that would protect endangered species and require sharing research and profits with nations whose genetic resources were used. It also made small financial commitments in comparison with other major industrial countries. However, the United States joined in consensus with 27 broad principles for environmental policy and on an 800-page blueprint to clean up the environment and encourage development.

Many environmental activists were disappointed at the results of the conference, but others seized on the 800-page agenda and principles approved at the conference as a basis for lobbying for legislative action to protect the environment.

Although it was not a UN conference, the World Summit for Children at the United Nations on September 29 and 30, 1990, accomplished the aims of a world conference. A record 71 heads of state attended the conference, which was held during the General Assembly meeting. They signed a Declaration and a Plan of Action that included goals of reducing under-five child mortality by 30 percent and reducing their malnutrition by one-half. They also urged ratification of the Convention on the Rights of the Child adopted by the General Assembly in 1989, which included goals of eliminating child labor and prostitution.

Other landmark conferences include: (1) The World Population Conference, which met in Bucharest in 1974. It adopted a World Population Plan of Action, which gave added impetus to countries with family planning programs but also at the insistence of a few governments included provisions for encouraging population growth. (2) The World Food Conference in 1974 called attention to malnutrition and starvation and instructed UN bodies such as the UNDP, the Food and Agriculture Organization, and the World Bank to increase their assistance to agriculture. This was more than an admonition, since the same countries making recommendations at the conference control the boards of directors of the other UN agencies. (3) The 1975 Conference on the Status of Women stressed the responsibility of governments to enable women to be fully integrated into society. (4) World conferences of 1978 and 1983 to combat racism added to the public pressures for sanctions against the racist government of South Africa. (5) World conferences on disarmament of 1978, 1982, and 1988 were part of the UN efforts that brought about the network of nuclear arms agreements described in Chapter V. (6) The International Conference on Drug Abuse and Illicit Trafficking of June 1987 adopted by acclamation a declaration expressing the commitment to take vigorous action in ending drug abuse.

The United Nations provides a framework for international cooperation in the economic and social field, including a means of delivering or coordinating a major part of the world's technical assistance and aid programs. The United Nations is an effective system because the many action agencies, including the Specialized Agencies, report to the Economic and Social Council and the General Assembly, which coordinate the programs and policies of these agencies. The agencies of the United Nations proper report to and take general guidance from the secretary general, although they have their own governing bodies and sources of funds. Many times, new programs and policies are debated and refined in several forums before being implemented in the UN System.

Administrative experts could be disturbed by the overlapping and duplication and could wish for a more rational organization. However, there is an advantage in allowing a number of bodies to exercise initiatives and search for funds. For example, operations of UNICEF could be incorporated in other bodies, but the UN System would then have about $200 million less for its programs every year, because UNICEF has developed its own imaginative appeals to the conscience of the world to help children.

There was relatively little superpower confrontation in these programs, because the Soviet Bloc contributed only nominal amounts of assistance. They used the UN forums to criticize the capitalist world, which disturbed customers of the mass media, but these rhetorical criticisms had little impact on the constructive work of the UN bodies.

Many countries use the UN bodies as a channel for their aid, so the UN programs are large in comparison to total bilateral aid programs. However, as indicated in Figure 6 (Chapter X), it takes a magnifying glass to see the total UN aid programs in comparison with the tremendous amounts spent on the defense budget of the United States or the Soviet Union. This reflected the dominance of power politics over international cooperation, a trend that was noted in previous chapters on the peacekeeping functions of the United Nations.

In recent years the United Nations has been in the forefront in addressing environmental and health problems of world concern. These problems cannot be addressed on an individual country basis, and as world interdependence grows, the functions of these international agencies have also expanded.

We now examine the activities of the World Bank and the IMF, which are the world's bankers and the largest source of loans for economic assistance, and activities of other Specialized Agencies in the UN System.

Notes to Chapter 8

1. A. Yoder, "U.N. Monitoring of Transnational Corporations," *Towson State Journal of International Affairs,* Spring 1981.

2. D. Acheson, *Present at the Creation* (New York: W.W. Norton, 1969), p. 231.

3. U.S. Department of State, *United States Contributions to International Organizations,* Report to the Congress for Fiscal Year 1984 (December 1985).

4. UNDP, 1991 UNDP Annual Report (New York: United Nations, 1992), p. 20.

5. UNDP, Document (DP/1984) 5/Add.2 (New York: United Nations, 1984).

6. *U.N. Chronicle,* June, 1982, pp. 96–98; J. Morse, "Statement Before the UNDP Governing Council," June 12, 1984.

7. Organization for Economic Cooperation and Development (Paris: OECD, 1983).

8. UNDP, 1984.

9. I. Gruhn, "The U.N. Maze Confounds African Development, *"International Organization,"* Spring 1979.

10. *U.N. Chronicle,* September, 1986, pp. i–xv.

11. *U.N. Observer,* April, 1988, p. 4.

12. *U.N. Chronicle,* November 1987, pp. 29–38; C. Boucher and W. Siebeck, "UNCTAD VII: New Spirit in North South Relations," *Finance and Development,* December 1987, pp. 14–16.

13. Yoder, "U.N."

14. U.N. Commission on Transnational Corporation, Document e/c.10/45, April 11, 1979 (New York: United Nations), p. 6.

15. *U.N. Chronicle,* 1987, pp. 60–62.

Chapter IX

THE IMF, WORLD BANK, AND OTHER SPECIALIZED AGENCIES

The Specialized Agencies of the United Nations have their own boards of directors and their own budgets. The heads of these organizations, therefore, are not appointed by or directed by the secretary general or the General Assembly, as are the organs in the previous chapter. The Specialized Agencies have negotiated agreements with the United Nations, so that they are closely associated in administrative practices, and they submit reports annually to ECOSOC. They closely cooperate with each other and with bodies of the United Nations proper, and the same governments direct their policies that pass resolutions in the General Assembly, ECOSOC, and other UN organs. Such resolutions do have an impact, since governments like to be consistent. It is considered a privilege to be a Specialized Agency, and organizations such as the World Intellectual Property Organization (WIPO) and the UN Industrial Development Organization (UNIDO) lobbied for many years to be accepted by the General Assembly as a Specialized Agency of the UN System.

The International Bank for Reconstruction and Development (IBRD) and the International Monetary Fund (IMF) are the two most powerful Specialized Agencies of the UN System and the two least dependent on the UN for policy guidance. Their articles of agreement with the United Nations specify that they do not take policy directions from it, but they do coordinate their administrative policies with the UN and report to it every year. When appropriate they also work closely with other bodies of the UN System.

The articles of agreement of the two organizations were drafted at Bretton Woods, New Hampshire, in 1944 before the UN Charter itself was approved. The fact that these complicated agreements were approved by the

U.S. Congress with little trouble is a tribute to the care with which the secretary of the treasury, Henry Morgenthau, prepared the Congress, foreign governments, and the public for accepting them. It also reflects the fact that major attention at that time was focused on World War II. The two key individuals in drafting the agreement were Lord Keynes of Great Britain and Harry Dexter White of the United States. Keynes, the famous economist, gained fame with his prediction of the disastrous consequences of the reparation and debt burdens of the World War I Versailles Treaty, as well as with his monetary theories. Most historians and economists agree that reparations and debts were largely responsible for the Great Depression. Keynes helped design the IMF and the IBRD so that the post-World War II arrangements would prevent such disorder. White was later charged with having Communist sympathies, whereas John Maynard Keynes was regarded by many as a radical economist. Nevertheless, the institutions they helped create were bastions of conservatism and still the target of attack of liberal and radical economists.[1]

Their charters and policies reflect a determination of Secretary of State Hull to support free international trade. Their conservatism has won the confidence of financial advisers and bankers of the major countries of the world. After World War I there had been no international organization to prevent a severe international financial crisis that was triggered by the U.S. stock market crash in 1929. More than 40 years after World War II, with the help of the IMF and IBRD there has been no comparable financial crisis, despite the strains of post-war reconstruction, several major wars, the skyrocketing of oil prices, and the heavy burdens of international debt payments that had accumulated by the 1980s. By the 1980s, the IBRD and the IMF had become powerful financial institutions on the world scene with the IMF controlling over $100 billion of foreign currencies and the World Bank lending close to $16 billion a year for development. Nevertheless, there were distributing signs that many developing countries had accumulated more debt than they could service, and for the first time countries began to default on their debts to the IMF.

We first look at their organization and the way they operate before discussing the ways they have addressed major challenges to international financial stability and development. We then examine the other Specialized Agencies of the UN System.

THE INTERNATIONAL MONETARY FUND

The IMF to a very limited extent performs the function of a Federal Reserve System to the world. The IMF uses a major portion of its $100 billion in potential resources to buy and sell world currencies and to make balance-of-payments loans in order to help countries with short- and medium-term balance of payments problems, but it does not dispense development loans as such. As we see below, however, it comes close to this with its lending for structural adjustments.

In the early 1970s it foresaw the problems created by a limited supply of gold and a rapidly expanding international trade, so it created a new international reserve asset to back international transactions. This special drawing right (SDR) to some extent has replaced gold as a reserve asset. In fact, the new paper gold is better than gold because countries can accumulate these SDRs above original allocations and draw interest on them, whereas countries that lose allocations of this asset pay interest. By 1986 countries had created and allocated almost $30 billion (SDR 21 billion) of paper gold on the basis of their level of world trade. To compensate the developing countries, which believed they should get a larger SDR allocation because they needed it more, the IMF finally sold much of its gold stock and distributed the profits on the basis of need rather than on economic strength. The IMF also gives them lower interest rates on certain types of loans, such as those for "structural adjustment."

The assets of the IMF are the pool of currencies provided by about 150 member nations. To assist in its complicated financial transactions, the IMF publishes the most current and comprehensive financial statistics in the world.

The IMF is a major repository of reserves of members, facilitating the financial transactions it undertakes. The IMF also cooperates with the World Bank in providing technical assistance, in developing financial statistics, and in dealing with financial problems. The other major function is to cooperate with the World Bank in arranging meetings of the "Paris Club" to help creditors and debtors adjust international debts when a default is threatened. Until recently the IMF did not have to worry about collecting debts owed to it, because its member countries are anxious to keep a good credit rating with the IMF and World Bank, which are a major source of balance-of-payments aid and development aid.

Each member of the IMF is given a quota based on a complicated formula of GNP, reserves, and trade potential. The member pays the quotas in its own currency or with acceptable reserve assets including the SDRs. This quota determines a member's voting power, which is used in electing the board of governors and the 22 executive directors and in decisions on loans. The quota also determines a member's maximum access to the resources of the IMF, and its share in the allocation of SDRs when they are created. The assets (mostly members' currencies) amounted to about $130 billion in 1991. Normally, only about half of the currencies of the Fund would be used for lending. In 1991 total outstanding IMF loans were about $35 billion.

When the IMF helps a country beyond its original quota, the IMF applies conditionalities. Instead of collateral, the IMF insists on correcting the situation that gave rise to the borrowing. Basic principles for conditionalities are free trade and ending of foreign exchange restrictions.

The IMF has created two funds for structural adjustment, which are loans on easy terms designed to strengthen the economy. Policies financed by these funds include liberalizing trade controls, lifting price controls, and balancing budgets. The IMF seal of approval for structural adjustment is often accompanied by loans from others, which are called parallel financing. The IMF has provided such loans to most African countries.[2]

The IMF and the International Bank were in a unique position to encourage the Eastern European countries and the former Soviet republics to adopt market-oriented reforms after the revolutions of 1989. The newly independent governments were anxious to join the IMF and the IBRD to get access to billions of dollars of credits. Seven had been admitted by July 1992 and the rest were completing procedures for memberships. Loans to new members were tied to conditionalities, and these were endorsed on April 26, 1992, by finance ministers and central bank governors of major industrial countries, which were the major source of funds and voting power of the IMF.

The IMF and IBRD sent experts to the former Soviet republics and to Eastern European countries. The teams prepared frank economic reports on these former Communist countries and provided experts for legal, banking, and public finance reforms. About two-thirds of the IMFs structural loans, or $5 billion, were to Eastern Europe in 1990/1991. The IMF and IBRD also designed a $24 billion package to help Russia's economic reform; the IMF would finance $4.5 billion. In July 1992 Michel Camdessus, the managing director of IMF, reached agreement in Moscow for Russia to hold back inflation in return for a $1 billion loan from the $24 billion package. He praised the Russians for their courageous reform program.

The IMF exercises a great deal of leverage on economic policies of its clients. It gives its advice discreetly and avoids the nationalist reaction that would occur if a country such as the United States imposed the same kind of conditions. The IMF as an international institution has an unbiased reputation, which is impossible for a great power to have. The IMF is gaining in stature as it provides loans that help countries adjust to market-oriented policies and help the world economic system adjust to shocks such as those caused by rises in oil prices.

As indicated below, the debt burdens reached a new dimension after

1985, and new policies were considered for meeting the threat to world financial stability.

THE WORLD BANK

The World Bank is a group of three institutions—The International Bank for Reconstruction and Development (IBRD), the International Development Association (IDA), and the International Finance Corporation (IFC). The IBRD and the IDA have the same officers and staff—about 5,000—although their operations are legally and financially separated. The IDA assistance is concentrated on the poor countries, and its loans are up to 50 years with very low or no interest. These loans amount to a small proportion of total loans of the World Bank group.

The IFC is closely associated to the World Bank and the IDA, but the IFC staff and funds are different. Its purpose is to provide risk capital for private enterprise, and its commitments are a small percentage of the total commitments of the World Bank group.

The World Bank has about 166 members, which subscribe to its capital according to a complicated formula based on GNP and trade. The member governments delegate direction of its operations to 21 full-time executive directors. Five are appointed by the largest shareholders, and each of the rest represent more than one member.

The World Bank group's total of long-term development loans is more than that of any other institution. Following is a summary of major activities:

The International Bank for Reconstruction and Development, which is often called the World Bank, makes loans for infrastructure and development projects at low market rates of interest to developing countries. In the first decades after World War II, its policies were relatively conservative. It designed most loans to cover only foreign exchange costs and to finance only specific projects. Loans were to be repaid in hard currencies, and interest costs were close to market rates. Total loans to developing countries up to June 30, 1952 amounted to just $582 million.

The developing countries began lobbying for a new international organization to finance development in 1949 in the UN Economic and Social Council. In 1955 the United States and the Soviet Union compromised on admitting new members to the United Nations, and by the end of the second decade UN membership had more than doubled to 122 members. The increased leverage of the developing nations in the UN System was reflected in a liberalization of the lending policies of the World Bank, which wanted to head off the movement to establish a new institution to lend to the developing countries. These pressures helped bring about the establishment of the

International Finance Corporation (1956) and the International Development Association (1960), as well as the UNDP. There was also a greater emphasis on aid to developing countries in the bilateral aid programs. The shift of the focus of the Cold War to the developing world contributed to this increasing attention to those countries.[3]

In 1985 the International Bank made loan commitments of over $11 billion to 44 countries. By 1987 it had about $90 billion in outstanding loans. In the 40 years since its founding, it had approved over $100 billion in loans. Most of its funds came from borrowing on the private capital markets, and it relent the funds at low rates of interest. Virtually all loans have been to developing countries with some countries passing into the developed country category. Although the International Bank has been the major single source of lending for development, the total development assistance by individual countries has been over three times as great.

By 1988 it was apparent that the Bank's plans for lending for 1989 of $17 billion would exceed its resources, and it obtained an authorization to increase its capital by $74.8 billion over the statutory level of about $95 billion. This would allow it eventually to almost double its loans. However, the portion of capital actually paid in amounted to only about $5 billion, and it was borrowing about $11 billion a year to get the funds to meet its lending commitments. The excess of authorized capital over paid-up capital represented guarantees of governments to pay in their capital if required to make good on the IBRD guarantees of loans.

Originally its loans were devoted mostly to infrastructure projects such as large dams and irrigation projects. Each of these loans was guaranteed by the governments concerned. Since the era of Robert McNamara's presidency, the World Bank has greatly increased loans for project and sector assistance. Sector assistance means that the World Bank makes loans to institutions in developing countries that relend the money to farmers, business people, and entrepreneurs in other economic sectors for types of projects specified in the original loan agreement. Such loans include loans to institutions that are helping with family planning.

The World Bank makes engineering and economic feasibility studies and helps coordinate assistance programs from many sources. It also works closely with the UN Development Program (UNDP) and with other organs of the UN System. The World Bank provides considerable technical assistance to developing countries to help them improve feasibility studies and supervise their loans. Its Economic Development Institute has trained thousands of officials from developing countries.

The World Bank's aims of recent years have been to emphasize improving access of the poor to better food, shelter, health, and schooling as well as protecting the environment.[4]

The International Development Association was established in 1960 to provide long-term loans at low rates of interest to the poor countries that could not afford conventional loans. The IDA committed more than $3 billion to 45 countries in fiscal year 1985, and its cumulative loans amounted to $37 billion.

The International Finance Corporation since 1956 has mobilized resources for development in the private sector. In fiscal year 1985 the IFC channeled almost $1 billion in loans and equity capital directly to private businesses in 38 developing countries. Cumulative commitments were $5.6 billion.

Until 1984 the World Bank had a perfect record on collecting loans, but from 1984 to 1988 eight borrowers fell more than six months in arrears. Together they owed $3.24 billion, or about 3.6 percent of its $90 billion of loans outstanding at the end of 1987. The eight borrowers were Nicaragua, Guyana, Liberia, Syria, Peru, Sierra Leone, Zambia, and Panama. The World Bank announced that it expects them to pay, but it was increasing its reserves against these loans.[5]

The major function of the World Bank and the IMF is to provide a framework for preventing the vicious circle of financial crises that led to the world depression of the 1930s. In the 1980s there were some economists who were predicting serious financial crises arising out of the excessive foreign debt burden of certain countries. The IMF and the World Bank were in the middle of the action to prevent this.

THE WORLD DEBT CRISIS

In the late 1980s the world was still reeling from wildly fluctuating oil prices, which began in the early 1970s. Petroleum, of course, is a principle source of energy, and the great increases of oil prices of the 1970s affected entire economies. Initially the skyrocketing prices caused a recession in the developed countries and also put many developing countries heavily in debt. Their debt rose from $130 billion in 1973 to $343 billion in 1978, to over a trillion dollars by 1988.[6] World oil prices more than doubled in each of these two periods, which stimulated inflation. During this period, the IBRD and the IMF played a leadership role in rescheduling debts of developing countries in over 50 meetings of the so-called Paris Club, an organization set up to adjust debt burdens. The rescheduling was designed to spread out repayments over a period of years to prevent debt burdens from bunching up.

By 1985 the world's bankers were so alarmed with their overcommitment of loans that their credits dried up to 1 percent of the 1984 level. Somehow the creditors and debtors, including those most heavily in debt in Latin

America, muddled through. It was clear, however, that some new initiatives were needed. Some relief occurred with falling oil prices and the revival of economic activity in 1985 in the industrial countries, which increased their demands for exports from the developing countries that helped them meet their debt payments. There was also some easing of the interest rates. However, late in 1985 there was a slackening of recovery and an adverse turn in the terms of trade (the relative cost of developing countries pay for their imports compared to the price of their exports), which added about $40 billion to the burden of debt of the countries. Moreover, real interest rates (the margin of interest rates over inflation) were still much higher than historical levels. These developments hurt countries heavily in debt, such as Argentina, Mexico, and Brazil, which were undergoing belt-tightening measures to try to pay off their foreign debts. Political groups from these countries tended to blame the conditionalities (conditions of new loans) of the World Bank and the IMF, and were unwilling to face up to stringent measures to cut back unnecessary spending, since such measures could cause unemployment.

Although the IMF refrains from making specific recommendations on social services and income distribution in a country, critics blamed it for being too restrictive in its conditions for loans and for discouraging democratic developments in debtor nations. Critics have proposed expansionary policies that would increase production and improve the economic base for paying off debt. This sounded somewhat like Reaganomics, which brought about an expanding U.S. economy fueled by high budget deficits after the slump of the early 1980s.

In debates over economic policies, the IMF tended to take the conservative position and impose fairly uniform conditionality provisions. The World Bank officials, on the other hand, who were oriented toward development, tended to want to make sound loans that would improve the productive base of the debtor nations.

At the annual meeting of the World Bank and the IMF in Seoul in 1985, U.S. Secretary of Treasury Baker made some general proposals for addressing the world debt crisis. He suggested that governments, and not just the creditors and debtors, get involved in discussion of world debts. He proposed that everyone pull together with sound development policies, that the World Bank and other international institutions should increase loans about $20 billion to 15 countries, and that the private sector should provide another $20 billion. Critics pointed out that this would be only a drop in the bucket compared to about $1 trillion of world debt. Supporters of the "Baker Initiative" pointed out that the major causes of the excessive debts were governmental policies such as those that lead to high interest rates and policies that cause deterioration in terms of trade, which are outside the control of the debtor nations. Critics replied that the United States was more interested in preserving its major banks, which were heavily overextended in loans to developing countries, than it was in helping these countries through reducing their interest rates and writing off debts.

The debtor countries continued to lobby for relief in the Group of 24 and other committees of the IMF and World Bank. Their efforts bore fruit in the June 21, 1988, Toronto meeting of the "Group of Seven" of major industrial countries (West Germany, Britain, France, Italy, Canada, Japan, and the United States). The summit agreed to grant low-interest rates and write-offs of debts, and urged the Paris Club to work out technicalities.

In March 1989 the U.S. Secretary of the Treasury, Nicholas Brady, proposed a plan for private bankers to help debtor nations reduce interest and principal payments, in return for their reducing inflation and opening their economies to foreign investment and foreign trade. The Paris Club followed through in negotiations reducing debt payments up to 50 percent.

On July 9, after 3 years of negotiations, agreement was reached with Brazil, the largest debtor in the developing world, for steps to reduce its $44 billion debt. Representatives of hundreds of private lenders reached agreement on six options that included reducing the principal or the interest rates by 35 percent. A loan guarantee fund was set up. Brazil, on the other hand, would be required to implement IMF conditionalities.

The agreement capped 5 years of similar negotiations with other countries. Paul Volcker, former chairman of the U.S. Federal Reserve Board, said that the "Latin American debt crisis is no longer a crisis . . . and should not be a threat to the financial system." Large U.S. banks in previous years had written down the value of their Latin American loans, which had dominated their balance sheets. The developing countries still owed large amounts to governments, but those debts now appeared manageable and not a threat to the world's private banking system.[7]

With the help of the World Bank and the IMF, financial officials are addressing the world debt problems. These institutions are committed to discouraging and preventing restrictions that would clog up world trade and encourage a vicious circle of retaliation. In the 1990s it appeared that there was a good chance of continued success with these institutions in contrast to the 1930s, when officials watched helplessly as a few ad hoc international meetings struggled in vain to prevent the Great Depression.

Both conservative and liberal economists agree that the world economy is tied together and that neither developing nor developed countries can prosper alone. World economic policies are not a zero-sum game in which gains on one side balance losses on the other. Rather, all tend to prosper or suffer together, and it is the job of the World Bank and the IMF to preserve a favorable climate to permit international prosperity.

OTHER ORGANIZATIONS OF THE UN FAMILY

There is a long list of international organizations closely associated with the United Nations, and their work has steadily expanded since its founding. These so-called Specialized Agencies, which are formally associated in administrative agreements with the UN, do not gain much publicity, because their work generally is noncontroversial and is more-or-less taken for granted. They exchange information with the UN proper, and they agree to report to the UN on any action taken as a result of UN recommendations. (See Appendix E.)

Following is a summary of their work and description of how they relate to other parts of the UN System.[8]

FAO

The Food and Agricultural Organization (FAO) was founded in 1945 with the aim of raising the levels of nutrition and food production and bettering the conditions of rural populations. It was made a Specialized Agency in 1946. FAO has more than 160 member nations, which elect its governing council of 49 members. Its predecessor was the International Institute of Agriculture, founded in Rome in 1905.

FAO carries out extensive research and technical assistance programs in the fields of agriculture, livestock, fisheries, and forestry. In 1986, for example, it assisted 2,500 projects. Its regular budget, supplemented by other sources including UNDP technical assistance funds, is larger than that of the United Nations. By 1984 it had helped channel more than $26 billion to the agricultural sectors of 90 developing countries.

FAO, at a U.S. suggestion, established the World Food Program in 1963 to provide food relief and assist development projects. In 1977 the International Fund for Agricultural Development was established as a UN Specialized Agency to promote food production in developing countries. They both work with the International Bank and other parts of the UN System.

Spurred on by the General Assembly these organizations have tried to use food aid to encourage food production in developing countries. The problems of food production include unwise development policies with a lack of incentives as well as poor weather. Also, wealthier countries have cut back on agricultural production to keep prices up and protect their farmers' incomes, while poorer countries suffer from food shortages, particularly in drought areas of Africa and in Asia. Therefore, root problems of world food shortages are distribution and poverty, not just production.

UNESCO

The major purpose of the UN Economic, Social and Cultural Organization (UNESCO), as defined in its constitution, is to "contribute to peace and security by promoting collaboration among the nations through education, science and culture" in order to further respect for justice, the rule of law, and human rights. The General Conference of UNESCO with representatives from each state meets every two years to formulate policies. National commissions representing both government and nongovernmental organizations link UNESCO with the educational, scientific, and cultural organizations in each country. It has provided funds for programs of literacy and of teacher training, scientific research in developing countries, cultural exchanges, and technical assistance in the news media field.

One of its major functions in recent years has been to back an African news agency (PANA) to correct African dependence on Western news agencies, which African officials called negative and culturally biased. After 5 years of experience PANA's new director conceded that officially censored news, which was the source of PANA's releases, must give way to free access to news sources. He noted that his editors were forced to use government press agencies, which were often silent when political crises occurred. For example, there were no official news releases for days during the Algerian riots of October 1987, or when thousands were killed in massacres in Burundi in August 1987, while the Western news media were reporting the crises. PANA is also saddled with serious equipment and money problems, so that its output is only a small fraction of Western news media output.[8]

UNESCO, like other UN bodies, has become involved in political issues. The United States strongly opposed UNESCO resolutions condemning Israeli policies in the occupied territories and the proposed new world information order, and complained about UNESCO's poor management. In 1984 the United States withdrew from UNESCO, followed by the United Kingdom and Singapore. This forced the agency to start implementing a plan to cut back almost 600 positions in order to save about $44 million. In 1987 under pressure from the United States and a threat from others to withdraw, the head of UNESCO stepped down, and Frederico Mayor Zaragoza of Spain, an official more acceptable to the United States, Britain, and others, was elected. The new head announced as one of his aims the return of the United States, the United Kingdom, and Singapore to the agency.

ILO

The International Labor Organization's original constitution was part of the Treaty of Versailles. It is an intergovernmental agency with each country having four representatives, two from government, one from labor, and one from business. The ILO Conference of all representatives elects the executive council, with both bodies having the same proportional representation of government, labor, and industry. The ILO Conference sets the budget and the general lines of policy.

One of the primary functions of ILO is to raise labor standards, and to this end it has adopted over 300 conventions and recommendations with over 5,000 ratifications. Each convention represents a new extension of international law. After ratification the states concerned report periodically on implementation of these agreements. In addition, the ILO provides technical assistance, usually through UNDP, on questions relating to productivity, small industries, social security, occupation safety, labor standards, and occupation training.

The annual ILO Conference, which is attended by about 2,000 delegates, takes up controversial issues such as the treatment of the Polish Solidarity Union, apartheid, and the Palestine issue. There is no opposition to the Conference condemning apartheid, but the Polish Solidarity and Palestine issues usually generate heated debates.

The United States withdrew from the ILO for a number of years in the late 1970s because George Meany, head of the AFL/CIO labor union, objected to participation by Soviet trade unions, which he claimed were not genuine trade unions. After Meany's death, the United States resumed its membership in February 1980. The focus of U.S. activities in recent years has been to fight off resolutions that would condemn Israel.

WHO

The World Health Organization, which was founded in 1948, carried forward the work of the League of Nations Health Organization. The World Health Organization and its governing board coordinate the work of six major regional offices, each having its own governing committee.

A major aim of WHO since 1977 has been "health for all" by the year 2000, which embraces education, proper food, safe water, sanitation, maternal health, family planning, and immunization and treatment of diseases. One major part of this program is a UNDP/WHO/World Bank program, which focuses on six major tropical diseases with the help of about 3,500 scientists. Also, WHO has had success in eradication of smallpox in the world and in its program to try to eradicate the six major diseases of childhood by 1990. (See pages 143–144.) WHO has also promoted the use of an inexpensive solution of salts to cure children of diarrhea. It estimated this oral rehydration saved the lives of 1.1 million children in 1988. WHO and FAO have eradicated the screwworm, a larval disease that affects humans and animals in Africa, by dropping sterile flies from aircraft, which mate with fertile flies, resulting in an increasing population of infertile flies.

In recent years WHO has campaigned against the tobacco industry and sought to find ways to combat AIDS. In 1987 WHO adopted the Global AIDS Plan. In that year it trained more than 350 laboratory workers in 100 countries on how to test and diagnose the disease. It helps governments set up national plans and coordinate assistance. In 1987 WHO reported the alarming news that 5–10 million people were probably infected. As many as 5–10 percent in some countries were infected, with women and men being equally infected. WHO coordinated efforts by UNFPA, UNESCO, UNICEF, and the World Bank to educate people and carry out research on AIDS.

WHO operates on the principle of decentralization. It uses networks of physicians and other health centers, and it has no laboratories of its own. Its future targets include eradicating tropical diseases, pneumonia, and leprosy, and reducing lifestyle diseases in developed countries by promoting known methods of prevention.[9]

ICAO

The International Civil Aviation Organization, as already noted, has made successful efforts to contain skyjacking. Its major purpose is to set up standards to foster development of safe air transport and promote the development of airports and air navigation facilities. The 27-member Council has adopted many standards and practices that are constantly reviewed and amended. In addition, it has promoted conventions that spell out rules and standards for air carriage. It has provided technical assistance to over 100 developing countries. The ICAO was thrust into a political controversy following the September 1, 1983 destruction by Soviet fighters of a Korean Air Line Boeing 747. The ICAO Council condemned the downing of the airliner and appointed a team to conduct an inquiry. The report concluded that the aircraft deviated from its course as a result of a navigational error. A special ICAO assembly approved an amendment to the ICAO treaty banning the use of military force against civilian aircraft.

UPU

The Universal Postal Union, which has been in existence since 1865, has only a small budget of $10 million, but it has more members than any other Specialized Agency. Its major aim is to promote postal services, and its 168 members form a single postal territory for the reciprocal exchange of correspondence. It also assists training programs for modernizing postal services.

ITU

The International Telecommunication Union, which was founded in 1865, has established standards to keep up with the rapidly changing telecommunications industry. With the revolution in computer and fax services, it has established standards to permit machines to talk to each other across national boundaries. It allocates frequencies, promotes safety, and promotes telecommunications in developing countries. The United States has objected to ITU's efforts to regulate U.S. telecommunications satellites and opposed ITU's opinions against Radio Marti, which aims broadcasts at Cuba.

WMO

The World Meteorological Organization, established in 1978, facilitates exchanging weather information and standardizing of observations, and encourages research and training in meteorology. It works through six regional organizations that coordinate information. With a small budget it has been able to standardize weather reports of over 8,000 weather stations and a similar number of aircraft and surface ships throughout the world. It disseminates weather information with computers. It also carries out extensive research on environmental pollution and provides technical assistance on developing water resources. It and the UNDP established the International Panel for Climate Change, which has made authoritative reports on global warming used by international conferences taking action on the issue. WMO also supports environmental research on the oceans.

IMO

The aim of the International Marine Organization (formerly called the Inter-Governmental Maritime Consultative Organization) is to exchange information on technical matters affecting shipping, with special attention to safety of life at sea. The IMO has promoted the adoption of codes on ship construction and obtained approval of treaties and agreements to prevent oil pollution of the sea. The codes include prohibition of the former practice of washing out oil tanks with sea water in the open ocean.

GATT

The General Agreement on Tariffs and Trade (GATT) was originally a stop-gap set of rules for negotiating tariff concessions that were to serve only until a specialized agency called the International Trade Organization (ITO) was established. The ITO was never approved, and countries have continued to use the GATT arrangements for trade negotiations. It has a secretariat of about 200 that about every 10 years facilitates comprehensive negotiations of tariff and trade concessions. GATT has formulated a code based on the principles of nondiscrimination, protection only by tariffs instead of quotas and other trade restrictions, consultation to avoid damage to trade interests, and reduction of tariffs and trade barriers. The rounds of tariff negotiations are complicated, involving over 100 members and taking place over several years. In the fall of 1986 the United States was successful in getting GATT to consider removing restrictions on banking and insurance in addition to those on commodity trade.

The Uruguay Round of GATT negotiations began in 1987, and agreements were reached on many issues. However, the United States proposed the "zero option" of removal of all agricultural subsidies by the year 2000. This was opposed by the European Community, and became the last major issue for intense negotiations in 1992.

WIPO

The World Intellectual Property Organization after many years achieved the status of a Specialized Agency through approval of the General Assembly. Its mission is to promote international agreements to protect copyrights, patents, and other intellectual property. Its patent center in Vienna, Austria, registers over one million patents a year on its computer and makes data on them available to patent offices and other institutions. Many developing and Communist countries have accepted the idea that such protection promotes responsible trade in products and prevents irresponsible pirating and disrupting of normal trade channels.

UNIDO

The most recent Specialized Agency is the UN Industrial Development Organization. It took about 20 years for the General Assembly to approve the status of this body in 1986. It originated in the United Nations as a Committee for Industrial Development and later a Center for Industrial Development to coordinate UN activities in the field of industrial development and promote technical assistance and the exchange of information. It has been supported by the developing countries, but the industrial nations have not been enthusiastic supporters of this organization, believing that industrial technology can best be promoted through private business operations. The annual budget for 1986 was $56 million.

The Specialized Agencies carry out many of the goals of solving international problems of "an economic, social, cultural, or humanitarian character" specified in Article 1 of the UN Charter. Although the United Nations proper does not directly control these organizations, they have been brought into a close relationship with the UN System. The Specialized Agencies have negotiated agreements with the Secretariat that provide for reciprocal representation at meetings, exchange of information, and coordination of statistical and administrative arrangements. Each Specialized Agency has agreed to consider recommendations to it by the United Nations and report back on action taken. These arrangements have been particularly effective in coordinating technical assistance under the leadership of UNDP, providing aid to alleviate wars, famines, and other disasters, attacking problems of pollution, and facilitating world commerce and transportation.

The problems of trade, development, debt burdens, AIDS, the environment, pollution, and many others demand international cooperation. The UN System has provided the administrative framework to address them. The Specialized Agencies have expanded with the growing interdependence of countries. Their governing bodies occasionally dabbled in politics with resolutions against Israel and against apartheid. Such controversies attracted media attention, but these resolutions are of minor importance in comparison with the vast amount of constructive activities carried on by the organizations. They have promoted a network of codes, treaties, and other international agreements that provide a sound basis for international cooperation.

The dream of the founders of the United Nations was that some day this network of agreements and operations would make the world so interdependent that war would be inconceivable. National rivalries still dominate the international system, but technicians and experts cooperated and worked together in these international bodies, and their work expanded despite pressure by the United States and others for economies in operation.

Notes to Chapter 9

1. Anand G. Chandazarkar's account of how the IMF operates opens with this quotation from John Maynard Keynes: "This is not a Red Cross altruistic relief scheme, by which rich countries come to the rescue of the poor. It is a piece of highly necessary business mechanism which is at least as useful to the creditor as the debtor." *The International Monetary Fund: Its Financial Organization and Activities* (Washington, DC: IMF, 1984).

2. *IMF Survey,* March 21, 1988; A. Outarra, "Fund is Helping to Resolve Africa's Debt Problem by Supporting Growth-Oriented Economic Reforms," IMF Survey, June 13, 1988.

3. J. Spero, *The Politics of International Economic Relations* (New York: St. Martins, 1985).

4. S. Stern, "World Bank's General Capital Increase," *Finance and Development,* June 1988.

5. *New York Times,* July 11, 1988, first business page.

6. H. Eduard and B. Puckahtickom, "Export Credit Policy" (Washington, DC: IMF, 1985).

7. *New York Times*, July 9, 1992, pp. 1, C2; International Monetary Fund, *World Economic Outlook—May 1992*, pp. 22–23.

8. For information on the UN and Specialized Agencies see *Everyone's United Nations* (New York: United Nations, 1986); the *U.N. Chronicle*; United Nations Association of the United Nations; *A Global Agenda—Issues before the General Assembly of the United Nations* (New York: United Nations); and the annual U.S. Department of State, *United States Participation in the UN*, a Department of State Publication.

9. *UN Chronicle*, September 1992, pp. 43–48.

Chapter X

MANAGING THE UN SYSTEM

The UN record of accomplishments in peacemaking noted in previous chapters is due largely to the ability and dedication of the secretaries general and the officials under them in the UN Secretariat. They have worked effectively in many crises despite strong nationalistic pressures opposing them. The secretaries general have grown with their job and have expanded the role of the Secretariat.

THE SECRETARY GENERAL

The secretary general does not head an executive branch in the ordinary sense. He does not submit detailed proposals to legislative organs, solicit public support for them, and then carry out the resulting programs within legislative guidelines. His Secretariat is primarily a service organization for meetings and for carrying out instructions of UN bodies. However, in a crisis and in difficult situations the secretary general can take initiatives behind the scenes and make proposals for settling issues. He also makes informal suggestions on economic and social issues, and the Secretariat does detailed work on them. The Security Council and other organs can assign the secretary general duties, such as peacekeeping, to enable him to act as a conventional executive. When members cannot reach agreement on problems, they can turn them over to the secretary general (Figure 4). As explained below, Dag Hammarskjold extended the power of the secretary general by filling a vacuum in the Charter. However, the secretary general is still directed by UN organs, and the secretary general is not a crisis manager like a president or prime minister.

175

(a)   (b)   (c)

(d)   (e)   (f)

Figure 4. Six Secretaries-General of the United Nations. (a) Trygve Lie (Norway) February 1, 1946–April 10, 1953; (b) Dag Hammarskjold (Sweden) April 10, 1953–September 18, 1961; (c) U Thant (Burma) November 3, 1961–December 22, 1971; (d) Kurt Waldheim (Austria) December 22, 1971–December 15, 1981; (e) Javier Perez de Cuellar (Peru) December 15, 1981–January 1, 1992; (f) Boutros Boutros-Ghali (Egypt) January 1, 1992–. (*Courtesy:* UN Photos 165430 and 178980/M. Grant)

The secretary general is appointed by the General Assembly upon the recommendation of the Security Council. His appointment is subject to the veto of any one of the permanent members, and he also must be acceptable to developing nations, which could block his nomination. Candidates are questioned and interviewed by the members to elicit their views on controversial issues. Traditionally, the secretary general is selected after a number of votes in the Security Council in which one or more candidates are vetoed.

Chapter 15 of the UN Charter reflects the desire of the sponsoring governments to give adequate authority to the secretary general to perform the many duties assigned to him. There was a great deal of discussion about whether the General Assembly and the Security Council should appoint the deputies of the secretary general, but it was finally decided after much debate that this could undermine the authority of the secretary general and the international character of the Secretariat. Therefore, the secretary general was given the authority to appoint his deputies under regulations established by the General Assembly. This is desirable, because if members of the Secretariat tried to promote national views, this would rapidly bring a halt to meaningful action.[1] The oath of office of the staff commits a member of the staff "not to seek or accept instructions in regard to the performance of my duties from any government or other authority external to the Organization."

Listing the duties of the secretary general indicates the great scope of the job. The position is responsible for a tremendous number of reports requested by the General Assembly, the Economic and Social Council, and other bodies of the UN. These reports range from verbatim accounts of the Security Council meetings to a thoughtful analysis of the activities of multinational corporations. Normally the Secretariat plays a major role in helping committees draft reports on their activities and investigations. These reports should be prepared in a timely fashion in the six official languages of the United Nations.

In line with Article 98, the secretary general is responsible for administrative support of the meetings of the many commissions, and committees of the United Nations. Most of these meetings take place in New York, Geneva, and in the headquarters of the five regional commissions around the world. He participates in the major meetings and, in addition, when special meetings or conferences are called for other locations, the secretary general often attends them.

The secretary general also is responsible for the budget, personnel, and other administrative support for the many bodies of the UN proper. There are many unusual complications arising from the fact that he is assisting 175 different countries, dealing with many foreign languages and many currencies. He is instructed to meet quotas for hiring, so that the staff represents the countries of the United Nations. As explained below, he has to fight for his regular budget of over $19.1 billion a year, and in addition must help solicit special contributions amounting to much more than this for the budgets of the organizations like UNDP under him. He has to provide support for meetings in many countries and that support includes interpreters in many languages. He, of course, has to delegate extensively, but he will come under sharp criticism if facilities are not provided or if there is evidence of waste.

His most important function is to exercise quiet diplomacy in world crisis situations to help prevent catastrophic confrontations between the major power blocs of the world. Article 99 gives him a little leverage in carrying out this task by permitting him to call to the attention of the Security Council any matter that may threaten the maintenance of international peace and security. The secretary general has used this power rarely. He normally is forced to rely primarily on the force of his own personality and diplomacy behind the scenes to try to settle disputes.

During the first major crisis faced by the United Nations to discuss the continued occupation of Iran by the Soviet Union, Secretary General Trygve Lie issued a memorandum on whether or not the issue should remain on the agenda of the Security Council. Although the Security Council overruled him, the secretary general with the above precedent has continued to contribute to political debates before the Council.

Lie was an activist, particularly in mediating the Arab-Israel issues. When North Korea invaded South Korea, he opened the debate by reporting that the UN Commission on Korea had reported that North Korea was invading the South and that the Security Council should act. He proposed even more authority for the United Nations than the U.S. government would agree to, since the Pentagon was anxious not to dilute its control over American forces, which were doing most of the fighting.[2]

As a result of Lie's actions on the Korean issue, the Soviets attacked him as acting illegally and as being an "abettor of aggression." Originally in 1946 for the first term, Soviet Foreign Minister Vyshinsky had said Lie was the only candidate they would support, but Russia vetoed his candidacy for a second term. After numerous meetings, the Security Council informed the General Assembly that it could not reach agreement on a candidate. The General Assembly then finessed the veto problem by passing a resolution by a vote of 46 to 5 extending his term for three years, noting that he had been recommended by the Security Council in 1946. The Charter does not specify the length of his term, and the decision held. This satisfied Lie, who originally had indicated that he wanted to retire after the first term, but stubbornly stayed on to protect the position of the secretary general from the Russian attempt to weaken it.[3]

Dag Hammarskjold was also an activist, particularly in the Suez crisis of 1956 and the Congo crisis in the 1960s. Hammarskjold, at the General Assembly's request, organized the UN Emergency Force for the Sinai in 48 hours. This was the United Nation's first major peacekeeping force.

In the Lebanese crisis that followed, the secretary general announced a policy of "helping to fill a vacuum" if the General Assembly or Security Council did not give him guidance in safeguarding peace and security. The United States had moved troops into Lebanon at its request when its independence and Jordan's appeared threatened by coups. The United States indicated that it would be willing to withdraw troops if the UN Observer Group in Lebanon (UNOGIL) were expanded. The Soviets vetoed a Security Council resolution on this because it appeared to justify the United States sending troops there in the first place. At this point the secretary general indicated that he would fill the vacuum and expand UNOGIL, which he did. The United States and Russia agreed on an emergency meeting of the General Assembly, and in the debate the United States indicated willingness to withdraw its troops if the United Nations took steps to establish peace and security. The General Assembly then passed an Arab League resolution calling for an end to the crisis and a withdrawal of troops, and the crisis passed.[4] The U.S. troops were quickly withdrawn.

This set the stage for a high point of activism of the secretary general in the Congo crisis and subsequently a major challenge to the position's authority. When Belgian troops threatened to intervene in their former colony of the Congo to restore order and protect their citizens, Ralph Bunche, who was there representing the United Nations at the Congo's independence celebration, informally helped the government request the United Nations for assistance. Secretary General Hammarskjold then invited the members of the Security Council to lunch and proposed the sending of a UN peacekeeping force as well as emergency food supplies. That evening, on July 14, 1960, he convened the Security Council and by prearrangement a resolution was introduced calling for such a peacekeeping force. The resolution passed 8 to 0 with 3 abstentions.

During the crisis Hammarskjold used the initial grant of authority to create a military force of 20,000 and to close the airports of the Congo to oppose intervention by the Soviet Union and others. This infuriated the Soviets, and they refused to cooperate with him, but they could not withdraw the authority granted to him in the original Security Council resolution.

Khrushchev's reaction was to propose a three-person troika to replace the secretary general. It would represent the Communists, the Western powers, and the Third World. This would give the Soviets a veto on actions of the Secretariat. At one point Khrushchev attacked Hammarskjold in the General Assembly as an agent of imperialist countries. Hammarskjold's reply stating his intention to remain in his post in order to protect the position of the secretary general received a standing ovation. Strangely enough, an hour later Hammarskjold was invited to a Soviet reception where he was received warmly by Khrushchev.[5]

Hammarskjold's actions weakened the veto of the five permanent members. In the Congo operation, after the secretary general was authorized to intervene as commander-in-chief of the UN force, the Soviets or other permanent member of the Council could not withdraw the authorization and stop him with the veto. This was different from the Korean War case when action was shifted from the Security Council to the General Assembly to get around the veto. In the Lebanon case, the secretary general took action in a vacuum to carry out the general intent of the Security Council and the UN Charter without explicit authorization of the Security Council or General

Assembly. These three cases represented a marked increase in the authority of the secretary general.

Later Hammarskjold was killed in an airplane crash while visiting the UN forces, and Secretary General U Thant took over. The bitter civil war continued, which the United Nations tried to referee, and a government was finally established that was able to bring about peace.

U Thant was the first secretary general who had come from the Third World, which gave him an advantage in dealing with the colonialism issues. He was instrumental in helping resolve the dispute between the Netherlands and Indonesia over Dutch New Guinea (West Irian), the 1962 civil conflict in Yemen, the dispute between the Philippines and Malaya over Sarawak and North Borneo, and in ending the disputes over the Congo.

Many observers criticized him unjustly over his role in the 1967 war crisis in the Sinai. He brought the matter up in its early stages before the advisory committee of members contributing to the peacekeeping force. Some of these insisted on agreeing to Egypt's demand for withdrawing the UNEF units. U Thant warned the Security Council of the dangers of the situation, but it did not act. Any one of the UN members could have brought the matter before the General Assembly, which was meeting at that time, but they did not. U Thant has been made the scapegoat for the failure of major powers, including the United States, to prevent the war, although it had been forewarned of Israel's intentions. As noted in Chapter IV, three weeks elapsed between Egypt's demand for the UNEF force to withdraw and the attack of Israel against the Egyptian and Syrian forces.

Legally the secretary general was on solid ground to withdraw the forces. UNEF was established by the General Assembly, which did not have the power of "enforcement" given by the Charter to the Security Council. This meant that legally UNEF was required to withdraw when requested by the host state, Egypt. UNEF withdrew and war broke out about two weeks later. As a result of the disastrous effect of the 1967 war, the peacekeeping forces since that time have been authorized by the Security Council. This did not solve the problem of financing the 1956 UNEF forces, since the Soviets did not help pay the cost. Finally in 1988 the Soviets agreed to pay assessments for peacekeeping forces. By that time there was a new financial crisis with the United States withholding over $500 million in assessments.

The fact that the Security Council after the 1967 war was willing to authorize peacekeeping forces in the Middle East made the task easier for Secretary General Waldheim, U Thant's successor. Waldheim also took initiatives in mediating conflicts in Cyprus, between India and Pakistan, and in Vietnam. His critical comments about American bombing of North Vietnam resulted in a public denouncement by President Nixon. Waldheim, like his predecessors, decried the failure of nations to refer disputes to the United Nations in their early stages before they break out in war.

After 10 years Waldheim stepped down. His successor, Javier Perez de Cuellar, helped bring an end to the Iran-Iraq war, the Afghanistan war, and the Cambodian war, monitor elections in Namibia and Nicaragua, and end the war in El Salvador. He did not succeed in mediating the Falklands war, since Britain's quick attack brought the conflict to an end after Argentina refused to negotiate. The U.S. news media began to report positively about the United Nations, a change from the UN bashing of previous years. He set a precedent by being reelected for a second term without a controversy.

On January 1, 1992, with unanimous approval of the General Assembly, the new secretary general, Boutros Boutros-Ghali, took office. A former Egyptian prime minister, he had played a major role in the Camp David breakthrough on the Arab-Israel disputes. In the 1992 Yugoslav crises his representative Cyrus Vance managed to get cease-fires in Slovenia and Croatia, after the European Community failed. In response to a Security Council request to keep the possibility of deploying a peacekeeping force in Bosnia-Herzegovina under review, Boutros-Ghali recommended that the Security Council consider "other means" to deliver aid to blockaded Sarajevo, which implied the use of force. The Security Council president on June 26, 1992, after consulting with the Security Council publicly endorsed the recommendations and the blockade was broken. This was a precedent for UN peacekeeping forces intervening in a civil war.

In July 1992, in response to a request from Nelson Mandela, head of the African National Congress, and South Africa's president, the Security Council authorized Cyrus Vance to visit South Africa and report on the situation because of its concern that negotiations had broken down on ending apartheid. The secretary general also sent ten UN observers there to give an unbiased report on demonstrations. He later requested the Security Council authority for sending 30 more. Their objective was to defuse violence and help create conditions for negotiations. The above actions were another precedent for the Security Council action on human rights issues.

In sum, the secretaries general, despite lack of support and even opposition of major powers and despite attacks on the United Nations by the American news media, have been able to mediate major disputes while administering a large and complicated bureaucracy. Their peacekeeping units have performed a service that governments individually or collectively could not match. Their recent successes, including helping settle the Afghanistan and the Iran-Iraq wars, suggest that the United Nations could be much more effective in settling international disputes if it had consistent support from major powers.

THE UN DEBT CRISIS

In addition to the above duties, the secretary general has the onerous duty of obtaining financing for the budget of the UN proper. The regular UN budget has grown to $1.1 billion a year. Contributions are based on a formula that includes such factors as national income and the ability of members to obtain foreign currencies. The poorest members pay a minimum of .01 percent of this budget, whereas the 10 largest members pay about three-fourths of the budget. In the early 1970s criticism mounted in the U.S. Congress that the U.S. share of the budget, about one-third, was too large. At that time the assessment was about 31 percent based on the above formula. After a tremendous lobbying effort by the United States, the General Assembly members were persuaded to reduce the U.S. assessment to 25 percent.

The Soviet Union with 10 percent, Japan with 11.4 percent, and Germany with 8 percent of the UN budget were the next largest contributors in 1990. In terms of a percentage of national income, Gambia was the largest contributor with .6 percent of its national income; the United States was close to the bottom of the list, contributing only .03 of its national income to the budget.[6]

The major debt crisis of the United Nations arose from the failure of the Soviet Union, France, and later the United States, to pay their assessments for peacekeeping forces. This included the UNEF forces that replaced the British and French troops in the Sinai in 1956, and the ONUC forces that closed the airports to Soviet forces in the Congo during the 1960s. As an emergency measure, in 1961 the General Assembly authorized $200 million in UN bonds that matured in 25 years. The United States, at that time under President Kennedy, subscribed 50 percent of the UN bonds to tide it over the financial crisis. In July 1962 the World Court, in an advisory opinion by a 9 to 5 vote, declared that the assessments for peacekeeping were regular expenses of the UN within the context of Article 17 and that members would have to pay their peacekeeping assessments or lose their votes. The Soviets still refused to pay. During the 1964 session of the General Assembly, its president with support of its members, in order to avoid an open confrontation with the Soviet Union, passed resolutions without formal votes. In the following year the Soviet Union won since it was not challenged on its vote, although it continued to withhold its share of assessments for Middle East and other peacekeeping operations. Its rationale was that the crisis was caused by the "imperialist" powers and that the Soviet Union and the Communist countries were not responsible for these expenses.

In the spring of 1986 a special General Assembly meeting was called to meet what the secretary general called "the most serious financial crisis in its history." He asserted that unless the 159 member governments paid what they owed the United Nations, it might go the way of the League of Nations. The secretary general pointed out that the financial problems of the UN were greatly intensified by the threat of the United States to withhold $90 to $100 million from its assessed contributions in 1985 and 1986. This threat arose out of U.S. congressional action to limit contributions to 20 percent of the total budget unless the UN voting procedures were changed to give the United States a weighted vote, taking into account its large financial contributions. Under the regular formula the United States would contribute over 28 percent of the total, which had been cut to 25 percent by the concession noted above. Western Europe countries and others indicated, however, that they were not willing to change the voting procedure.

As the demands for peacekeeping and monitoring elections mounted, political support for the UN budget increased. In 1988 President Reagan's White House spokesperson announced it would request Congress to pay arrearages to the United Nations. This did not end the crisis because Senator Helms managed to hold up appropriations.[7] In 1990 President Bush got congressional support to pay arrearages over a period of five years. By that time member states owed the UN about $1 billion, with the United States in debt over $500 million. Moreover, the United States would pay its assessment at the end rather than the beginning of the UN fiscal year.

In 1991 the General Assembly approved the regular two-year budget of $2.3 billion by consensus for the first time in history. In addition there were peacekeeping costs, which skyrocketed. Permanent Security Council members are assessed for peacekeeping 20 percent above their normal share of the regular budget, which meant the U.S. share was 30 percent. The secretary general in dealing with the cash flow problem requested an increase in the working capital fund to $250 million, as well as a peacekeeping reserve fund of $50 million and an emergency humanitarian fund of $50 million. The relief of the financial crisis, however, had been brought with an agreement that U.S. or major contributors could veto the budget in committee. On April 30, 1992 the United States was in arrears $555 million for the regular budget and $308 million for peacekeeping operations.

By 1992 it was obvious that additional action would have to be taken to relieve the situation, particularly in the peacekeeping areas. The costs were estimated to triple in 1992 from their 1991 level of $700 million (Table 5). A move was underway in the U.S. Congress to put peacekeeping in the Defense Department budget, where its proportion would be minuscule, instead of the State Department budget, where it is a major item.

In addition to peacekeeping and the regular budget the secretary general is responsible for UN voluntary budgets such as the UNDP and UNICEF, which total much more than the regular UN budget. (See Appendix E.)

Table 5
Cost of UN Peacekeeping Operations (in millions)

Country or Area	Cost
Cambodia*	$1,900.0
Yugoslavia[†]	634.0
Lebanon	151.5
Western Sahara	140.9
Iraq and Kuwait	80.2
Angola	52.1
Golan Heights	37.8
Cyprus	31.0
Arab-Israeli conflict	31.0
El Salvador	13.2
India and Pakistan	5.0

Source: United Nations.
*Projection for 1992/1993.
[†]1992 projection. Other figures for 1991.

THE SECRETARIAT

The UN Secretariat is designated under Article 7 as one of the principal organs of the United Nations to assist the secretary general. The Secretariat's staff in 1992 consisted of about 14,700 professional and clerical staff. This included staff in Geneva and of the regional commissions as well as the technical experts who oversee field operations.

The hiring of about 3,800 professionals is affected by country quotas (desirable range), based on the member state's contribution to the budget and the size of its population. In 1990 the number of Americans in posts subject to country quotas amounted to about 13 percent, which was below the desirable range. The United States has a special office in the Department of State to recruit for the United Nations, but the Department of State has difficulty in finding qualified personnel willing to serve at the salary levels of the United Nations. This gives some perspective to the charge of critics that UN salary levels are too high. The salaries are comparable to those earned by federal employees of the U.S. government, which are used by the United Nations as a standard of the best-paid national civil service. The idea of such a civil service standard was accepted by the League of Nations in 1920.

Paragraphs 1 and 3 of Article 101 of the UN Charter reads:

> 1. The staff shall be appointed by the Secretary-General under regulations established by the General Assembly.

> 3. The paramount consideration in the employment of the staff in the determination of the conditions of service shall be the necessity of securing the highest

standards of efficiency, competence, and integrity. Due regard shall be paid to the importance of recruiting the staff on as wide as geographical basis as possible.

The major powers, and particularly the Russians, led the attack on these provisions at the San Francisco conference. They wanted four deputies of the secretary general to be elected by the General Assembly on recommendation of the Security Council. Canada successfully led opposition to this proposal, insisting that the secretary general should appoint his own deputies free from the control of the political organs of the United Nations.[8]

The United States tried to compromise the independence of the Secretariat during the McCarthy era. In the 1950s Secretary General Lie, under pressure of U.S. congressional investigations, dismissed employees and even allowed the Federal Bureau of Investigation to set up shop in the UN building to interview American employees of the United Nations to see if they were Communists. The dismissed employees were compensated, but the UN Secretariat lost face.

The Soviet's attempts to undermine the authority of the Secretariat were more effective, if less blatant. The Soviets controlled appointees from the Soviet Union and how long they would serve. After the Congo crisis, the Soviets failed to have a troika of undersecretaries appointed by the Security Council and the General Assembly, but they succeeded in balancing second-level positions with Communist, free-market, and neutral philosophies. Also, some countries including the United States seconded top officials to the Secretariat, which meant that they served for a limited time and then returned to their career posts at home. This undermined their international status. Soviet officials made no secret of the fact that their officials received instructions from the Russian ambassador in New York or from Moscow. In 1988 the Soviets agreed to limit seconding.

The International Court of Justice has strengthened the status of the Secretariat by ruling that it has the right to bring a case before the court. Other public international organizations and individuals cannot bring cases before the court; only governments can do so. In an advisory opinion concerning compensation for the death of Count Folk Bernadotte, who was killed by Israeli terrorists, the court stated that the United Nations is an international person that could bring suit and receive compensation. Moreover, in 1964 the court ruled that the General Assembly did not have the right to prevent the Secretariat from awarding compensation to an employee judged by a UN administrative tribunal to have been unjustly dismissed.

Thomas M. Franck, after serious study and evaluation of his own experience as head of the UN Institute for Training and Research (UNITAR), concludes that the effect of quotas and politicking by governments for positions in the Secretariat has been "profoundly negative."[9] It still should be possible for the secretary general to develop an effective personnel service subject to national quotas if a large proportion of the key policy staff would stay employed as career officials. Such officials could remain independent of financial and career pressures that could affect their decisions if they were seconded.

THE PERMANENT MISSIONS

The members of the United Nations have established permanent missions close to the UN headquarters in New York City. Most of them have similar missions at Geneva, where the European headquarters are located. The United Nations inherited the League of Nations buildings in Geneva, which ironically were completed in the late 1930s as the League reached its nadir and closed out its operations. The Economic Commission for Europe and many of the Specialized Agents have their headquarters in Geneva, and the Economic and Social Council and other UN organs hold meetings there.

The missions in New York City are governed by a 1947 agreement dealing with privileges and immunities of the UN headquarters staff and of the diplomatic missions assigned to that headquarters. The City of New York has found protection of the Israeli and certain other missions and its diplomats a serious burden, but has managed to keep terrorist activities to a minimum.

In March 1986 the Reagan administration ordered the Soviets to reduce their missions to the United Nations by more than one-third because of alleged spying activities. Most observers recognized that the Russian mission included KGB officials. At about the same time, Zakharov, a physicist on the staff of the United Nations, was accused of trying to buy classified information about a U.S. military aircraft engine. The Soviets reacted indignantly to the arrest, but by October 1 had complied with the order to reduce their staff. The UN secretary general's press spokesman stated that the U.S. order to reduce the staff was not in accord with the 1947 agreement with the United Nations, and that the United Nations would try to settle the dispute informally before sending the issue to a three-person tribunal to be nominated by the secretary general.

The Soviets reacted by arresting Nicholas Daniloff, a *New York Times* reporter, for allegedly taking secret documents from a Soviet citizen. Many observers viewed this as a set-up; the KGB in the past has set up someone like Daniloff by having one of their agents shove secret papers at the victim and then arresting him. After secret bargaining Daniloff and Zakharov were sent home. The United States and the Soviets then traded further reductions of their diplomatic staff before the incident blew over.

The UN Legal Counsel commented that the sending states did have a duty to assure that the size of their mission did not exceed what was reasonable, and that issue with the host country should be settled by consultation. The Soviets met the deadline of reducing their staff from 275 to 170 by March 1988.

In 1987 the U.S. Department of Justice, over the opposition of the U.S. Department of State, requested the PLO to close its New York City mission to the United Nations. In 1988 the U.S. courts ruled that the Justice action was illegal. Nevertheless, in December 1988 Secretary of State Shultz denied permission of Yasar Arafat to speak to the United Nations. The General Assembly in a resolution condemned this as a violation of the 1947 agreement with the United Nations and arranged a special session in Geneva to hear Arafat speak. This seemed to clear the air, and the United States then agreed for the first time to open discussions with the PLO on Mideast peace issues.

Secretaries general have carried out their many responsibilities with remarkable efficiency. They delegate to subordinates a great deal of authority, and some of the UN organs are relatively autonomous. Nevertheless, their budgets and administrative data are compiled and organized by computers, which help in coordination of their activities, many of which overlap.

The great powers often carp at the extravagance of the UN operations, overlooking the fact that UN spending for peace literally is microscopic in comparison with the tremendous amounts spent on armaments, even by one country, the United States (see Figure 5). The United States joined with the Soviet Bloc and Israel as the only votes against the 1986/87 budget.[10] The criticisms help restrain waste in the UN System, but they also help undermine its prestige and effectiveness.

The Secretariat was burdened by the national quota system and great power pressures in trying to create a truly independent international career service. Nevertheless, there are many dedicated employees on the UN staff. Ambassadors and other members of the missions to the United Nations take international law and diplomacy seriously and opposed, at least with resolutions, the power politics of the superpowers and governments not committed to international law and peaceful solutions of international issues. In the summer of 1988 as the secretary general's efforts to achieve peace in the Afghanistan and Iran-Iraq wars bore fruit, the pendulum of popular support in the United States swung back to support the United Nations.

Secretary General Perez de Cuellar played a central role in the revival of UN prestige during the 1980s. Few realized this because he avoided controversial statements and headlines. Most of the Security Council operations that mediated and monitored conflicts were mounted during his tenure. He

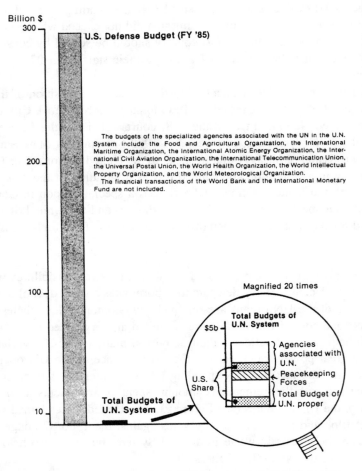

Figure 5. A Comparison of the Budgets for the UN System and the U.S. Defense Department.

took initiatives despite mounting UN deficits, and somehow managed to keep it solvent despite huge U.S. arrearages.

His successor, Boutros-Ghali, was an activist. He quickly made administrative reforms by cutting under-secretaries reporting to him from 14 to 8. In the Yugoslav conflicts he followed the Charter, holding back until the regional organization, the European Community, failed. His mediator, Cyrus Vance, a former U.S. secretary of state, then negotiated a truce in the two northern provinces of Croatia and Slovenia. Fighting continued in Bosnia-Herzegovina. The Security Council in August 1992, in line with the secretary general's suggestion, authorized force to deliver relief supplies to its capital, Sarajevo. This created another UN precedent of using force in a civil war, where attacks on civilians had outraged much of the world community. At his suggestion the Security Council also sent more units to Somalia to protect relief supplies. In his first year Boutros-Ghali was keeping the United Nations in the center of the international action.

Notes to Chapter 10

1. S. Bailey, *The Secretariat of the United Nations* (New York: Praeger; 1964), pp. 5–13.

2. J. Murphy, *The United Nations and the Control of International Violence* (Totowa, NJ: Towman and Allenheld, 1982), p. 30.

3. T. Lie, *In the Cause of Peace* (New York: Macmillan, 1954), Chap. xx.

4. B. Urquart, *Hammarskjold* (New York: Harper, 1972), pp. 277–299.

5. Urquart, *Hammarskjold*, Chaps. 15, 16.

6. *Everyone's United Nations* (New York: United Nations, 1988), pp. 29–30.

7. *Christian Science Monitor,* June 29, 1988; *New York Times,* July 26, 1988.

8. *Congressional Quarterly,* October 29, 1988, pp. 3142–3143; *New York Times,* October 15, 1988, p. 1; October 24, 1988, p. 4.

9. T. Franck, *Nations Against Nations* (New York: Oxford University Press, 1985), p. 113.

10. *U.N. Chronicle,* February 1986, p. 99.

Chapter XI

CRITICISMS, ACHIEVEMENTS, AND PROSPECTS

Previous chapters assess the achievements of the League of Nations and of the United Nations, particularly in ending wars. For most of the period after World War II, however, the superpowers used the UN System only when it suited their purposes, whereas the Soviet Union, particularly, committed aggression in violation of the UN Charter. The United States at first gave strong support to the United Nations but later also violated the Charter, criticized the United Nations, and hindered its work by withholding its share of budgets. Since the end of 1987, however, the United States and the Soviet Union (now Russia) renewed support for the United Nations. This concluding chapter analyzes major criticisms of the UN System, reviews its accomplishments, and assesses its prospects.

MAJOR CRITICISMS OF THE UNITED NATIONS

Critics often assert the United Nations has been dominated by Third World countries. Criticism has come both from the right, from such groups as the Heritage Foundation, and from the left, from such magazines as the *New Republic*. They assert that although the United States contributed 25 percent of the UN budget, the United States has only one vote in the General Assembly. Critics point to its resolutions passed over our objections, including ones critical of the United States. It is true the General Assembly and other UN organs alienated the U.S. government and powerful political groups as indicated below:

1. The U.S. government. In the 1970s the United States was frequently attacked in UN forums for CIA attacks against the Allende government of

Chile and the CIA's alleged connection with the International Telephone and Telegraph Corporation (ITT). At that time the leader of the Latin American caucus in UN organs was Ambassador Santa Cruz of Chile, who contributed to the unfavorable publicity. When President Allende of Chile was assassinated by an opposition group, which had previously had connections with the CIA, the American reputation was further damaged.

Later, Latin American countries in the United Nations and in the Organization of American States (OAS) attacked the United States for its invasion of a sovereign country, Grenada, after it aligned with Cuba and the Soviet Union. Similarly, the United States was criticized in UN resolutions as well as the OAS for CIA-supported attacks against Nicaragua, and the International Court of Justice gave support to the criticism with a ruling that the United States should desist. These actions by the United States, which violated international law, were supported from the White House, which at one point said it would not be bound by the International Court ruling.

The above criticisms, as well as broad-gauge criticisms in UN resolutions discussed below, undermined U.S. executive branch support for the UN System. The situation was exacerbated by the fact that for the first six years of the Reagan administration important officials in UN affairs in the State Department were from the Heritage Foundation, a political action group that had frequently attacked the United Nations.[1] The key official resigned in 1987 perhaps from pressure from Secretary of State Shultz, who was beginning to find the United Nations useful for American foreign policy.

2. The Jews. The Arab caucus in the United Nations has naturally aligned with other developing countries and was able to get support for anti-Israel resolutions. One of the most gratuitous insults was the "Zionism is Racism" resolution, which was passed in 1976 despite abstentions and opposition of major powers. This resolution was particularly insulting because of the Jews' memory of Hitler's Holocaust. Subsidiary UN organs and some of the Specialized Agencies also passed resolutions condemning Israel's occupation of the West Bank and its suppression of the Palestinians. In December 1988 after the United States denied a visa to Arafat to visit the United Nations, which many observers noted as violating the U.S. agreement with the United Nations, the General Assembly by a vote of 152 to 2 (the United States and Israel) criticized the United States for that action and then voted to move the General Assembly session to Geneva to hear Arafat. This was not the first time the United States was left as the sole supporter of Israel in a UN forum.

3. Business groups. In the 1970s there was much support in ECOSOC, UNCTAD, the General Assembly, and other UN forums for the idea of a New International Economic Order (NIEO), which implies more state management of trade and financial relationships. UNESCO was a vehicle for promotion of the ideas for the NIEO, and Secretary of State Shultz accused

UNESCO of being statist. The multinational corporations also came under attack and were even associated with the criticisms of ITT noted above. Business groups resented criticism of the multinationals in UN bodies. Since the early 1970s this criticism has moderated as a result of the report of the Group of the Eminent Persons and the monitoring of international corporations by the UN Commission on Transnational Corporations noted in Chapter VIII.

4. *Labor.* Labor unions of the United States for many years had major problems with the ILO, because it recognized the state-controlled labor unions of the Communist Bloc on the same basis as the free labor unions of the West. George Meany, former head of the American Federation of Labor/ Congress of Industrial Organization (AFL/CIO), pressured the United States to withdraw in the late 1970s, but after his death the United States resumed membership in February 1980.

5. *Right to life groups.* The UN Fund for Population Activities has supported programs in countries with population control programs that promote abortions. This association with such programs, particularly with a program in China, has drawn fire from the right to life groups, which resulted in Congress cutting funding for the UNFPA.

6. *News media.* UNESCO has also led the attack on biased reporting of the Western news media, which dominate the world's news. As noted in Chapter IX, it proposed a New World Information Order (NWIO) subsidized by governments to give more attention to the problems and viewpoints of developing countries. The United States and Western countries opposed the idea, fearing it would become a vehicle for propaganda that would curb the activities of the free press. The developing countries' criticism of the Western news services during this controversy helped alienate the influential news services. Moreover, there is a natural tendency of the American news media to feature the exciting controversies in the United Nations, rather than the routine constructive work in the UN System. The development activities of UNDP and the lending and technical work of the IMF and IBRD, for example, rarely get into the news, except for an occasional item on the business pages. Therefore, the media often present an unfavorable, distorted view of the activities of the United Nations.

Richard Gardner, a former State Department official, notes in a *Foreign Affairs* article on practical internationalism, that the UN organs could not have chosen any more influential and active U.S. interest groups to alienate.[1] The above groups have influence with Congress and have helped build up pressures to cut back on U.S. appropriations for the United Nations. The pressure to cut back the U.S. budget was a major political concern of Congress in the 1980s, and the UN programs were a tempting target. Moreover, the administrative sections of the Department of State and the congressional staffs form a natural alliance in attacking the budgets of the UN System. In practice, this cooperation has conflicted with policies of other State Department officials who have called on the United Nations to expand its activities, such as peacekeeping.

Figure 6 in Chapter X puts the actions to cut the UN budget in perspective.[2] One needs a magnifying glass to analyze the U.S. contribution to total UN expenditures in comparison with the U.S. military budget. Even total expenditures of the entire UN System are minuscule in comparison with the U.S. military budget. Yet Congress, the news media, and even U.S. officials express great concern about the waste in the UN budget, whereas there had been overwhelming support for greatly increased Pentagon spending, despite many examples of waste. The next section addresses the question of what has been accomplished with the spending for UN programs.

The above critics of the influence of the smaller countries on the UN policies often neglect to discuss the strong influence exercised by major contributors to the UN System, and particularly that of the United States, that is built into the system. The strong U.S. leverage includes the following:

1. The UN Charter gives five permanent members of the Security Council a veto on action for maintaining international peace and security. This veto has been used many times by these members, and particularly by the Soviet Union and the United States. The veto has been effective, and no significant UN action has been taken against the United States, although as noted above it has been criticized in the Security Council, General Assembly, and other UN organs.

2. In recognition of the great power status of the United States, it has been a continuing member of the Economic and Social Council and other UN bodies, instead of being forced to take turns like the smaller nations. Similarly, the United States is one of the few outside members of the regional commissions of the United Nations in Europe (ECE), South America (ECLA), Asia (ESCAP), and Africa (ECA).

3. The UN Secretariat has established quotas for hiring officials based in part on the size of the contribution to the UN budget. The U.S. informal quota is about 17 percent. Moreover, in recognition of the major U.S. contributions to the UN Development Program (UNDP), a U.S. national has headed this organization, which coordinates development and assists relief efforts in the UN System.

4. In many of the Specialized Agencies, the United States has a weighted vote or is a continuing member of its boards of directors. In the powerful IMF and IBRD, the United States has a weighted vote of about 17 percent, reflecting the size of its gross national product and trade.

5. The great economic and political power of the United States is recognized

informally throughout the UN System when efforts are made to compromise *important* resolutions and directives to get the support of the United
States and other Western nations. Those who work in the UN System
realize that resolutions have little influence unless they have the endorsement of the United States and other great powers. The resolutions that are
passed without such support have little more than rhetorical value and often
are forgotten.

The next question is what have been the accomplishments of the UN System in the light of the criticisms of powerful political groups in the United
States?

ACHIEVEMENTS OF THE UN SYSTEM

In 1988 there was a major revival of interest in the UN System, particularly
in its peacekeeping function. The secretary general estimated that the demands emerging for peacekeeping units in Namibia, Western Sahara, and
Kampuchea, in addition to the new requirements for peacekeeping in Afghanistan and Iran-Iraq war, would require as many as 44,000 peacekeeping
forces rather than the 10,000 already in place. The cost could be as much as
$2.7 billion annually. Following is an analysis of how the pendulum of popu-
lar support is swinging back toward support of the United Nations.

The United Nations was born with excessive popular support and expecta-
tions. Officials were determined to build a new world organization that would
correct the weaknesses of the League of Nations. The League had been created after World War I with similar enthusiasm by officials determined not to
repeat the mistakes that led to World War I. The diplomats of the World War I
era and many historians believed that the great powers could have prevented
that war if there had been an established forum where they could have met to
prevent escalation of the crisis that arose when terrorists assassinated the heir
to the Austro-Hungarian throne. After that war the diplomats, with the leadership of President Wilson of the United States, met to form the League of
Nations hoping to prevent the world from blundering into another world war
and to restrain Germany from obtaining revenge from a harsh peace. They
failed as Japan, Italy, and Germany in the 1930s attacked countries one by
one.

The fact that the League of Nations had worked effectively in its first
decade has been lost in the mists of history. Historians skip over the 1920s,
when the League settled many territorial disputes arising out of World War I,
carried out outstanding work in combating epidemics, and helped in the financial reconstruction of Austria and Hungary. They tend to focus on the trage-
dies of the 1930s, when Hitler rose to power and the German-Japanese-Italian
Axis destroyed the League and world order.

The League of Nations, with the United States cooperating, did censure Japan for its aggression against China in 1931 so that Japan withdrew from the League. In the next major challenge, the League mobilized economic sanctions against Italy for aggression against Ethiopia (Abyssinia), but diplomatic maneuvers outside the League by the French and British foreign ministers undercut the League's efforts and encouraged the Axis powers to continue on the road that led to World War II. During the 1930s Russia vainly tried in the League to mobilize further opposition to aggression. Russia failed and turned toward appeasement of Hitler and aggression. Today the League, rather than the power brokers outside the League who appeased Hitler, is often blamed for the failures of the 1930s.

Hitler's invasion of Poland was the final blow to the Versailles system, and the League of Nations disbanded in the first years of World War II. Leaders who managed the war, however, including power brokers like Prime Minister Churchill and President Roosevelt, were convinced that a stronger international organization should be created to maintain peace after World War II. At the end of the war Secretary of State Cordell Hull and President Harry Truman, who were liberal internationalists, led the way in bringing this idea to fruition, aided by widespread popular support for plans for the United Nations.

As World War II was ending, world leaders met in San Francisco to establish a stronger world organization, the United Nations, with the aim of supporting collective security and preventing another world catastrophe. As the United Nations was founded, the world entered the nuclear era, and leaders realized another failure could mean the end of civilization and even the end of intelligent life on earth.

Conservatives, liberals, Socialists, and Communists in many countries joined in support of the UN Charter. The drafters of the Charter were determined that it should be a universal organization including the great powers of the world. For a while there were plans to create a strong UN military force capable of enforcing UN rulings. However, the basic ideological split between the Soviets and Western nations prevented the unanimity among great powers necessary to implement that part of the Charter. This distrust was embodied in the veto, which required the affirmative vote of the five major powers for Security Council actions on other than procedural matters. The veto did not apply to discussions or attempts at peaceful settlements of disputes, and it did not apply to the General Assembly, which could act on a two-thirds majority.

The differences between the Soviets and the Western world were so fundamental that the United Nations did not have a 10-year honeymoon as did the League. In the first meeting of the Security Council in January 1946, Iran charged the Soviet Union with committing aggression in a northern province. World opinion was soon mobilized successfully to put pressure on the Soviets to withdraw direct support to insurgent forces there. Greece later made similar charges that the neighboring Communist countries were supporting an insurgency in Greece. The United Nations investigated and condemned this aggression. The major factors solving this crisis were international pressures, the aid programs of the United States, and the withdrawal of Yugoslavia from the Communist bloc, which ended the support of guerrillas from Yugoslavia's long border with Greece.

The Korean War provided the major challenge of the first decade to the collective security system of the UN Charter. President Truman immediately called on the Security Council to act, and U.S. forces started to defend South Korea as authorized in Article 51 of the Charter. Later, when Security Council action was blocked by the Soviet Union's veto, the United States transferred action to the General Assembly, where the non-Communist nations, who were a large majority, gave UN military action strong support. After 3 years of bitter fighting a truce was established, and North Korea was forced to stop fighting with a minor loss of territory.

Initially there was strong domestic support for Truman's action, but in the last cruel years of the war before the truce, his popularity sank to an all-time low, because there seemed to be no end to the fighting. Some important U.S. political and military leaders became disillusioned with the strains of working with 16 other allies. Consequently, about 10 years later when the United States came to the aid of South Vietnam, which was being attacked by rebels and irregular forces from North Vietnam, President Johnson decided to support South Vietnam without using the United Nations. South Korea, Thailand, and Australia joined in the effort, assisted by logistical support by the United States. Other U.S. friends and allies watched from the sidelines, regarding the conflict primarily as a civil war. At the end, when the attack changed from insurgency to open military attacks by the North against South Vietnam, the United States could not mobilize enough international or domestic support to continue the fight, and U.S. forces were forced to withdraw. Few observers recognized that the U.S.-South Vietnam defeat in the main was a failure of power brokers acting outside the United Nations, in contrast to the success of the UN action in Korea.

In contrast to the relative success of the Korean War and the failure of the United States and South Vietnam in Vietnam, the Middle East wars have been long and painful with no final decision. The United Nations has been in the center of action since the first war in 1948. The United Kingdom in 1948 was forced by the internal conflict between Jews and Arabs in Palestine to turn over to the United Nations the problems originating in its old League of Nations mandate. A special UN committee, and then the General Assembly, decided to split Palestine into two opposing areas, which would form a Jewish and an Arab state. The Arab nations opposed this Solomon's solution and tried to crush the new Jewish state. The effort failed. The United Nations mediated the conflict, and the new Jewish state of Israel was formed at the end of the 1948 war with more territory than it had under the original UN partition plan.

The Arab states were irreconcilable, and major wars followed. The first, in 1956, was started by France, Britain, and Israel, with the major aim of forcing Egypt to give back the Suez Canal, which it had nationalized. President Eisenhower acted as a liberal internationalist supporting international law and opposing aggression, even though it meant opposing two close NATO allies, Britain and France, who planned and initiated the aggression. In retrospect, this was a wise policy that prevented a serious break with Arab states, and yet permitted the United States to heal the temporary breach with Britain, France, and Israel. The second war was triggered in 1967 when Egypt mobilized to threaten Israel, whereas the third was initiated in 1973 when Egypt attacked to gain back territory lost in the 1967 war. In each case the wars were ended with mediation within the UN framework, with the help of UN peacekeeping forces and with major political and material assistance by the United States and other major powers.

The first breakthrough in ending this cycle of wars was made outside the United Nations with the mediation of President Carter at Camp David. Carter, Prime Minister Begin of Israel, and President Sadat of Egypt, after 13 days of intensive meetings, agreed on a framework for a peace treaty between Israel and Egypt. The treaty returned all the territory that Israel took from Egypt in the 1967 war and established normal diplomatic relations between Egypt and Israel, the two major antagonists of the Arab-Israel wars. This treaty was within the framework of international law and was based on Security Council Resolution 242 of 1967 (Appendix C). Since Egypt was and is by far the largest and most powerful Arab neighbor of Israel, this treaty greatly reduced the chances for another major war between Israel and its Arab neighbors, although terrorist actions from Lebanon and retaliation by Israel continued.

The United Nations continued to help contain such violence. In 1978 and again in 1983, Israel invaded Lebanon to retaliate against terrorists and to force the PLO out of southern Lebanon, where it had built up its military strength to the point that the PLO was outside the control of the Lebanese government. The Israelis under pressure from the United States and with the support of UN peacekeeping forces along the border of Syria (UNDOF) and of UN patrols in southern Lebanon (UNIFIL), withdrew their troops from Lebanon. However, Israel continued patrols in a "security zone" along Lebanon's southern border and made occasional strikes against targets in Lebanon. The United States, Britain, and France for a while outside the UN framework inserted forces to patrol the Beirut area, but they were driven out by terrorist action, and particularly when terrorists bombed the U.S. Marine headquarters and killed 241 marines. Syria, a neighbor and Soviet ally, took over the thankless task of trying to enforce peace in the chaotic civil conflicts in Lebanon.

This brief review of UN activities in the Middle East demonstrates that the United Nations was in the middle of the action except when the United States tried to settle the Lebanon crisis without it. The Security Council continued to authorize peacekeeping forces to patrol Syria's and Lebanon's borders. Truces were achieved for the major Mideast wars and the wars were contained by the United Nations within a framework of international law, when the United States worked in cooperation with it. When President Reagan applied power with little regard for international law, his attempts to establish peace in Lebanon failed.

The conflicts in the Middle East involved major interests of the superpowers—proximity of the Soviet Union to the area, and the non-Communist world's dependence on Arab oil resources. With the Camp David agreements and with the continued patrols of the UNDOF and UNIFIL forces along Israel's border, the chances for another major war between Israel and its Arab neighbors were greatly diminished. There still is no peace, however, because of Israel's repression of the Palestinians on the West Bank and Gaza, as well as terrorist actions by Arab groups and periodic Israeli retaliatory strikes.

In 1991, after long negotiations, Secretary of State Baker managed to convince Israel and the Arab states to discuss outstanding issues. At Israel's insistence they met outside a UN framework. With the exception of Egypt, this was the first time that Arab countries had recognized the existence of Israel in formal talks. Israel's moderate Labor Party won in June 1992 elections, and there was hope when the talks resumed, they would make progress. The United Nations would probably be involved in any settlement.

The United Nations also played a leading role in the settlement of other wars including the Congo war that began in 1960, the India-Pakistan wars, the Afghanistan War, and the Iran-Iraq war. It still plays a minor role in maintaining the peace with its observer group in the Kashmir area between India and Pakistan and a major role with the UN peacekeeping forces maintaining a truce in Cyprus. In 1962 President Kennedy secretly prepared as a last resort to use the United Nations to settle the Cuban missile crisis that threatened nuclear war. The United Nations also monitored elections and helped settle conflicts in Cambodia, Central America, and Africa.

Presidents Truman and Eisenhower were liberal internationalists who led the world in using the United Nations for crises. President Kennedy used power more than UN procedures. President Johnson ignored the United Nations in failing to save South Vietnam. President Nixon used the United Nations in the Middle East and Pakistan wars, and for nuclear weapons agreements. President Carter's major initiatives were in line with international law. President Reagan up until the last year of his presidency paid little attention to the United Nations. President Bush and Secretary of State Baker, however, made extensive use of the UN System.

Major failures of the power brokers occurred under Johnson in the Vietnam War, and under Reagan in conflicts in Lebanon and Central America. This does not necessarily mean the United Nations could have solved those problems, but at least the United States would not have suffered such obvious defeats. The above defeats and successes were not reflected as such in the American news media, largely because forceful actions tend to get favorable headlines and public reaction, whereas patient, long-drawn-out negotiations get yawns and disdain.

Other major UN efforts for peace have been promotion of a network of nuclear arms agreements. Most such agreements are directly associated with UN initiatives. Until 1986 the most important of these were the agreement for the International Atomic Energy Agency (IAEA) of 1956, the Nuclear Non-Proliferation Treaty (NPT) of 1970, the Limited Test Ban Treaty of 1963, and the nuclear-free zone in Latin America. The Anti-Ballistic Missile Treaty of 1972, and the SALT I and II agreements of 1972 and 1978 were indirectly associated with the NPT. By 1986 all except the IAEA agreements were in jeopardy, because the Reagan administration believed that the keystone SALT agreement enabled the Soviets to forge ahead in the nuclear arms race and that the Soviets were not observing the key agreements. In October 1986, however, President Reagan and General Secretary Gorbachev, in a two-day meeting in Iceland, apparently resolved most negotiating issues on nuclear arms control except for the Star Wars (Strategic Defense Initiative) issue. In 1987 and 1988 Reagan reached agreement with Gorbachev for completely eliminating from Europe medium and shorter range nuclear missiles with a range of 300 to 3,400 miles. In the summer of 1988 Russian and American inspectors began detailed monitoring of missile sites and the destruction of missiles. These negotiations and subsequent negotiations on agreements to destroy the majority of each side's strategic missiles took place outside the UN framework, but they were linked to the Non-Proliferation Treaty. They prepared the way for a Soviet-American detente that would help bring the United Nations to center stage.

American foreign policy had been dominated by the Cold War, and this intensified under Reagan who saw a Communist threat in the new leftist government of Nicaragua. He was determined to reverse gains that he thought the Communist movement had made in Central America and Afghanistan, Angola, Ethiopia, and other areas. U.S. forces invaded Grenada in 1983 to remove a Communist-supported government in that small Caribbean island, and the United States supported Contra forces in their attacks against Nicaragua, another government supported by the Communist nations. Congress temporarily endorsed this U.S. support to the Contras with a $100 million appropriation, despite the fact that the above U.S. actions were condemned by the World Court, the United Nations, and the Organization of American States.

During this period, as Congress desperately tried to cut spending, it even withdrew financial support from UNIFIL, despite the pleas of Lebanon to maintain UNIFIL patrols along the border with Israel, and it held up over $500 million for the U.S. share of the budgets for the United Nations and its peacekeeping forces.

The Soviet invasion of Afghanistan in 1979 also helped erode U.S. support for the United Nations. This was a flagrant violation of the UN Charter like the Soviet support for the Korean War, its invasion of Hungary in 1956, and its invasion of Czechoslovakia in 1968 to keep them in the Soviet camp. Opponents of the Soviet Union argued that the United States should not tie its hand with the constraints of international law and should fight spreading Communist influence by supporting Contras and other insurgents. Only in the case of U.S. support for the mujahidin of Afghanistan, who were opposing Soviet aggression, could a good argument be made that such support was defensive and did not violate international law. A good case could not be made for U.S. support to other insurgents fighting recognized governments.

In the mid-1980s both major power blocs had taken off the gloves of international law and were opposing each other indirectly in opposing forces in Nicaragua, El Salvador, Afghanistan, Cambodia, Angola, and other areas. The Soviets were at fault in Afghanistan with their flagrant invasion of a neighboring country. The United States was at fault in indirectly supporting rebel forces against recognized governments of Angola and Nicaragua.

After 1988 dramatic changes took place on the world scene that reverberated from reforms of the new Soviet leader, Mikhail Gorbachev. After he indicated that the Eastern European satellites could determine their own future, democratic revolutions broke out in Eastern Europe. In November 1989 the Berlin Wall came down, signalling the end of the Cold War. Meanwhile, undreamed of reductions of nuclear arms were negotiated by the superpowers.

As cooperation replaced conflict, the United Nations brokered the end of the war in Afghanistan and mediated the end of the Iran-Iraq war. The UN Secretary General helped mediate the end of the conflicts in Nicaragua and El Salvador. Pressure from Gorbachev helped get Vietnamese troops out of Cambodia, and the UN established the largest peacekeeping force in history to help end its vicious war and supervise the setting up of a new government. A top UN official achieved release of Western hostages from Lebanon after frustrating failures of U.S. threats and power politics. The United Nations helped bring about cease-fires in northern Croatia and Slovenia and in 1992 was deeply involved in trying to end the war in Bosnia-Herezegovina. At the same time, at the urging of the secretary general, the United Nations intervened to try to end the civil war and famine in Somalia. It also helped bring an end to the war in Angola. After decades of pressure on the South African government the United Nations helped support efforts to end apartheid in South Africa. The above efforts were done with financial legerdemain because of severe budget restraints reflecting U.S. arrears of over $500 million.

The most dramatic action took place in helping meet the challenge of Iraq's invasion of Kuwait which threatened the major oil resources of the world. In a series of 12 resolutions culminating in a deadline of withdrawal, the Security Council authorized severe sanctions and the use of force. After Iraq's defeat by a coalition led by the United States, IAEA inspectors backed by Security Council threats destroyed Iraq's weapons of mass destruction. The U.S. news media and pundits not only stopped their UN bashing but asserted that the United Nations was acting as its founders had envisaged.

Although the principal aim of the United Nations is to support peace, over 80 percent of its funds and efforts are devoted to long-term goals of promoting human rights, social progress, and better standards of life. While the superpowers and the news media focused on actions of the Security Council, progress continued in the economic and social realm. Many nations approved the Covenants on Human Rights, which cover the same general area as the U.S. Bill of Rights. Like great principles of constitutions, the covenants were not strictly enforced, but they were used as guidelines for new governments supported by the United Nations and for pressure on other governments to live up to their commitments.

The most powerful economic institution of the UN System is the International Monetary Fund, which has supervised the world's financial system since World War II. Its loans and other activities have helped prevent the type of economic crises that occurred without such an institution to promote cooperation after World War I. The IMF together with the World Bank has also helped readjust the heavy debt burdens of dozens of debtor countries, and thereby has avoided serious defaults. The debts still threaten the world's financial stability, and nations continue to work with the IMF on this problem. Meanwhile, the World Bank, which is the major source of development lending, has lent money to debtor countries for sound economic projects. Both major institutions worked effectively to prevent trade restrictions, which could encourage a vicious cycle of retaliation like that which led to the Great Depression of the 1930s. Both encouraged the private sector to make sound international loans that could ease adjustment processes and strengthen the economies of developing nations.

Both the IMF and the World Bank are conservative institutions that impose conditions on their aid called "conditionality." This conditionality, without being specific, usually requires the country to take measures to balance its budget and avoid trade restrictions. The IMF and the World Bank eagerly accepted the invitations of Eastern European countries and former Soviet republics to help them design market-oriented reforms, and began helping the adjustments with billions of dollars of loans.

The United Nations supports one of the world's largest technical assistance programs under the UN Development Program (UNDP). Its projects emphasize problem solving and provide a channel for countries providing aid but not wanting to go to the expense of setting up their own delivery systems. The UNDP draws on the expertise of other parts of the UN System. The United States and other industrial countries of the West are major donors, whereas the Communist countries have provided very little for such aid programs. The United States and other Western countries also give strong support to other UN programs such as UNICEF and UN population programs, the UN High Commissioner for Refugees, the world environment programs, refugee aid to the Middle East, and disaster relief.

In recent years the General Assembly has approved agreements to cooperate against international terrorism, to protect diplomats, and to establish legal standards for settling maritime issues such as boundary disputes. Generally, these agreements are observed. The major Law of the Sea treaty, however, was rejected by the Reagan administration, even though it was signed by 150 nations. The U.S. government observed most of the legal norms of the treaty but insisted that U.S. companies should not be limited in mining resources of the open seas. In 1992 the United Nations sponsored a world conference on the environment. Although the United States held back on specific targets and financial pledges, the agreements approved by the Conference along with top news media coverage gave a major impetus to the environment movements' drives for specific legislation.

The UN secretary general supervises the above economic and social programs, which are within the framework of the United Nations proper, but is forced to delegate major responsibility to subordinates and to governing boards dominated by the major donors. The secretaries general have given most of their personal attention to security issues.

The other UN Specialized Agencies, which have separate constitutions, also establish international norms and carry out major programs of international cooperation and assistance. Air commerce is regulated and protected under the International Civil Aviation Organization, which has had major success in reducing air piracy. International postal services are facilitated under the Universal Postal Union. The World Meteorological Organization provides for the exchange of weather information. The World Intellectual Property Organization establishes standards for protecting patents and copyrights. The General Agreement on Tariff and Trade organizes international conferences to reduce trade and tariff barriers. The World Health Organization carries on the work of the League of Nations Health Organization in ridding the world of epidemics and disease. The Food and Agricultural Organization promotes agricultural assistance, particularly to developing countries. The International Labor Organization promotes international labor standards. UNESCO promotes international educational and cultural programs including literacy. The International Telecommunications Organization facilitates international electronic communication. The UN Industrial Development Organization, a new Specialized Agency, promotes industrial development in the developing world. The International Maritime Organization provides standards for ships and ocean trade and helps clean up the oceans. The UN Environment Program coordinates efforts to protect the world's environment, including preventing the loss of the ozone layer and the "greenhouse effect."

The above international organizations are providing worldwide communication and economic services that developed countries tend to take for granted. They also provide forums and services to meet global threats to health and to the air and oceans. All the above organizations report to the General Assembly and observe standard UN administrative practices. They generally do not take policy directions from the General Assembly and ECOSOC, but often policy discussions and resolutions of these bodies and in other parts of the UN System influence decisions of the Specialized Agencies. The same governments are involved in the various bodies of the UN System, and debates and resolutions in one part of the system affect final decisions in other parts of the system, although voting weights are different in the various bodies.

The above is a remarkable record of accomplishment in the UN System at a negligible cost, when one compares it with military spending (Figure 6).[3] The UN System is recognized by most nations as indispensable for peacekeeping and addressing the world's economic and social problems.

PROSPECTS

Despite the increasing activities and successes of the UN System, the forces of nationalism still dominate international affairs. Some critics have asserted the United Nations is so weak that the United States should rely on power politics to protect its interests. They tend to view the United Nations as a nuisance dominated by smaller countries. Other critics are impatient because the United Nations has not been given enough military and political power to be a supergovernment. Both sets of critics do not recognize the nature of governing. There have been few governments in history with the absolute power to enforce peace for more than a short period. Many powerful governments have been wracked by civil wars, and many governments are still faced by conflicts. Great Britain has its Irish rebellion. The Soviet Union, a superpower, could not mobilize force to hold together. The United States had its civil war, and still has internal riots. It does not automatically move federal troops in to enforce peace, but lets local and state officials act and waits for their requests before deciding whether or not to assist them. Most national governments are not powerful organizations that move armies or police against individuals to enforce laws strictly. Their successful governing depends mostly on compromise and on a process of building up respect for law and for the government that provides services. In a broad sense this applies to the United Nations.

The use of power to enforce rulings of the United Nations is delegated primarily to the Security Council, which depends on unanimity of the five permanent members plus four of the remaining 10 members. Like national governments the Security Council negotiates with the parties, and only as a last resort mobilizes forces to try to enforce its rulings. It has had remarkable successes when the permanent members cooperate, and there have been disasters when some of these countries have acted outside the United Nations and international law.

Although pundits have given world opinion and economic sanctions little credit in the past, such non-military measures had a major impact in crises we discussed. Mussolini was hurt by the League of Nations economic sanctions, until the diplomats outside the League ended them. Japan's attack at Pearl Harbor was triggered by the pain of a U.S. oil embargo.[4] South Africa's reforms of apartheid reflected years of trade and political sanctions by the United Nations. UN sanctions against Iraq after the war forced it to open its installations to UN inspection. Sanctions caused pain in Libya and forced it to offer compromises on releasing men for trial for terrorism. The great revolutions in Eastern Europe and the Soviet Union and its withdrawal from Afghanistan reflected the force of people's opinions and their yearning for freedom. Diplomacy, sanctions, and patience are more cost effective in terms of lives and money than the impatient use of force. The United Nations was designed for moderate approaches before applying force.

The Security Council as envisaged in the Charter has been in the center of the action in world crises, but the other organs have also played important roles. The General Assembly has proven to be much more than a debating society. It is authorized to act when the Security Council cannot make a decision. It did this in crises such as the Korean War and the 1956 Suez War. Also, it has registered overwhelming world opinion against aggression in other cases including the Soviet attacks on Hungary, Czechoslovakia, and Afghanistan. Similarly it has opposed apartheid in South Africa and U.S. intervention in Panama and Nicaragua. If the world moves into a new order where there is respect for international law, the General Assembly will continue to show the way along with the Security Council. The General Assembly also approves the UN budget. It authorizes actions of the Economic and Social Council, and endorses activities of UNDP, UNICEF, UNHCR, and other organs of the UN proper which promote social and economic development.

The United Nations has been served by dedicated secretary generals who exercised firm, although often behind-the-scenes, leadership in a world of powerful nationalistic governments. Boutros-Ghali in his first months of office in 1992 took a leading role in getting support for the United Nations to contain conflicts in Yugoslavia after the European Community representatives failed in achieving cease-fires. At the same time, he took issue with the great powers by insisting they also increase aid to the civil war and starvation in Somalia. They responded and world attention turned to the terrible starvation there that was intensified by the fighting and failure of opposing forces to permit deliveries of aid. Although the UN representatives had negotiated cease-fires with Somalian leaders in February and again in September, their troops continued to block deliveries of relief supplies and to loot warehouses. On November 25, 1992, President Bush made a dramatic offer to provide 15,000 to 30,000 U.S. troops as part of a multinational force to protect such deliveries. Secretary General Boutros-Ghali indicated he would ask the Security Council for authorization for such military units, with an option to use force if necessary.

Also, the Security Council on November 24 approved President Bush's proposal to send a UN observer force to Macedonia to forestall escalation of fighting between Christians and Muslims as well as Serbian attacks in that southern republic of Yugoslavia. Greece, Bulgaria, and Albania also have ancient claims on that territory. As indicated below this was the sort of preventive action Secretary Perez de Cuellar and Boutros-Ghali had been recommending. These actions in the fall of 1992 substantially extended the scope of UN action on matters formerly considered under domestic jurisdiction.

As the Cold War ended, the UN System led the world in the new era of reform and internaitonal cooperation. Gorbachev and then Yeltsin accepted the international law principles of non-intervention in the countries of Eastern Europe, and then also allowed self-determination for the republics of the Soviet Union. These nations moved rapidly to support democratic and then free market reforms, encouraged by the IMF and World Bank. The United States and the Soviet Union (later Russia) began to use the UN Security Council as intended for ending wars. The most dramatic action of the Security Council involved Soviet and Chinese cooperation in the Security Council authorizing a coalition to defeat Iraq's aggression in Kuwait.

There was less public attention to their cooperation in using UN units to end Vietnam's aggression in Cambodia, the local wars in Angola and Namibia, the wars in Nicaragua and El Salvador, the Afghanistan war, and the Iran-Iraq war. In 1992 the Security Council extended its scope of action to try to end civil wars in former Yugoslavia.

Leaders' fear of a nuclear holocaust, the burdens of the arms race, and the growing interdependence of the world brought them to the UN System to solve their problems. Even power brokers were enticed to use the United Nations because of its relative effectiveness in addressing issues.

On January 30, 1992, Prime Minister Major of Britain in an unprecedented gesture of support for the United Nations called a meeting of heads of government of the UN Security Council. At this meeting the Security Council requested the secretary general to propose ways of improving its peacekeeping role. In response Boutros-Ghali, the new secretary general, prepared recommendations that were released on June 23. His report reflected farewell recommendations of Perez de Cuellar, who had played a key role in the revival of UN prestige, but who had retired at the end of 1991.[5] The recommendations also reflected the desire of Prime Minister Major and other leaders for strengthening the UN capacity for "preventive diplomacy, for peacemaking and for peacekeeping." The June 23 report included the following principal proposals:

1. *Preventive Diplomacy.* The report proposed measures of preventive diplomacy including better fact-finding, an early warning system of threats to the peace, and preventive deployment of UN forces to deter attacks. Perez de Cuellar had noted the swift response of the Security Council to repel the invasion of Kuwait, but he deplored the failure of collective diplomacy to prevent untold loss of innocent lives and the appalling dangers to public health. The information available in advance of international crises had been wholly inadequate. He had no UN surveillance systems and inadequate field representation abroad. He also asked the General Assembly to give the secretary general authority to ask the International Court of Justice for a ruling, prior to an invasion, on issues such as the Iraq-Kuwait border dispute.

2. *Peacemaking and Peacekeeping.* The report proposed creation of a new category of UN peacemaking forces more heavily armed than peacekeeping forces. They could be deployed to maintain cease-fires or help guarantee international security. Boutros-Ghali proposed that such forces be made available to the Security Council on a permanent basis. This recommendation went beyond the farewell recommendations of Perez de Cuellar. He had noted the wide variety of tasks of UN units and how the secretary general could improvise to obtain forces for particular jobs. This reflected Perez de Cuellar's realism, that realized, for example, President Bush would not have placed U.S. forces under a UN command in an operation such as Desert Storm.[6]

3. *Peacebuilding.* The report proposed measures for disarming belligerents, monitoring elections, and strengthening government and democratic institutions. The latter proposals reflected UN activities in Cambodia. Perez de Cuellar had included proposals for reporting to the UN on details of arms transactions. This "transparency" of arms sales was in line with a 1991 General Assembly resolution requesting registration of such sales at the UN with the aim of encouraging voluntary restraints on such sales. Also Perez de Cuellar placed more emphasis on human rights as one of the "keystones in the arch of peace." While cautioning about modifying principles of states' sovereignty, he said this does not include the right of mass

slaughter or the forced exodus of civilian populations, an obvious reference to Yugoslavia.

Both secretary generals noted the chasm that existed between the tasks assigned to the United Nations and the funds assigned to it. Their budget requests had included funds for emergencies to permit the Secretariat to respond quickly to tasks assigned to it.[7]

President Bush's proposed "new order" in connection with committing U.S. troops to the Gulf War under UN resolutions indicated a commitment to the United Nations. Subsequently, on November 25, 1992, he reinforced a liberal internationalist policy by offering U.S. troops for a multinational peacemaking force to protect deliveries of food to the starving people of Somalia. The UN Security Council approved the proposal unanimously on December 3. Although U.S. forces were not placed under direct UN command, President Bush made it clear that the force would stay strictly within UN Security Council guidelines as the forces did in the Gulf War. Nonpermanent members of the Security council helped shape the Somalia resolution to make this clear, although they indicated they would have preferred a UN force. Both they and the United States agreed that the job of reconstructing a government in Somalia would be turned over later to a UN peacekeeping force. France, Belgium, Zimbabwe, Nigeria, and Kenya immediately also offered troops for the Somalia peacemaking force.

Secretary generals in the past have stayed on a short leash careful to check with the Security Council each step of the way. Although they have had remarkable successes, they were not provided the authority or resources to act as commanders-in-chief in certain conflict situations. In the Gulf and Somalia crises it was realistic for the Security Council to delegate the combat command to the United States, which provided most of the troops. Secretary generals have had their hands full recruiting such forces from many nations and administering the growing number of peacekeeping forces. The United States, in any event, would not have been willing to place its forces under the direct command of the secretary general.

Bush's actions in the Gulf, Yugoslavia, and Somalia crises helped expand the scope of action of the United Nations and reinforced a new liberal internationalist policy for the United States. However, the United States was still deeply in debt to the United Nations, and the United States still had not made as strong a commitment to liberal internationalism as Presidents Wilson and Truman did.

Bush indicated his intention to withdraw U.S. forces and turn the peacekeeping task over the UN units by the time to the new president took office in two months. President-elect Clinton praised President Bush's decision for Somalia as a historic action. He had already indicated that he supported the liberal internationalist role for the United Nations that President Roosevelt and President Truman had envisaged.[8] The United Nations would need the new president's support to meet challenges of a world lashed by ethnic and nationalist storms.

The world still has many conflicts and economic and social problems. With the end of the Cold War leaving the United States as the only superpower, old power politics concepts have become obsolete. A new world order is being built on support for the United Nations and respect for international law. Roland Dumas, Minister of State and Minister of Foreign Affairs for France, in the summer of 1992 proposed that the United States should give such support to the new international order: "The United Nations is the sole legitimate multiparty organization. American must commit itself to the world body unhesitatingly and provide it with all the resources it needs."[9] After World War I the League of Nations had failed without United States support, and the United Nations needs the unhesitating support of the United States. With such support there would be a realistic hope for the first time to achieve the UN Charter's goals "to save succeeding generations from the scourage of war," "to maintain obligations . . . of international law," and "to promote social programs and better standards of life in larger freedom."

Notes to Chapter 11

1. *Interdependent,* Feb./March 1988, p. 3.

2. *Foreign Affairs,* Spring 1988, pp. 827–845.

3. I used the original version of this graph in 1973 in an internal memorandum to try to persuade the assistant secretary of International Organization Affair of the Department of State to agree to vote for the UN budget, rather than abstain, as was being urged by his administrative staff.

4. A. Yoder, *World Politics and the Causes of War* (Boston: University Press of America, 1986), Chapter IV.

5. Testimony of Secretary of State Baker before the Senate Foreign Relations Committee, June 22, 1992. Senator Pell, Chairman of the Foreign Relations Committee, in the hearings suggested that perhaps the time had come for such a UN peacekeeping force.

6. Perez de Cuellar's proposals were an extension of preventive diplomacy beyond that suggested by Secretary General Hammarskjold, who saw it as a means of settling disputes before they were escalated by the Cold War confrontation. Brian Urquart, *Hammarskjold* (New York: Harper & Row, 1972), pp. 256–257.

7. *UN Chronicle,* September 1992, pp. 2–4: J. Perez de Cuellar, "Report of the Secretary General on the Work of the Organization" (New York: United Nations, 1991); *New York Times,* January 31, 1992, p. 4.

8. B. Clinton, "A Democrat Lays Out His Plan: A New Covenant for American Security." *Harvard Business Review.* Summer 1992, pp. 28, 62.

9. R. Dumas, "Time to Share the Burden." *Harvard Business Review.* Summer 1992, pp. 18–20.

Appendices

Appendices

A. The Covenant of the League of Nations*

The High Contracting Parties

In order to promote international co-operation and to achieve international peace and security

by the acceptance of obligations not to resort to war,
by the prescription of open, just and honourable relations between nations,
by the firm establishment of the understandings of international law as the actual rule of conduct among Governments,
and by the maintenance of justice and a scrupulous respect for all treaty obligations in the dealings of organised peoples with one another,
Agree to this Covenant of the League of Nations.

Article 1

1. The original Members of the League of Nations shall be those of the Signatories which are named in the Annex to this Covenant and also such of those other States named in the Annex as shall accede without reservation to this Covenant. Such accession shall be effected by a Declaration deposited with the Secretariat within two months of the coming into force of the Covenant. Notice thereof shall be sent to all other Members of the League.

2. Any fully self-governing State, Dominion or Colony not named in the Annex may become a Member of the League if its admission is agreed to by two-thirds of the Assembly, provided that it shall give effective guarantees of its sincere intention to observe its international obligations, and shall accept such regulations as may be prescribed by the League in regard to its military, naval and air forces and armaments.

3. Any Member of the League may, after two years' notice of its intention so to do, withdraw from the League, provided that all its international obligations and all its obligations under this Covenant shall have been fulfilled at the time of its withdrawal.

---

*The texts printed in italics indicate amendments adopted by the League.

Article 2

The action of the League under this Covenant shall be effected through the instrumentality of an Assembly and of a Council, with a permanent Secretariat.

Article 3

1. The Assembly shall consist of Representatives of the Members of the League.

2. The Assembly shall meet at stated intervals and from time to time as occasion may require at the Seat of the League or at such other place as may be decided upon.

3. The Assembly may deal at its meetings with any matter within the sphere of action of the League or affecting the peace of the world.

4. At meetings of the Assembly, each Member of the League shall have one vote, and may have not more than three Representatives.

Article 4

1. The Council shall consist of Representatives of the Principal Allied and Associated Powers, together with Representatives of four other Members of the League. These four Members of the League shall be selected by the Assembly from time to time in its discretion. Until the appointment of the Representatives of the four Members of the League first selected by the Assembly, Representatives of Belgium, Brazil, Spain and Greece shall be Members of the Council.

2. With the approval of the majority of the Assembly, the Council may name additional Members of the League whose Representatives shall always be Members of the Council; the Council with like approval may increase the number of Members of the League to be selected by the Assembly for representation on the Council.

2. *bis. The Assembly shall fix by a two-thirds majority the rules dealing with the election of the non-permanent Members of the Council, and particularly such regulations as relate to their term of office and the conditions of re-eligiblity.*

3. The Council shall meet from time to time as occasion may require, and at least once a year, at the Seat of the League, or at such other place as may be decided upon.

4. The Council may deal at its meetings with any matter within the sphere of action of the League or affecting the peace of the world.

5. Any Member of the League not represented on the Council shall be invited to send a Representative to sit as a member at any meeting of the

Council during the consideration of matters specially affecting the interests of that Member of the League.

6. At meetings of the Council, each Member of the League represented on the Council shall have one vote, and may have not more than one Representative.

Article 5

1. Except where otherwise expressly provided in this Covenant or by the terms of the present Treaty, decisions at any meeting of the Assembly or of the Council shall require the agreement of all the Members of the League represented at the meeting.

2. All matters of procedure at meetings of the Assembly or of the Council, including the appointment of Committees to investigate particular matters, shall be regulated by the Assembly or by the Council and may be decided by a majority of the Members of the League represented at the meeting.

3. The first meeting of the Assembly and the first meeting of the Council shall be summoned by the President of the United States of America.

Article 6

1. The permanent Secretariat shall be established at the Seat of the League. The Secretariat shall comprise a Secretary-General and such secretaries and staff as may be required.

2. The first Secretary-General shall be the person named in the Annex; thereafter the Secretary-General shall be appointed by the Council with the approval of the majority of the Assembly.

3. The secretaries and staff of the Secretariat shall be appointed by the Secretary-General with the approval of the Council.

4. The Secretary-General shall act in that capacity at all meetings of the Assembly and of the Council.

5. *The expenses of the League shall be borne by the Members of the League in the proportion decided by the Assembly.*

Article 7

1. The Seat of the League is established at Geneva.

2. The Council may at any time decide that the Seat of the League shall be established elsewhere.

3. All positions under or in connection with the League, including the Secretariat, shall be open equally to men and women.

4. Representatives of the Members of the League and officials of the League when engaged in the business of the League shall enjoy diplomatic privileges and immunities.

5. The buildings and other property occupied by the League or its officials or by Representatives attending its meetings shall be inviolable.

Article 8

1. The Members of the League recognise that the maintenance of peace requires the reduction of national armaments to the lowest point consistent with national safety and the enforcement by common action of international obligations.

2. The Council, taking account of the geographical situation and circumstances of each State, shall formulate plans for such reduction for the consideration and action of the several Governments.

3. Such plans shall be subject to reconsideration and revision at least every ten years.

4. After these plans have been adopted by the several Governments, the limits of armaments therein fixed shall not be exceeded without the concurrence of the Council.

5. The Members of the League agree that the manufacture by private enterprise of munitions and implements of war is open to grave objections. The Council shall advise how the evil effects attendant upon such manufacture can be prevented, due regard being had to the necessities of those Members of the League which are not able to manufacture the munitions and implements of war necessary for their safety.

6. The Members of the League undertake to interchange full and frank information as to the scale of their armaments, their military, naval and air programmes and the condition of such of their industries as are adaptable to warlike purposes.

Article 9

A permanent Commission shall be constituted to advise the Council on the execution of the provisions of Articles 1 and 8 and on military, naval and air questions generally.

Article 10

The Members of the League undertake to respect and preserve as against external aggression the territorial integrity and existing political independence of all Members of the League. In case of any such aggression or in case of any threat or danger of such aggression, the Council shall advise upon the means by which this obligation shall be fulfilled.

Article 11

1. Any war or threat of war, whether immediately affecting any of the Members of the League or not, is hereby declared a matter of concern to

the whole League, and the League shall take any action that may be deemed wise and effectual to safeguard the peace of nations. In case any such emergency should arise, the Secretary-General shall, on the request of any Member of the League, forthwith summon a meeting of the Council.

2. It is also declared to be the friendly right of each Member of the League to bring to the attention of the Assembly or of the Council any circumstance whatever affecting international relations which threatens to disturb international peace or the good understanding between nations upon which peace depends.

Article 12

1. The Members of the League agree that if there should arise between them any dispute likely to lead to a rupture they will submit the matter either to arbitration *or judicial settlement* or to enquiry by the Council, and they agree in no case to resort to war until three months after the award by the arbitrators *or the judicial decision* or the report by the Council.

2. In any case under this article the award of the arbitrators *or the judicial decision* shall be made within a reasonable time, and the report of the Council shall be made within six months after the submission of the dispute.

Article 13

1. The Members of the League agree that whenever any dispute shall arise between them which they recognise to be suitable for submission to arbitration *or judicial settlement,* and which cannot be satisfactorily settled by diplomacy, they will submit the whole subject-matter to arbitration *or judicial settlement.*

2. Disputes as to the interpretation of a treaty, as to any question of international law, as to the existence of any fact which, if established, would constitute a breach of any international obligation, or as to the extent and nature of the reparation to be made for any such breach, are declared to be among those which are generally suitable for submission to arbitration *or judicial settlement.*

3. *For the consideration of any such dispute, the court to which the case is referred shall be the Permanent Court of International Justice, established in accordance with Article 14, or any tribunal agreed on by the parties to the dispute or stipulated in any Convention existing between them.*

4. The Members of the League agree that they will carry out in full good faith any award *or decision* that may be rendered, and that they will not resort to war against a Member of the League which complies therewith. In the event of any failure to carry out such an award *or decision,* the Council shall propose what steps should be taken to give effect thereto.

Article 14

The Council shall formulate and submit to the Members of the League for adoption plans for the establishment of a Permanent Court of International Justice. The Court shall be competent to hear and determine any dispute of an international character which the parties thereto submit to it. The Court may also give an advisory opinion upon any disputd or question referred to it by the Council or by the Assembly.

Article 15

1. If there should arise between Members of the League any dispute likely to lead to a rupture, which is not submitted to arbitration *or judicial settlement* in accordance with Article 13, the Members of the League agree that they will submit the matter to the Council. Any party to the dispute may effect such submission by giving notice of the existence of the dispute to the Secretary-General, who will make all necessary arrangements for a full investigation and consideration thereof.

2. For this purpose, the parties to the dispute will communicate to the Secretary-General, as promptly as possible, statements of their case with all the relevant facts and papers, and the Council may forthwith direct the publication thereof.

3. The Council shall endeavour to effect a settlement of the dispute, and if such efforts are successful, a statement shall be made public giving such facts and explanations regarding the dispute and the terms of settlement thereof as the Council may deem appropriate.

4. If the dispute is not thus settled, the Council either unanimously or by a majority vote shall make and publish a report containing a statement of the facts of the dispute and the recommendations which are deemed just and proper in regard thereto.

5. Any Member of the League represented on the Council may make public a statement of the facts of the dispute and of its conclusions regarding the same.

6. If a report by the Council is unanimously agreed to by the members thereof other than the Representatives of one or more of the parties to the dispute, the Members of the League agree that they will not go to war with any party to the dispute which complies with the recommendations of the report.

7. If the Council fails to reach a report which is unanimously agreed to by the members thereof, other than the Representatives of one or more of the parties to the dispute, the Members of the League reserve to themselves the right to take such action as they shall consider necessary for the maintenance of right and justice.

8. If the dispute between the parties is claimed by one of them, and is found by the Council, to arise out of a matter which by international law is solely within the domestic jurisdiction of that party, the Council shall so report, and shall make no recommendation as to its settlement.

9. The Council may in any case under this article refer the dispute to the Assembly. The dispute shall be so referred at the request of either party to the dispute provided that such request be made within fourteen days after the submission of the dispute to the Council.

10. In any case referred to the Assembly, all the provisions of this article and of Article 12 relating to the action and powers of the Council shall apply to the action and powers of the Assembly, provided that a report made by the Assembly, if concurred in by the Representatives of those Members of the League represented on the Council and of a majority of the other Members of the League, exclusive in each case of the Representatives of the parties to the dispute, shall have the same force as a report by the Council concurred in by all the members thereof other than the Representatives of one or more of the parties to the dispute.

Article 16

1. Should any Member of the League resort to war in disregard of its covenants under Articles 12, 13, or 15, it shall, *ipso facto,* be deemed to have committed an act of war against all other Members of the League, which hereby undertake immediately to subject it to the severance of all trade or financial relations, the prohibition of all intercourse between their nationals and the nationals of the Covenant-breaking State, and the prevention of all financial, commercial or personal intercourse between the nationals of the Covenant-breaking State and the nationals of any other State, whether a Member of the League or not.

2. It shall be the duty of the Council in such case to recommend to the several Governments concerned what effective military, naval or air force the Members of the League shall severally contribute to the armed forces to be used to protect the covenants of the League.

3. The Members of the League agree, further, that they will mutually support one another in the financial and economic measures which are taken under this article, in order to minimise the loss and inconvenience resulting from the above measures, and that they will mutually support one another in resisting any special measures aimed at one of their number by the Covenant-breaking State, and that they will take the necessary steps to afford passage through their territory to the forces of any of the Members of the League which are co-operating to protect the covenants of the League.

4. Any member of the League which has violated any covenant of the League may be declared to be no longer a Member of the League by a vote

of the Council concurred in by the Representatives of all the other Members of the League represented thereon.

Article 17

1. In the event of a dispute between a Member of the League and a State which is not a member of the League or between States not members of the League, the State or States not members of the League shall be invited to accept the obligations of membership in the League for the purposes of such dispute, upon such conditions as the Council may deem just. If such invitation is accepted, the provisions of Article 12 to 16 inclusive shall be applied with such modifications as may be deemed necessary by the Council.

2. Upon such invitation being given, the Council shall immediately institute an enquiry into the circumstances of the dispute and recommend such action as may seem best and most effectual in the circumstances.

3. If a State so invited shall refuse to accept the obligations of membership in the League for the purposes of such dispute, and shall resort to war against a Member of the League, the provisions of Article 16 shall be applicable as against the State taking such action.

4. If both parties to the dispute when so invited refuse to accept the obligations of membership in the League for the purposes of such dispute, the Council may take such measures and make such recommendations as will prevent hostilities and will result in the settlement of the dispute.

Article 18

Every treaty or international engagement entered into hererafter by any Member of the League shall be forthwith registered with the Secretariat and shall, as soon as possible, be published by it. No such treaty or international engagement shall be binding until so registered.

Article 19

The Assembly may from time to time advise the reconsideration by Members of the League of treaties which have become inapplicable and the consideration of international conditions whose continuance might endanger the peace of the world.

Article 20

1. The Members of the Legue severally agree that this Covenant is accepted as abrogating all obligations or understandings *inter se* which are inconsistent with the terms thereof, and solemnly undertake that they will not hereafter enter into any engagements inconsistent with the terms thereof.

2. In case any Member of the League shall, before becoming a Member of the League, have undertaken any obligations inconsistent with the terms of this Covenant, it shall be the duty of such Member to take immediate steps to procure its release from such obligations.

Article 21

Nothing in this Covenant shall be deemed to affect the validity of international engagements, such as treaties of arbitration or regional understandings like the Monroe doctrine, for securing the maintenance of peace.

Article 22

1. To those colonies and territories which as a consequence of the late war have ceased to be under the sovereignty of the States which formerly governed them and which are inhabited by peoples not yet able to stand by themselves under the strenuous conditions of the modern world, there should be applied the principle that the well-being and development of such peoples form a sacred trust of civilisation and that securities for the performance of this trust should be embodied in this Covenant.

2. The best method of giving practical effect to this principle is that the tutelage of such peoples should be entrusted to advanced nations who, by reason of their resources, their experience or their geographical position, can best undertake this responsibility, and who are willing to accept it, and that this tutelage should be exercised by them as Mandatories on behalf of the League.

3. The character of the mandate must differ according to the stage of the development of the people, the geographical situation of the territory, its economic conditions and other similar circumstances.

4. Certain communities formerly belonging to the Turkish Empire have reached a stage of development where their existence as independent nations can be provisionally recognised subject to the rendering of administrative advice and assistance by a Mandatory until such time as they are able to stand alone. The wishes of these communities must be a principal consideration in the selection of the Mandatory.

5. Other peoples, especially those of Central Africa, are at such a stage that the Mandatory must be responsible for the administration of the territory under conditions which will guarantee freedom of conscience and religion, subject only to the maintenance of public order and morals, the prohibition of abuses such as the slave trade, the arms traffic and the liquor traffic, and the prevention of the establishment of fortifications or military and naval bases and of military training of the natives for other than police purposes and the defence of territory, and will also secure equal opportunities for the trade and commerce of other Members of the League.

6. There are territories, such as South West Africa and certain of the

South Pacific Islands, which, owing to the sparseness of their population, or their small size, or their remoteness from the centres of civilisation, or their geographical contiguity to the territory of the Mandatory, and other circumstances, can be best administered under the laws of the Mandatory as integral portions of its territory, subject to the safeguards above mentioned in the interests of the indigenous population.

7. In every case of mandate, the Mandatory shall render to the Council an annual report in reference to the territory committed to its charge.

8. The degree of authority, control or administration to be exercised by the Mandatory shall, if not previously agreed upon by the Members of the League, be explicitly defined in each case by the Council.

9. A permanent Commission shall be constituted to receive and examine the annual reports of the Mandatories and to advise the Council on all matters relating to the observance of the mandates.

Article 23

Subject to and in accordance with the provisions of international Conventions existing or hereafter to be agreed upon, the Members of the League:

> (a) will endeavour to secure and maintain fair and humane conditions of labour for men, women and children, both in their own countries and in all countries to which their commercial and industrial relations extend, and for that purpose will establish and maintain the necessary international organisations;
>
> (b) undertake to secure just treatment of the native inhabitants of territories under their control;
>
> (c) will entrust the League with the general supervision over the execution of agreements with regard to the traffic in women and children, and the traffic in opium and other dangerous drugs;
>
> (d) will entrust the League with the general supervision of the trade in arms and ammunition with the countries in which the control of this traffic is necessary in the common interest;
>
> (e) will make provision to secure and maintain freedom of communications and of transit and equitable treatment for the commerce of all Members of the League. In this connection, the special necessities of the regions devastated during the war of 1914–1918 shall be borne in mind;
>
> (f) will endeavour to take steps in matters of international concern for the prevention and control of disease.

Article 24

1. There shall be placed under the direction of the League all international bureaux already established by general treaties if the parties to such treaties

consent. All such international bureaux and all commissions for the regulation of matters of international interest hereafter constituted shall be placed under the direction of the League.

2. In all matters of international interest which are regulated by general Conventions but which are not placed under the control of international bureaux or commissions, the Secretariat of the League shall, subject to the consent of the Council and if desired by the parties, collect and distribute all relevant information and shall render any other assistance which may be necessary or desirable.

3. The Council may include as part of the expenses of the Secretariat the expenses of any bureau or commission which is placed under the direction of the League.

Article 25

The Members of the League agree to encourage and promote the establishment and co-operation of duly authorised voluntary national Red Cross organisations having as purposes the improvement of health, the prevention of disease and the mitigation of suffering throughout the world.

Article 26

1. Amendments to this Covenant will take effect when ratified by the Members of the League whose Representatives compose the Council and by a majority of the Members of the League whose Representatives compose the Assembly.

2. No such amendments shall bind any Member of the League which signifies its dissent therefrom, but in that case it shall cease to be a Member of the League.

B.   The Charter of the United Nations*

We the peoples of the United Nations determined

to save succeeding generations from the scourge of war, which twice in our lifetime has brought untold sorrow to mankind, and to reaffirm faith in fundamental human rights, in the dignity and worth of the human person, in the equal rights of men and women and of nations large and small, and

to establish conditions under which justice and respect for the obligations arising from treaties and other sources of international law can be maintained, and

to promote social progress and better standards of life in larger freedom, and for these ends

to practice tolerance and live together in peace with one another as good neighbors, and

to unite our strength to maintain international peace and security, and

to ensure, by the acceptance of principles and the institution of methods, that armed force shall not be used, save in the common interest, and

to employ international machinery for the promotion of the economic and social advancement of all peoples,

have resolved to combine our efforts to accomplish these aims.

Accordingly, our respective Governments, through representatives assembled in the city of San Francisco, who have exhibited their full powers found to be in good and due form, have agreed to the present Charter of the United Nations and do hereby establish an international organization to be known as the United Nations.

CHAPTER I. PURPOSES AND PRINCIPLES

Article 1

The Purposes of the United Nations are:

1. To maintain international peace and security, and to that end: to take

---

*Articles 23, 27, and 61 were revised by amendments, proposed by the General Assembly in its Resolution 1991 A & B (XVIII) of December 17, 1963, which entered into force on August 31, 1965. Article 109 was amended by a process that began with General Assembly Resolution 2101 (XX) of December 20, 1965, and was concluded on June 12, 1968.

In these articles, portions deleted by amendment are enclosed in parentheses, and new provisions are printed in italics.

effective collective measures for the prevention and removal of threats to the peace, and for the suppression of acts of aggression or other breaches of the peace, and to bring about by peaceful means, and in conformity with the principles of justice and international law, adjustment or settlement of international disputes or situations which might lead to a breach of the peace;

2. To develop friendly relations among nations based on respect for the principle of equal rights and self-determination of peoples, and to take other appropriate measures to strengthen universal peace;

3. To achieve international cooperation in solving international problems of an economic, social, cultural, or humanitarian character, and in promoting and encouraging respect for human rights and for fundamental freedoms for all without distinction as to race, sex, language, or religion; and

4. To be a center for harmonizing the actions of nations in the attainment of these common ends.

Article 2

The Organization and its Members, in pursuit of the Purposes stated in Article 1, shall act in accordance with the following Principles.

1. The Organization is based on the principle of the sovereign equality of all its Members.

2. All Members, in order to ensure to all of them the rights and benefits resulting from membership, shall fulfill in good faith the obligations assumed by them in accordance with the present Charter.

3. All Members shall settle their international disputes by peaceful means in such a manner that international peace and security, and justice, are not endangered.

4. All Members shall refrain in their international relations from the threat or use of force against the territorial integrity or political independence of any state, or in any other manner inconsistent with the Purposes of the United Nations.

5. All Members shall give the United Nations every assistance in any action it takes in accordance with the present Charter, and shall refrain from giving assistance to any state against which the United Nations is taking preventive or enforcement action.

6. The Organization shall ensure that states which are not Members of the United Nations act in accordance with these Principles so far as may be necessary for the maintenance of international peace and security.

7. Nothing contained in the present Charter shall authorize the United Nations to intervene in matters which are essentially within the domestic jurisdiction of any state or shall require the Members to submit such matters to settlement under the present Charter; but this principle shall not prejudice the application of enforcement measures under Chapter VII.

CHAPTER II. MEMBERSHIP

Article 3

The original Members of the United Nations shall be the states which, having participated in the United Nations Conference on International Organization at San Francisco, or having previously signed the Declaration by United Nations of January 1, 1942, sign the present Charter and ratify it in accordance with Article 110.

Article 4

1. Membership in the United Nations is open to all other peace-loving states which accept the obligations contained in the present Charter and, in the judgment of the Organization, are able and willing to carry out these obligations.

2. The admission of any such state to membership in the United Nations will be effected by a decision of the General Assembly upon the recommendation of the Security Council.

Article 5

A Member of the United Nations against which preventive or enforcement action has been taken by the Security Council may be suspended from the exercise of the rights and privileges of membership by the General Assembly upon the recommendation of the Security Council. The exercise of these rights and privileges may be restored by the Security Council.

Article 6

A Member of the United Nations which has persistently violated the Principles contained in the present Charter may be expelled from the Organization by the General Assembly upon the recommendation of the Security Council.

CHAPTER III. ORGANS

Article 7

1. There are established as the principal organs of the United Nations: a General Assembly, a Security Council, an Economic and Social Council, a Trusteeship Council, an International Court of Justice, and a Secretariat.

2. Such subsidiary organs as may be found necessary may be established in accordance with the present Charter.

Article 8

The United Nations shall place no restrictions on the eligibility of men and women to participate in any capacity and under conditions of equality in its principal and subsidiary organs.

CHAPTER IV. THE GENERAL ASSEMBLY

Composition

Article 9

1. The General Assembly shall consist of all the Members of the United Nations.

2. Each Member shall have not more than five representatives in the General Assembly.

Functions and Powers

Article 10

The General Assembly may discuss any questions or any matters within the scope of the present Charter or relating to the powers and functions of any organs provided for in the present Charter, and, except as provided in Article 12, may make recommendations to the Members of the United Nations or to the Security Council or to both on any such questions or matters.

Article 11

1 The General Assembly may consider the general principles of cooperation in the maintenance of international peace and security, including the principles governing disarmament and the regulation of armaments, and may make recommendations with regard to such principles to the Members or to the Security Council or to both.

2. The General Assembly may discuss any questions relating to the maintenance of international peace and security brought before it by any Member of the United Nations, or by the Security Council, or by a state which is not a Member of the United Nations in accordance with Article 35, paragraph 2, and, except as provided in Article 12, may make recommendations with regard to any such questions to the state or states concerned or to the Security Council or to both. Any such question on which action is necessary shall be referred to the Security Council by the General Assembly either before or after discussion.

3. The General Assembly may call the attention of the Security Council to situations which are likely to endanger international peace and security.

4. The powers of the General Assembly set forth in this Article shall not limit the general scope of Article 10.

Article 12

1. While the Security Council is exercising in respect of any dispute or situation the functions assigned to it in the present Charter, the General Assembly shall not make any recommendations with regard to that dispute or situation unless the Security Council so requests.

2. The Secretary-General, with the consent of the Security Council, shall notify the General Assembly at each session of any matters relative to the maintenance of international peace and security which are being dealt with by the Security Council and shall similarly notify the General Assembly, or the Members of the United Nations if the General Assembly is not in session, immediately the Security Council ceases to deal with such matters.

Article 13

1. The General Assembly shall initiate studies and make recommendations for the purpose of:

a. promoting international cooperation in the political field and encouraging the progressive development of international law and its codification;

b. promoting international cooperation in the economic, social, cultural, educational, and health fields, and assisting in the realization of human rights and fundamental freedoms for all without distinction as to race, sex, language, or religion.

2. The further responsibilities, functions, and powers of the General Assembly with respect to matters mentioned in paragraph 1 (b) above are set forth in Chapters IX and X.

Article 14

Subject to the provisions of Article 12, the General Assembly may recommend measures for the peaceful adjustment of any situation, regardless of origin, which it deems likely to impair the general welfare or friendly relations among nations, including situations resulting from a violation of the provisions of the present Charter setting forth the Purposes and Principles of the United Nations.

Article 15

1. The General Assembly shall receive and consider annual and special reports from the Security Council; these reports shall include an account of

the measures that the Security Council has decided upon or taken to maintain international peace and security.

2. The General Assembly shall receive and consider reports from the other organs of the United Nations.

Article 16

The General Assembly shall perform such functions with respect to the international trusteeship system as are assigned to it under Chapters XII and XIII, including the approval of the trusteeship agreements for areas not designated as strategic.

Article 17

1. The General Assembly shall consider and approve the budget of the Organization.

2. The expenses of the Organization shall be borne by the Members as apportioned by the General Assembly.

3. The General Assembly shall consider and approve any financial and budgetary arrangements with specialized agencies referred to in Article 57 and shall examine the administrative budgets of such specialized agencies with a view to making recommendations to the agencies concerned.

Voting

Article 18

1. Each member of the General Assembly shall have one vote.

2. Decisions of the General Assembly on important questions shall be made by a two-thirds majority of the members present and voting. These questions shall include: recommendations with respect to the maintenance of international peace and security, the election of the non-permanent members of the Security Council, the election of the members of the Economic and Social Council, the election of members of the Trusteeship Council in accordance with paragraph 1 (c) of Article 86, the admission of new Members to the United Nations, the suspension of the rights and privileges of membership, the expulsion of Members, questions relating to the operation of the trusteeship system, and budgetary questions.

3. Decisions on other questions, including the determination of additional categories of questions to be decided by a two-thirds majority, shall be made by a majority of the members present and voting.

Article 19

A Member of the United Nations which is in arrears in the payment of its financial contributions to the Organization shall have no vote in the General Assembly if the amount of its arrears equals or exceeds the amount of the contributions due from it for the preceding two full years. The General Assembly may, nevertheless, permit such a Member to vote if it is satisfied that the failure to pay is due to conditions beyond the control of the Member.

Procedure

Article 20

The General Assembly shall meet in regular annual sessions and in such special sessions as occasion may require. Special sessions shall be convoked by the Secretary-General at the request of the Security Council or of a majority of the Members of the United Nations.

Article 21

The General Assembly shall adopt its own rules of procedure. It shall elect its President for each session.

Article 22

The General Assembly may establish such subsidiary organs as it deems necessary for the performance of its functions.

CHAPTER V. THE SECURITY COUNCIL

Composition

Article 23

1. The Security Council shall consist of (eleven) *fifteen* Members of the United Nations. The Republic of China, France, the Union of Soviet Socialist Republics, the United Kingdom of Great Britain and Northern Ireland, and the United States of America shall be permanent members of the Security Council. The General Assembly shall elect (six) *ten* other Members of the United Nations to be non-permanent members of the Security Council, due regard being specially paid, in the first instance to the contribution of Members of the United Nations to the maintenance of international peace and security and to the other purposes of the Organization, and also to equitable geographical distribution.

2. The non-permanent members of the Security Council shall be elected for a term of two years. In the first election of the non-permanent members (however, three shall be chosen for a term of one year) *after the increase*

of the membership of the Security Council from eleven to fifteen, two of the four additional members shall be chosen for a term of one year. A retiring member shall not be eligible for immediate re-election.

3. Each member of the Security Council shall have one representative.

Functions and Powers

Article 24

1. In order to ensure prompt and effective action by the United Nations, its Members confer on the Security Council primary responsibility for the maintenance of international peace and security, and agree that in carrying out its duties under this responsibility the Security Council acts on their behalf.

2. In discharging these duties the Security Council shall act in accordance with the Purposes and Principles of the United Nations. The specific powers granted to the Security Council for the discharge of these duties are laid down in Chapters VI, VII, VIII, and XII.

3. The Security Council shall submit annual and, when necessary, special reports to the General Assembly for its consideration.

Article 25

The Members of the United Nations agree to accept and carry out the decisions of the Security Council in accordance with the present Charter.

Article 26

In order to promote the establishment and maintenance of international peace and security with the least diversion for armaments of the world's human and economic resources, the Security Council shall be responsible for formulating, with the assistance of the Military Staff Committee referred to in Article 47, plans to be submitted to the Members of the United Nations for the establishment of a system for the regulation of armaments.

Voting

Article 27

1. Each member of the Security Council shall have one vote.

2. Decisions of the Security Council on procedural matters shall be made by an affirmative vote of (seven) *nine* members.

3. Decisions of the Security Council on all other matters shall be made

by an affirmative vote of (seven) *nine* members including the concurring votes of the permanent members; provided that, in decisions under Chapter VI, and under paragraph 3 of Article 52, a party to a dispute shall abstain from voting.

Procedure

Article 28

1. The Security Council shall be so organized as to be able to function continuously. Each member of the Security Council shall for this purpose be represented at all times at the seat of the Organization.
2. The Security Council shall hold periodic meetings at which each of its members may, if it so desires, be represented by a member of the government or by some other specially designated representative.
3. The Security Council may hold meetings at such places other than the seat of the Organization as in its judgment will best facilitate its work.

Article 29

The Security Council may establish such subsidiary organs as it deems necessary for the performance of its functions.

Article 30

The Security Council shall adopt its own rules of procedure, including the method of selecting its President.

Article 31

Any Member of the United Nations which is not a member of the Security Council may participate, without vote, in the discussion of any question brought before the Security Council whenever the latter considers that the interests of that Member are specially affected.

Article 32

Any Member of the United Nations which is not a member of the Security Council or any state which is not a Member of the United Nations, if it is a party to a dispute under consideration by the Security Council, shall be invited to participate, wihtout vote, in the discussion relating to the dispute. The Security Council shall lay down such conditions as it deems just for the participation of a state which is not a Member of the United Nations.

CHAPTER VI. PACIFIC SETTLEMENT OF DISPUTES

Article 33

1. The parties to any dispute, the continuance of which is likely to endanger the maintenance of international peace and security, shall, first of all, seek a solution by negotiation, enquiry, mediation, conciliation, arbitration, judicial settlement, resort to regional agencies or arrangements, or other peaceful means of their own choice.

2. The Security Council shall, when it deems necessary, call upon the parties to settle their dispute by such means.

Article 34

The Security Council may investigate any dispute, or any situation which might lead to international friction or give rise to a dispute, in order to determine whether the continuance of the dispute or situation is likely to endanger the maintenance of international peace and security.

Article 35

1. Any Member of the United Nations may bring any dispute, or any situation of the nature referred to in Article 34, to the attention of the Security Council or of the General Assembly.

2. A state which is not a Member of the United Nations may bring to the attention of the Security Council or of the General Assembly any dispute to which it is a party if it accepts in advance, for the purposes of the dispute, the obligations of pacific settlement provided in the present Charter.

3. The proceedings of the General Assembly in respect of matters brought to its attention under this Article will be subject to the provisions of Articles 11 and 12.

Article 36

1. The Security Council may, at any stage of a dispute of the nature referred to in Article 33 or of a situation of like nature, recommend appropriate procedures or methods of adjustment.

2. The Security Council should take into consideration any procedures for the settlement of the dispute which have already been adopted by the parties.

3. In making recommendations under this Article the Security Council should also take into consideration that legal disputes should as a general rule be referred by the parties to the International Court of Justice in accordance with the provisions of the Statute of the Court.

Article 37

1. Should the parties to a dispute of the nature referred to in Article 33 fail to settle it by the means indicated in that Article, they shall refer it to the Security Council.

2. If the Security Council deems that the continuance of the dispute is in fact likely to endanger the maintenance of international peace and security, it shall decide whether to take action under Article 36 or to recommend such terms of settlement as it may consider appropriate.

Article 38

Without prejudice to the provisions of Articles 33 to 37, the Security Council may, if all the parties to any dispute so request, make recommendations to the parties with a view to a pacific settlement of the dispute.

CHAPTER VII. ACTION WITH RESPECT TO THREATS TO THE PEACE, BREACHES OF THE PEACE, PEACE, AND ACTS OF AGGRESSION

Article 39

The Security Council shall determine the existence of any threat to the peace, breach of the peace, or act of aggression and shall make recommendations, or decide what measures shall be taken in accordance with Articles 41 and 42, to maintain or restore international peace and security.

Article 40

In order to prevent an aggravation of the situation, the Security Council may, before making the recommendations or deciding upon the measures provided for in Article 39, call upon the parties concerned to comply with such provisional measures at it deems necessary or desirable. Such provisional measures shall be without prejudice to the rights, claims, or position of the parties concerned. The Security Council shall duly take account of failure to comply with such provisional measures.

Article 41

The Security Council may decide what measures not involving the use of armed force are to be employed to give effect to its decisions, and it may call upon the Members of the United Nations to apply such measures. These may include complete or partial interruption of economic relations and of rail, sea, air, postal, telegraphic, radio, and other means of communication, and the severance of diplomatic relations.

Article 42

Should the Security Council consider that measures provided for in Article 41 would be inadequate or have proved to be inadequate, it may take such action by air, sea, or land forces as may be necessary to maintain or restore international peace and security. Such action may include demonstrations, blockade, and other operations by air, sea, or land forces of Members of the United Nations.

Article 43

1. All Members of the United Nations, in order to contribute to the maintenance of international peace and security, undertake to make available to the Security Council, on its call and in accordance with a special agreement or agreements, armed forces, assistance, and facilities, including rights of passage, necessary for the purpose of maintaining international peace and security.

2. Such agreement or agreements shall govern the numbers and types of forces, their degree of readiness and general location, and the nature of the facilities and assistance to be provided.

3. The agreement or agreements shall be negotiated as soon as possible on the initiative of the Security Council. They shall be concluded between the Security Council and Members or between the Security Council and groups of Members and shall be subject to ratification by the signatory states in accordance with their respective constitutional processes.

Article 44

When the Security Council has decided to use force it shall, before calling upon a Member not represented on it to provide armed forces in fulfillment of the obligations assumed under Article 43, invite that Member, if the Member so desires, to participate in the decisions of the Security Council concerning the employment of contingents of that Member's armed forces.

Article 45

In order to enable the United Nations to take urgent military measures, Members shall hold immediately available national air-force contingents for combined international enforcement action. The strength and degree of readiness of these contingents and plans for their combined action shall be determined, within the limits laid down in the special agreement or agreements referred to in Article 43, by the Security Council with the assistance of the Military Staff Committee.

Article 46

Plans for the application of armed force shall be made by the Security Council with the assistance of the Military Staff Committee.

Article 47

1. There shall be established a Military Staff Committee to advise and assist the Security Council on all questions relating to the Security Council's military requirements for the maintenance of international peace and security, the employment and command of forces placed at its disposal, the regulation of armaments, and possible disarmament.

2. The Military Staff Committee shall consist of the Chiefs of Staff of the permanent members of the Security Council or their representatives. Any Member of the United Nations not permanently represented on the Committee shall be invited by the Committee to be associated with it when the efficient discharge of the Committee's responsibilities requires the participation of that Member in its work.

3. The Military Staff Committee shall be responsible under the Security Council for the strategic direction of any armed forces placed at the disposal of the Security Council. Questions relating to the command of such forces shall be worked out subsequently.

4. The Military Staff Committee, with the authorization of the Security Council and after consultation with appropriate regional agencies, may establish regional subcommittees.

Article 48

1. The action required to carry out the decisions of the Security Council for the maintenance of international peace and security shall be taken by all the Members of the United Nations or by some of them, as the Security Council may determine.

2. Such decisions shall be carried out by the Members of the United Nations directly and through their action in the appropriate international agencies of which they are members.

Article 49

The Members of the United Nations shall join in affording mutual assistance in carrying out the measures decided upon by the Security Council.

Article 50

If preventive or enforcement measures against any state are taken by the Security Council, any other state, whether a Member of the United Nations or not, which finds itself confronted with special economic problems arising from the carrying out of those measures shall have the right to consult the Security Council with regard to a solution of those problems.

Article 51

Nothing in the present Charter shall impair the inherent right of individual or collective self-defense if an armed attack occurs against a Member of the United Nations, until the Security Council has taken the measures necessary to maintain international peace and security. Measures taken by Members in the exercise of this right of self-defense shall be immediately reported to the Security Council and shall not in any way affect the authority and responsibility of the Security Council under the present Charter to take at any time such action as it deems necessary in order to maintain or restore international peace and security.

CHAPTER VIII. REGIONAL ARRANGEMENTS

Article 52

1. Nothing in the present Charter precludes the existence of regional arrangements or agencies for dealing with such matters relating to the maintenance of international peace and security as are appropriate for regional action, provided that such arrangements or agencies and their activities are consistent with the Purposes and Principles of the United Nations.

2. The Members of the United Nations entering into such arrangements or constituting such agencies shall make every effort to achieve pacific settlement of local disputes through such regional arrangements or by such regional agencies before referring them to the Security Council.

3. The Security Council shall encourage the development of pacific settlement of local disputes through such regional arrangements or by such regional agencies either on the initiative of the states concerned or by reference from the Security Council.

4. This Article in no way impairs the application of Articles 34 and 35.

Article 53

1. The Security Council shall, where appropriate, utilize such regional arrangements or agencies for enforcement action under its authority. But no enforcement action shall be taken under regional arrangements or by regional agencies without the authorization of the Security Council, with the exception of measures against any enemy state, as defined in paragraph 2 of this Article, provided for pursuant to Article 107 or in regional arrangements directed against renewal of aggressive policy on the part of any such

state, until such time as the Organization may, on request of the Governments concerned, be charged with the responsibility for preventing further aggression by such a state.

2. The term enemy state as used in paragraph 1 of this Article applies to any state which during the Second World War has been an enemy of any signatory of the present Charter.

Article 54

The Security Council shall at all times be kept fully informed of activities undertaken or in contemplation under regional arrangements or by regional agencies for the maintenance of international peace and security.

CHAPTER IX. INTERNATIONAL ECONOMIC AND SOCIAL COOPERATION

Article 55

With a view to the creation of conditions of stability and well-being which are necessary for peaceful and friendly relations among nations based on respect for the principle of equal rights and self-determination of peoples, the United Nations shall promote:

a. higher standards of living, full employment, and conditions of economic an social progress and development;

b. solutions of international economic, social health, and related problems; and international cultural and educational cooperation; and

c. universal respect for, and observance of, human rights and fundamental freedoms for all without distinction as to race, sex, language, or religion.

Article 56

All Members pledge themselves to take joint and separate action in cooperation with the Organization for the achievement of the purposes set forth in Article 55.

Article 57

1. The various specialized agencies, established by intergovernmental agreement and having wide international responsibilities, as defined in their basic instruments, in economic, social, cultural, educational, health, and related fields, shall be brought into relationship with the United Nations in accordance with the provisions of Article 63.

2. Such agencies thus brought into relationship with the United Nations are hereinafter referred to as specialized agencies.

Article 58

The Organization shall make recommendations for the coordination of the policies and activities of the specialized agencies.

Article 59

The Organization shall, where appropriate, initiate negotiations among the states concerned for the creation of any new specialized agencies required for the accomplishment of the purposes set forth in Article 55.

Article 60

Responsibility for the discharge of the functions of the Organization set forth in this Chapter shall be vested in the General Assembly and, under the authority of the General Assembly, in the Economic and Social Council, which shall have for this purpose the powers set forth in Chapter X.

CHAPTER X. THE ECONOMIC AND SOCIAL COUNCIL

Composition

Article 61

1. The Economic and Social Council shall consist of (eighteen) *fifty-four* Members of the United Nations elected by the General Assembly.

2. Subject to the provisions of paragraph 3, (six) *nine* members of the Economic and Social Council shall be elected each year for a term of three years. A retiring member shall be eligible for immediate re-election.

3. At the first election *after the increase in the membership of the Economic and Social Council from twenty-seven to fifty-four members, in addition to the members elected in place of the nine members whose term of office expires at the end of that year, twenty-seven additional members shall be elected. Of these twenty-seven additional members, the term of office of nine members so elected shall expire at the end of one year, and of nine other members at the end of two years,* in accordance with arrangements made by the General Assembly.

4. Each member of the Economic and Social Council shall have one representative.

Functions and Powers

Article 62

1. The Economic and Social Council may make or initiate studies and reports with respect to international economic, social, cultural, educational, health, and related matters and may make recommendations with respect to any such matters to the General Assembly, to the Members of the United Nations, and to the specialized agencies concerned.

2. It may make recommendations for the purpose of promoting respect for, and observance of, human rights and fundamental freedoms for all.

3. It may prepare draft conventions for submission to the General Assembly, with respect to matters falling within its competence.

4. It may call, in accordance with the rules prescribed by the United Nations, international conferences on matters falling within its competence.

Article 63

1. The Economic and Social Council may enter into agreements with any of the agencies referred to in Article 57, defining the terms on which the agency concerned shall be brought into relationship with the United Nations. Such agreements shall be subject to approval by the General Assembly.

2. It may coordinate the activities of the specialized agencies through consultation with and recommendations to such agencies and through recommendations to the General Assembly and to the Members of the United Nations.

Article 64

1. The Economic and Social Council may take appropriate steps to obtain regular reports from the specialized agencies. It may make arrangements with the Members of the United Nations and with the specialized agencies to obtain reports on the steps taken to give effect to its own recommendations and to recommendations on matters falling within its competence made by the General Assembly.

2. It may communicate its observations on these reports to the General Assembly.

Article 65

The Economic and Social Council may furnish information to the Security Council and shall assist the Security Council upon its request.

Article 66

1. The Economic and Social Council shall perform such functions as fall within its competence in connection with the carrying out of the recommendations of the General Assembly.

2. It may, with the approval of the General Assembly, perform services at the request of Members of the United Nations and at the request of specialized agencies.

3. It shall perform such other functions as are specified elsewhere in the present Charter or as may be assigned to it by the General Assembly.

Voting

Article 67

1. Each member of the Economic and Social Council shall have one vote.

2. Decisions of the Economic and Social Council shall be made by a majority of the members present and voting.

Procedure

Article 68

The Economic and Social Council shall set up commissions in economic and social fields and for the promotion of human rights, and such other commissions as may be required for the preformance of its functions.

Article 69

The Economic and Social Council shall invite any Member of the United Nations to participate, without vote, in its deliberations on any matter of particular concern to that Member.

Article 70

The Economic and Social Council may make arrangements for representatives of the specialized agencies to participate, without vote, in its deliberations and in those of the commissions established by it, and for its representatives to participate in the deliberations of the specialized agencies.

Article 71

The Economic and Social Council may make suitable arrangements for consultation with non-governmental organizations which are concerned with matters within its competence. Such arrangements may be made with international organizations and, where appropriate, with national organizations after consultation with the Member of the United Nations concerned.

Article 72

1. The Economic and Social Council shall adopt its own rules of procedure, including the method of selecting its President.

2. The Economic and Social Council shall meet as required in accordance with its rules, which shall include provision for the convening of meetings on the request of a majority of its members.

CHAPTER XI. DECLARATION REGARDING NON-SELF-GOVERNING TERRITORIES

Article 73

Members of the United Nations which have or assume responsibilities for the administration of territories whose peoples have not yet attained a full measure of self-government recognize the principle that the interests of the inhabitants of these territories are paramount, and accept as a sacred trust the obligation to promote to the utmost, within the system of international peace and security established by the present Charter, the well-being of the inhabitants of these territories, and, to this end:

a. to ensure, with due respect for the culture of the peoples concerned, their political, economic, social, and educational advancement, their just treatment, and their protection against abuses;

b. to develop self-government, to take due account of the political aspirations of the peoples, and to assist them in the progressive development of their free political institutions, according to the particular circumstances of each territory and its peoples and their varying stages of advancement;

c. to further international peace and security;

d. to promote constructive measures of development, to encourage research, and to cooperate with one another, and, when and where appropriate, with specialized international bodies with a view to the practical achievement of the social, economic, and scientific purposes set forth in this Article; and

e. to transmit regularly to the Secretary-General for information purposes, subject to such limitation as security and constitutional considerations may require, statistical and other information of a technical nature relating to economic, social, and educational conditions in the territories for which they are respectively responsible other than those territories to which Chapters XII and XIII apply.

Article 74

Members of the United Nations also agree that their policy in respect of the territories to which this Chapter applies, no less than in respect of their metropolitan areas, must be based on the general principle of good-neighborliness, due account being taken of the interests and well-being of the rest of the world, in social, economic, and commercial matters.

CHAPTER XII. INTERNATIONAL TRUSTEESHIP SYSTEM

Article 75

The United Nations shall establish under its authority an international trusteeship system for the administration and supervision of such territories as may be placed thereunder by subsequent individual agreements. These territories are hereinafter referred to as trust territories.

Article 76

The basic objectives of the trusteeship system, in accordance with the Purposes of the United Nations laid down in Article 1 of the present Charter, shall be:

a. to further international peace and security;

b. to promote the political, economic, social, and educational advancement of the inhabitants of the trust territories, and their progressive development towards self-government or independence as may be appropriate to the particular circumstances of each territory and its peoples and the freely expressed wishes of the people concerned, and as may be provided by the terms of each trusteeship agreement;

c. to encourage respect for human rights and for fundamental freedoms for all without distinction as to race, sex, language, and to encourage recognition of the interdependence of the peoples of the world; and

d. to ensure equal treatment in social, economic, and commercial matters for all Members of the United Nations and their nationals, and also equal treatment for the latter in the administration of justice, without prejudice to the attainment of the foregoing objectives and subject to the provisions of Article 80.

Article 77

1. The trusteeship system shall apply to such territories in the following categories as may be placed thereunder by means of trusteeship agreements:

a. territories now held under mandate;

b. territories which may be detached from enemy states as a result of the Second World War; and

c. territories voluntarily placed under the system by states responsible for their administration.

2. It will be a matter for subsequent agreement as to which territories in the foregoing categories will be brought under the trusteeship system and upon what terms.

Article 78

The trusteeship system shall not apply to territories which have become Members of the United Nations, relationship among which shall be based on respect for the principle of sovereign equality.

Article 79

The terms of trusteeship for each territory to be placed under the trusteeship system, including any alteration or amendments, shall be agreed upon by the states directly concerned, including the mandatory power in the case of territories held under mandate by a Member of the United Nations, and shall be approved as provided for in Article 83 and 85.

Article 80

1. Except as may be agreed upon in individual trusteeship agreements, made under Articles 77, 79, and 81, placing each territory under the trusteeship system, and until such agreements have been concluded, nothing in this Chapter shall be construed in or of itself to alter in any manner the rights whatsoever of any states or any peoples or the terms of existing international instruments to which Members of the United Nations may respectively be parties.

2. Paragraph 1 of this Article shall not be interpreted as giving grounds for delay or postponement of the negotiation and conclusion of agreements for placing mandated and other territories under the trusteeship system as provided for in Article 77.

Article 81

The trusteeship agreement shall in each case include the terms under which the trust territory will be administered and designate the authority which will exercise the administration of the trust territory. Such authority, hereinafter called the administering authority, may be one or more states or the Organization itself.

Article 82

There may be designated, in any trusteeship agreement, a strategic area or areas which may include part or all of the trust territory to which the agreement applies, without prejudice to any special agreement or agreements made under Article 43.

Article 83

1. All functions of the United Nations relating to strategic areas, including the approval of the terms of the trusteeship agreement and of their alteration or amendment, shall be exercised by the Security Council.

2. The basic objectives set forth in Article 76 shall be applicable to the people of each strategic area.

3. The Security Council shall, subject to the provisions of the trusteeship agreements and without prejudice to security considerations, avail itself of the assistance of the Trusteeship Council to perform those functions of the United Nations under the trusteeship system relating to political, economic, social, and educational matters in the strategic areas.

Article 84

It shall be the duty of the administering authority to ensure that the trust territory shall play its part in the maintenance of international peace and security. To this end the administering authority may make use of volunteer forces, facilities, and assistance from the trust territory in carrying out the obligations towards the Security Council undertaken in this regard by the administering authority, as well as for local defense and the maintenance of law and order within the trust territory.

Article 85

1. The functions of the United Nations with regard to trusteeship agreements for all areas not designated as strategic, including the approval of the terms of the trusteeship agreements and of their alteration or amendment, shall be exercised by the General Assembly.

2. The Trusteeship Council, operating under the authority of the General Assembly, shall assist the General Assembly in carrying out these functions.

CHAPTER XIII. THE TRUSTEESHIP COUNCIL

Composition

Article 86

1. The Trusteeship Council shall consist of the following Members of the United Nations:

a. those Members administering trust territories;

b. such of those Members mentioned by name in Article 23 as are not administering trusts territories; and

c. as many other Members elected for three-year terms by the General Assembly as may be necessary to ensure that the total number of members of the Trusteeship Council is equally divided between those Members of the United Nations which administer trust territories and those which do not.

2. Each member of the Trusteeship Council shall designate one specially qualified person to represent it therein.

Functions and Powers

Article 87

The General Assembly and, under its authority, the Trusteeship Council, in carrying out their functions, may:

a. consider reports submitted by the administering authority;

b. accept petitions and examine them in consultation with the administering authority;

c. provide for periodic visits to the respective trust territories at times agreed upon with the administering authority; and

d. take these and other actions in conformity with the terms of the trusteeship agreements.

Article 88

The Trusteeship Council shall formulate a questionnaire on the political, economic, social, and educational advancement of the inhabitants of each trust territory, and the administering authority for each trust territory within the competence of the General Assembly shall make an annual report to the General Assembly upon the basis of such questionnaire.

Voting

Article 89

1. Each member of the Trursteeship Council shall have one vote.

2. Decisions of the Trusteeship Council shall be made by a majority of the members present and voting.

Procedure

Article 90

1. The Trusteeship Council shall adopt its own rules of procedure, including the method of selecting its President.

2. The Trusteeship Council shall meet as required in accordance with its rules, which shall include provision for the convening of meetings on the request of a majority of its members.

Article 91

The Trusteeship Council shall, when appropriate, avail itself of the assistance of the Economic and Social Council and of the specialized agencies in regard to matters with which they are respectively concerned.

CHAPTER XIV. THE INTERNATIONAL COURT OF JUSTICE

Article 92

The International Court of Justice shall be the principal judicial organ of the United Nations. It shall function in accordance with the annexed Statute, which is based upon the Statute of the Permanent Court of International Justice and forms an integral part of the present Charter.

Article 93

1. All Members of the United Nations are *ipso facto* parties to the Statute of the International Court of Justice.
2. A state which is not a Member of the United Nations may become a party to the Statute of the International Court of Justice on conditions to be determined in each case by the General Assembly upon the recommendation of the Security Council.

Article 94

1. Each Member of the United Nations undertakes to comply with the decision of the International Court of Justice in any case to which it is a party.
2. If any party to a case fails to perform the obligations incumbent upon it under a judgment rendered by the Court, the other party may have recourse to the Security Council, which may, if it deems necessary, make recommendations or decide upon measures to be taken to give effect to the judgment.

Article 95

Nothing in the present Charter shall prevent Members of the United Nations from entrusting the solution of their differences to other tribunals by virtue of agreements already in existence or which may be concluded in the future.

Article 96

1. The General Assembly or the Security Council may request the International Court of Justice to give an advisory opinion on any legal question.

2. Other organs of the United Nations and specialized agencies, which may at any time be so authorized by the General Assembly, may also request advisory opinions of the Court on legal questions arising within the scope of their activities.

CHAPTER XV. THE SECRETARIAT

Article 97

The Secretariat shall comprise a Secretary-General and such staff as the Organization may require. The Secretary-General shall be appointed by the General Assembly upon the recommendation of the Security Council. He shall be the chief administrative officer of the Organization.

Article 98

The Secretary-General shall act in that capacity in all meetings of the General Assembly, of the Security Council, of the Economic and Social Council and of the Trusteeship Council, and shall perform such other functions as are entrusted to him by these organs. The Secretary-General shall make an annual report to the General Assembly on the work of the Organization.

Article 99

The Secretary-General may bring to the attention of the Security Council any matter which in his opinion may threaten the maintenance of international peace and security.

Article 100

1. In the performance of their duties the Secretary-General and the staff shall not seek or receive instructions from any government or from any other authority external to the Organization. They shall refrain from any action which might reflect on their position as international officials responsible only to the Organization.

2. Each Member of the United Nations undertakes to respect the exclu-

sively international character of the responsibilities of the Secretary-General and the staff and not to seek to influence them in the discharge of their responsibilities.

Article 101

1. The staff shall be appointed by the Secretary-General under regulations established by the General Assembly.

2. Appropriate staffs shall be permanently assigned to the Economic and Social Council, the Trusteeship Council, and, as required, to other organs of the United Nations. These staffs shall form a part of the Secretariat.

3. The paramount consideration in the employment of the staff and in the determination of the conditions of service shall be the necessity of securing the highest standards of efficiency, competence, and integrity. Due regard shall be paid to the importance of recruiting the staff on as wide a geographical basis as possible.

CHAPTER XVI. MISCELLANEOUS PROVISIONS

Article 102

1. Every treaty and every international agreement entered into by any Member of the United Nations after the present Charter comes into force shall as soon as possible be registered with the Secretariat and published by it.

2. No party to any such treaty or international agreement which has not been registered in accordance with the provisions of paragraph 1 of this Article may invoke that treaty or agreement before any organ of the United Nations.

Article 103

In the event of a conflict between the obligations of the Members of the United Nations under the present Charter and their obligations under any other international agreement, their obligations under the present Charter shall prevail.

Article 104

The Organization shall enjoy in the territory of each of its Members such legal capacity as may be necessary for the exercise of its functions and the fulfillment of its purposes.

Article 105

1. The Organization shall enjoy in the territory of each of its Members such privileges and immunities as are necessary for the fulfillment of its purposes.

2. Representatives of the Members of the United Nations and officials of the Organization shall similarly enjoy such privileges and immunities as are necessary for the independent exercise of their functions in connection with the Organization.

3. The General Assembly may make recommendations with a view to determining the details of the application of paragraphs 1 and 2 of this Article or may propose conventions to the Members of the United Nations for this purpose.

CHAPTER XVII. TRANSITIONAL SECURITY ARRANGEMENTS

Article 106

Pending the coming into force of such special agreements referred to in Article 43 as in the opinion of the Security Council enable it to begin the exercise of its responsibilities under Article 42, the parties to the Four-Nation Declaration, signed at Moscow, October 30, 1943, and France, shall, in accordance with the provisions of paragraph 5 of that Declaration, consult with one another and as occasion requires with other Members of the United Nations with a view to such joint action on behalf of the Organization as may be necessary for the purpose of maintaining international peace and security.

Article 107

Nothing in the present Charter shall invalidate or preclude action, in relation to any state which during the Second World War has been an enemy of any signatory to the present Charter, taken or authorized as a result of that war by the Governments having responsibility for such action.

CHAPTER XVIII. AMENDMENTS

Article 108

Amendments to the present Charter shall come into force for all Members of the United Nations when they have been adopted by a vote of two-thirds of the members of the General Assembly and ratified in accordance with their respective constitutional processes by two-thirds of the Members of the United Nations, including all the permanent members of the Security Council.

Article 109

1. A General Conference of the Members of the United Nations for the purpose of reviewing the present Charter may be held at a date and place to be fixed by a two thirds vote of the members of the General Assembly and by a vote of any (seven) *nine* members of the Security Council. Each Member of the United Nations shall have one vote in the conference.

2. Any alteration of the present Charter recommended by a two-thirds vote of the conference shall take effect when ratified in accordance with their respective constitutional processes by two-thirds of the Members of the United Nations including all the permanent members of the Security Council.

3. If such a conference has not been held before the tenth annual session of the General Assembly following the coming into force of the present Charter, the proposal to call such a conference shall be placed on the agenda of that session of the General Assembly, and the conference shall be held if so decided by a majority vote of the members of the General Assembly and by a vote of any seven members of the Security Council.

CHAPTER XIX. RATIFICATION AND SIGNATURE

Article 110

1. The present Charter shall be ratified by the signatory states in accordance with their respective constitutional processes.

2. The ratifications shall be deposited with the Government of the United States of America, which shall notify all the signatory states of each deposit as well as the Secretary-General of the Organization when he has been appointed.

3. The present Charter shall come into force upon the deposit of ratifications by the Republic of China, France, the Union of Soviet Socialist Republics, the United Kingdom of Great Britain and Northern Ireland, and the United States of America, and by a majority of the other signatory states. A protocol of the ratifications deposited shall thereupon be drawn up by the Government of the United States of America which shall communicate copies thereof to all the signatory states.

4. The states signatory to the present Charter which ratify it after it has

come into force will become original Members of the United Nations on the date of the deposit of their respective ratifications.

Article 111

The present Charter, of which the Chinese, French, Russian, English, and Spanish texts are equally authentic, shall remain deposited in the archives of the Government of the United States of America. Duly certified copies thereof shall be transmitted by that Government to the Governments of the other signatory states.

IN FAITH WHEREROF the representatives of the Governments of the United Nations have signed the present Charter.

DONE at the city of San Francisco the twenty-sixth day of June, one thousand nine hundred and forty-five.

C.   Resolution 242*

The Security Council,

Expressing its continuing concern with the grave situation in the Middle East,

Emphasizing the inadmissibility of the acquisition of territory by war and the need to work for a just and lasting peace in which every State in the area can live in security.

Emphasizing further that all Member States in their acceptance of the Charter of the United Nations have undertaken a commitment to act in accordance with Article 2 of the Charter,

1. *Affirms* that the fulfilment of Charter principles requires the establishment of a just and lasting peace in the Middle East which should include the application of both the following principles:

  (i) Withdrawal of Israeli armed forces from territories occupied in the recent conflict;

  (ii) Termination of all claims or states of belligerency and respect for and acknowledgement of the sovereignty, territorial integrity and political independence of every State in the area and their right to live in peace within secure and recognized boundaries free from threats or acts of force;

2. *Affirms further* the necessity

  (a) For guaranteeing freedom of navigation through international waterways in the area;

  (b) For achieving a just settlement of the refugee problem;

  (c) For guaranteeing the territorial inviolability and political independence of every State in the area, through measures including the establishment of demilitarized zones;

3. *Requests* the Secretary-General to designate a Special Representative to proceed to the Middle East to establish and maintain contacts with the States concerned in order to promote agreement and assist efforts to achieve a peaceful and accepted settlement in accordance with the provisions and principles in this resolution;

4. *Requests* the Secretary-General to report to the Security Council on the progress of the efforts of the Special Representative as soon as possible.

---

*Adopted by the Security Council at Its 1382d Meeting on November 22, 1967

D. A Security Council Exercise

The following UN Security Council exercise has been tried successfully in numerous classes. The professor sets forth in the syllabus the scenario, the time reserved for the exercise, and the ground rules. Generally, six sessions are sufficient. To give more authenticity, a meeting room rather than a regular classroom should be used. The room should be set up with tables in a U-shape for 15, plus room for the president of the Security Council, and the secretary general at the head. It is also desirable to have a cardboard name plaque for display in front of each participant at the table. The presidency can be rotated among delegates at each session.

The ideal number for the exercise is about 20 persons, with one each for the 15 members of the Security Council, plus one for each of the other countries directly involved in a crisis. If there are 40 students, the professor could have two separate exercises in succeeding weeks. All students should attend both exercises and prepare comments on both. This type of Security Council exercise is more educational than the big general assembly type with hundreds of students, which is too big to be authentic.

The Arab-Israel dispute provides good material for an exercise. Each student can play the role of an ambassador at the Security Council. He or she should be required to write a letter to the appropriate UN mission in New York, explaining that the student plans to represent that country in a model UN meeting and that any material on the country's view on the issue would be appreciated. The students should be required to give the professor a copy of the letter they have sent.

Early in the session the professor can circulate names with the countries they represent, and phone numbers of students to help them collaborate on resolutions. The professor should write to one of the UN information offices to obtain copies of verbatim minutes on the issue involved. The professor should offer to pay xeroxing costs if extra copies are not available. These minutes can be put on reserve for the students to use in preparing their speeches and resolutions. The *U.N. Chronicle* generally carries the texts of important current resolutions.

Students should be asked to prepare a speech of perhaps one or two pages on the issue with a deadline in advance for the first mock UN session. The professor can require that it be neatly typed, single spaced, so that it could be included in the verbatim minutes of the first meeting. Such speeches can be pasted together and xeroxed without retyping. Generally, the first session or two can be devoted to these speeches. The most intensive activity generally comes before and during the last meeting.

Students should be graded on the authenticity of their contributions to the Security Council session. This means they can plagiarize for their speeches from the material that they receive from the missions or from the other material.

The professor can act as the secretary general, advising the president of the Council for managing the meeting, if necessary. Copies of the rules of procedure of the Security Council can be purchased for $2 (Provisional Rules of Procedures of the Security Council) from the UN Bookshop, GA 32 b, New York, NY 10017. The exercise could be initiated with a report from the secretary general, such as the hypothetical one attached. (Only the first paragraph is hypothetical.) The resolutions by the delegates should be drafted in a UN format such as the draft resolution. By cutting and pasting, the "secretary general" can make the headings look authentic and then duplicate draft resolutions for distribution. A number of students generally take the initiative on drafting resolutions, but find they are hard to pass. They then get to bargaining, which can be very educational.

Summary minutes can be made with the aid of a tape recorder. The first sessions are not difficult for reporting because the minutes can be put together by xeroxing the speeches. There is added value to the exercise if each student critiques the sessions with a three- or four-page paper. The students' participation in the exercise can be graded and given the same weight as a term paper.

The exercise can be advertised with posters. Local newspapers and the student newspapers are usually interested in covering meetings.

Following is an example of an initial report of the secretary general and a resolution approved in the exercise.

Report of the Secretary General on the Threat of War in Lebanon

The secretary general has called this session of the Security Council to act on the threat of war between Israel and Lebanon. In the past week there have been two mortar attacks against Israeli settlements in northern Israel, apparently originating from southern Lebanon. Israel is threatening to attack southern Lebanon. UNIFIL and UNTSO observers report that Lebanon is moving troops into southern Lebanon, whereas Syria has indicated that it will help Lebanon defend its sovereignty. The Lebanese government has stated that it intends to exercise its authority in southern Lebanon assisted only by UNIFIL.

The UNIFIL forces do not patrol the area along the Israel border where the firing occurred. This area has been patrolled by forces friendly to Israel. UNIFIL observers report that Israeli forces are mobilizing along the border. Syrian forces in eastern Lebanon have been put on an alert status.

The UNIFIL six-month's mandate expires on April 17. There are now 5,822 military personnel in the force from 10 countries: Fiji, Finland, France, Ghana, Ireland, Italy, Nepal, Netherlands, Norway, and Sweden. The commander is Lieutenant-General William Callaghan of Ireland. Since its establishment, 103 members of the force have died, 42 from gunfire and mines, 48 in accidents, and 13 from natural causes. The cost of the force is about $13 million per month. The accumulated arrears due to nonpayment of assessments is about $220 million.

The UN Disengagement Force (UNDOF) maintaining the cease-fire in the Golan Heights has 1,331 military personnel from Austria, Canada, Finland, and Poland plus 8 military observers from the UN Truce Supervision Organization. Major General Gustav Hagglund of Finland commands the force. It costs about $2.9 million per month.

Lebanon: Draft Resolution

The Security Council
Expressing its extreme concern with the grave situation in the Middle East,

While Remembering and condemning terrorist acts against noncombatants,

Emphasizing that all Member States in their acceptance of the Charter of the United Nations have undertaken a commitment to act in accordance with Article 2 of the Charter,

Specifically stating in part that all Members shall settle their international disputes by peaceful means in such a manner that international peace, security, and justice are not endangered, and furthermore that all members shall refrain from threatening or using force against the territorial integrity or political independence of any State,

1. *Calls Upon* all States in the region to renounce aggression as a means of settling their disputes;

2. *Asks That* all necessary measures of sanctions be taken against aggressors in accordance with Article 41, Chapter 7 of the Charter of the United Nations, recalling that these sanctions do not involve the use of armed force;

3. *Reaffirms* the need for the UNIFIL forces to maintain their positions and extends their mandate until October 19, 1986;

4. *Requests* the termination of all claims or states of belligerency and supports the respect for and acknowledgment of the sovereignty, territorial integrity, and political independence of every State in the area and their right to live in peace within secure and recognized boundaries free from the threats or acts of force;

5. *Pleads* for rational, constructive, and inspired leadership from all parties in the dispute so that a just and lasting peace might be implemented, bringing to a successful conclusion the pursuit of the rightful aspirations of all parties;

6. *Requests* that the Secretary-General report to the Council the progress made in compliance with this resolution and its implementation, especially with regard to the needs for immediate and sufficient sanctions in order that the current aggression is halted.

E. U.S. Contributions to the United Nations and Specialized Agencies

Calendar Years 1949–1990
(Thousands of Dollars)

| | Estimate 1990 | | 1949–1990 Cumulative Total |
	Contribution	Percent	
United Nations, Specialized Agencies, and the			
International Atomic Energy Agency			
(assessed budgets)			
United Nations[1]	266,600	25.00	3,281,290
Food and Agriculture Organization	69,950	25.00	658,494
International Maritime Organization	1,243	5.38	9,982
International Atomic Energy Agency	46,032	25.13	405,702
International Civil Aviation Organization	7,933	25.00	129,275
Joint Financing Program	—	—	49,867
International Labor Organization	61,898	25.00	522,666
International Telecommunication Union	5,435	7.95	60,957
United Nations Educational, Scientific and			
Cultural Organization[2]	—	—	546,454
United Nations Industrial Development			
Organization	25,913	25.00	70,192
Universal Postal Union	859	5.27	9,705
World Health Organization	83,129	25.00	1,180,826
World Intellectual Property Organization	1,057	5.72	8,882
World Meteorological Organization	8,966	24.65	79,220
United Nations, Specialized Agencies, and the			
International Atomic Energy Agency	579,015	—	7,013,512
United Nations Peacekeeping Forces			
United Nations Emergency Force/United			
Nations Disengagement Observer Force/			
United Nations Interim Force in Lebanon			
Assessed	40,751	29.39	715,301
United Nations Force in Cyprus[3]	8,837	32.61	212,329
United Nations Iran-Iraq Military Observer			
Group (UNIIMOG)	12,489	31.24	12,489

| | Estimate 1990 | | 1949–1990 Cumulative Total |
	Contribution	Percent	
United Nations Peacekeeping Forces (Cont.)			
United Nations Observer Group in Central America (ONUCA)	17,730	48.41	17,730
Inactive Peacekeeping Organizations	—	—	231,851
Peacekeeping Forces	79,807	—	1,189,700
Special Voluntary Programs			
Fund for the Protection of the World Cultural and Natural Heritage (World Heritage Fund)	206	8.80	2,534
International Atomic Energy Agency Technical Assistance Fund[4]	21,546	26.29	228,847
International Fund for Agricultural Development	34,400	14.57	504,320
United Nations Afghanistan Emergency Trust Fund (UNOCA)	13,283	12.43	23,283
United Nations Children's Fund	63,950	16.46	1,014,474
United Nations Development Program	105,000	10.26	3,040,305
United Nations Capital Development Fund	1,476	3.77	21,666
United Nations Center for Human Settlements (HABITAT)	393	5.37	1,976
United Nations Educational and Training Program for Southern Africa	788	16.53	12,172
United Nations Environment Program	11,805	23.90	153,130
United Nations Industrial Development Organization (UNIDO-IPS Voluntary)	492	100.00	1,142
United Nations Trust Fund for South Africa	492	13.67	3,859
U.N./FAO World Food Program	163,000	19.73	2,411,572
United Nations Fund for Drug Abuse Control	4,000	7.64	56,872
United Nations Institute for Namibia	—	—	3,987
United Nations Fund for Population Activities	—	—	410,291
U.N. High Commissioner for Refugees Program:			
Regular Programs	74,318	21.24	1,063,974
Special Programs	52,668	23.00	600,269
United Nations Relief and Works Agency	57,000	23.18	1,542,883
UNRWA Special Projects	—	—	23,070
United Nations Development Fund for Women	787	9.63	10,163
United Nations Institute for Training and Research	—	—	7,966
United Nations Voluntary Fund for Victims of Torture	—	—	272
United Nations Volunteers Program	100	13.94	2,838
Voluntary Fund for United Nations World Assembly on Aging	—	—	400

| | Estimate 1990 | | 1949–1990 Cumulative Total |
	Contribu-tion	Percent	
Special Voluntary Programs (Cont.)			
WHO Special Programs	40,000	22.22	239,307
WIPO Voluntary Programs	—	—	922
WMO Voluntary Cooperation Program	1,986	26.62	37,400
Inactive Special Voluntary Programs	—	—	679,496
Special Voluntary Programs	647,690	—	12,100,390
Total U.S. Contributions	1,306,512	—	20,303,602

Source: United States Department of State, *United States Contributions to International Organizations, Report to the Congress for Fiscal Year 1990.* Department of State Publication 9912.

[1]The amounts shown do not reflect the amounts received in repayment of principal and interest on UN bonds.

[2]The United States withdrew its membership from UNESCO effective December 31, 1984.

[3]UNFICYP was established in March 1964. The amounts include cash contributions and airlift services of $1,254,107 for which the United States did not charge the United Nations. The U.S. pledges have been based on the initial cost estimates of the Force with the qualification that the amount ultimately contributed will depend upon the contributions made by other governments and confirmation of the cost estimates.

[4]Amounts shown include contributions in cash, services, equipment, and fellowship training. Percentage refers to cash only. This amount also includes contributions for the Safeguards Program.

References

Acheson, D. 1969. *Present at the Creation*. New York: W.W. Norton.

Akehurst, M. 1984. *A Modern Introduction to International Law*. London: George Allen and Unwin.

Alexander, Y. and Nanes, A. 1980. *The United States and Iran: A Documental History*. Frederick, MD: University Press of America.

Baer, G. W. 1976. *Test Case: Italy, Ethiopia and the League of Nations*. Stanford: Hoover Institution Press.

Bailey, S. 1964. *The Secretariat of the United Nations*. New York: Frederick Praeger.

Bailey, S. D. 1971. *Voting in the Security Council*. Bloomington: Indiana University Press.

Bailey, T. A. 1945. *A Diplomatic History of the American People*. New York: F. Crofts.

Baker, R. 1937. *Woodrow Wilson: Life and Letters*. New York: Doubleday.

Bassett, J. 1930. *The League of Nations*. New York: Longmans, Green.

Berdiner, E. 1975. *A Time for Angels*. New York: Alfred A. Knopf.

Boucher, C. and Siebeck, W. 1987. "UNCTAD VII: New Spirit in North South Relations." *Finance and Development*.

Campbell, A. 1901. *The Rights of War and Peace*. Washington, DC: M. Walt Dunne.

Campbell, T. M. and Herring, G. C. 1975. *The Diaries of Edward R. Stettinius J*. New York: New Viewpoints.

Carter, J. 1982. *Keeping Faith*. New York: Bantam.

Chandazorkur, A. 1984. "The International Monetary Fund: Its Financial Organization and Activities." Washington, DC: IMF.

Chayes, A. 1974. *The Cuban Missile Crisis*. New York: Oxford University Press.

Churchill, W. 1948. *The Gathering Storm*. Cambridge: Houghton-Mifflin.

Claude, Inez, Jr. 1991. *Swords Into Plowshares*. New York: Random House.

Collins, L. and Lapierre, D. 1973. *O Jerusalem*. New York: Pocket Books.

Cordier, A. *Public Papers of the Secretaries General of the United Nations*. New York: Columbia University Press, 8 vols. Trygve Lie through U Thant.

Current History. Published monthly.

Dawisha, A. 1981. "Iraq: The West's Opportunity." *Foreign Policy,* Winter.

Dayan, M. 1966. *The Story of My Life*. New York: Werner Books.

Driscoll, David. *What is the International Monetary Fund.* Washington, DC: International Monetary Fund.

de Cuellar, Javier Perez. 1991. "Report of the Secretary-General on the Work of the Organization 1991. New York: United Nations.

de Vries, M. 1986. *The IMF in a Changing World—1945–85.* Washington, DC: IMF.

Devine, R. 1981. *The Cuban Missile Crisis.* Chicago: Quadrangle.

Dillon, K. B. 1985. *Recent Developments and External Debt Restructuring.* Washington, DC: IMF, August.

Economist (London). July 26, 1986.

Eduard, H. and Puckahtickom, B. 1985. *Export Credit Policy.* Washington, DC: IMF, August.

Eisenhower, D. 1963. *Mandate for Change.* New York: Doubleday.

————. 1965. *Waging Peace.* New York: Doubleday.

Falk, R., Kratochivil, F., and Mendlovitz, S. (eds). 1985. *International Law.* Boulder: Westview Press.

Feld, W. 1980. *Multinational Corporations and U.N. Politics.* New York: Pergamon.

Foreign Affairs. 1992. *America and the World 1992.* Published annually.

Franck, T. 1985. *Nations Against Nation.* New York: Oxford University Press.

Garthoff, R. 1987. *Reflections on the Cuban Missile Crisis.* Washington, DC: Brookings.

Gelb, L. and Betts, R. 1979. *The Irony of Vietnam: The System Worked.* Washington, DC: Brookings.

Goodrich, L. and Hambro E. 1946. *Charter of the United Nations: Commentary and Documents.* Boston: World Peace Foundation.

Gravel, M. 1971. *The Pentagon Papers.* Boston: Bacon Press.

Gruhn, I. 1979. "The U.N. Maze Compounds Development." *International Organization,* Spring.

Haig, A. 1984. *Caveat—Realism, Reagan and Foreign Policy.* New York: Macmillan.

Halberstam, D. 1969. *The Best and the Brightest.* New York: Random House.

Hardie, F. 1976. *The Abyssinian Crisis.* Hamdon, TN: Archon.

Harriman, W. and Abel, E. 1979. *Special Envoy to Churchill.* New York: Random House.

Heiberg, H. and Holst, J. 1986. "Peacekeeping in Lebanon—Comparing UNIFIL and the MNF." *Survival.* London: September/October.

Louis Henkin et al. 1989. *Right v. Might.* New York: Council on Foreign Relations.

Herring, G. 1979. *America's Longest War.* New York: John Wiley.

Hoopes, T. 1973. *The Devil and John Foster Dulles.* Boston: Little, Brown.

Hull, C. 1948. *The Memoirs of Cordell Hull.* New York: Macmillan (2 vols.).

International Labor Office Geneva. 1992. *World Labor Report 1992.* Geneva: International Labor Office.

International Monetary Fund. 1992. *Annual Report 1991.* Washington, DC: IMF. Published annually.

International Monetary Fund. *IMF Survey.* Published biweekly.

International Monetary Fund. *World Economic Outlook: May 1992*. Published biannually.

Janis, M. 1988. *An Introduction to International Law*. Boston: Little, Brown.

Jenkins, B. 1983. "International Cooperation in Locating and Recovering Stolen Nuclear Materials." *Terrorism*, Vol. 6, no. 4, pp. 561–576.

Johnson, L. 1971. *The Vantage Point*. New York: Popular Library.

Khalilzad, Z. July/August 1980. "Afghanistan and the Crisis in American Foreign Policy." *Survival*.

Khomeini, A. 1979. "Issues Related to the Struggle of Muslim People of Iran." San Francisco: Consulate General of the Islam Republic of Iran.

Khrushchev, N. 1970. *Khrushchev Remembers*. Boston: Little, Brown.

———. 1976. *Khrushchev Remembers, the Last Testament*. Boston: Little, Brown.

Kissinger, H. 1979. *White House Years*. Boston: Little, Brown.

———. 1982. *Years of Upheaval*. Boston: Little, Brown.

Lall, A. 1970. *The U.N. and the Middle East Crisis—1967*. New York: Columbia University Press.

Lauterpaucht, H. 19__. "The Grotian Tradition in International Law." In H. Falk et al., *International Law*. Boulder: Westview Press.

League of Nations, Information Section. 1926 to 1938. *The League from Year to Year*. Annual volumes. Geneva.

League of Nations. *League of Nations—A Survey 1920–26*. Geneva.

League of Nations. *Official Journal, 1922–24*. Geneva.

League of Nations. *Report of the Work of the League*. Annual reports.

League of Nations Secretariat. 1930. *Ten Years of World Cooperation*.

Lie, T. 1954. *In the Cause of Peace*. New York: Macmillan.

Link, A. 1965. *Wilson: Campaign for Progressivism and Peace 1916–1919*. Princeton: Princeton University Press.

Lowenthal, A. 1972. *The Dominican Intervention*. Cambridge: Harvard University Press.

McDonald, J. 1983. "The U.N. Convention Against Hostage-Taking." *Terrorism*. Vol. 6, no. 4, pp. 545–560.

McKenna, M. 1961. *Borah*. Ann Arbor: University of Michigan Press.

Mitrany, D. 1966. *A Working Peace System*. Chicago: Quadrangle Books.

Modelski, G., ed. 1979. *Transnational Corporations and World Order*. San Francisco: Freeman.

Morse, B. June 12, 1984. "Statement Before the UNDP Governing Council." United Nations, New York.

Murphy, J. M. 1982. *The United Nations and the Control of International Violence*. Totowa, NJ: Towman and Allenheld.

Newhouse, J. 1973. *Cold Dawn, The Story of SALT*. New York: Holt, Rinehart.

Nixon, R. 1979. *The Memoirs of Richard Nixon*. New York: Grosset & Dunlap (2 vols.).

Northedge, F. S. 1986. *The League of Nations*. New York: Holms and Meier.

Ouattara, A. 1988. "Fund is Helping to Resolve Africa's Debt Problem by Supporting Growth-Oriented Economic Reforms." *IMF Survey,* June 13.

Organization for Economic Cooperation and Development. 1983. *1983 Review.* Paris: OECD.

Organization for Economic Cooperation and Development. 1984. Paris: OECD. DP/ 1984/5/Add.2.

Pachter, H. M. 1963. *Collision Course.* New York: Praeger.

Pasha, G. 1957. *A Soldier with the Arabs.* London: Hoddar and Slaughton.

Pentagon Papers. 1976. New York Times Edition.

Peterson, M. 1986. *The General Assembly in World Politics.* Boston: Allen and Unwin.

Phillips, D. 1977. *The Night Watch.* New York: Ballantine.

Poole, P. 1973. *The United States and Indochina from FDR to Nixon.* Hinsdale, IL: Dryden.

Porter, G. 1978. "The Sino-Soviet Conflict in Southeast Asia." *Current History,* December.

Romulo, C. 1986. *Forty Years: A Third World Soldier at the UN.* New York: Greenwood Press.

Russell, R. 1958. *A History of the United Nations' Charter.* Washington, DC: Brookings.

Sadat, A. 1977. *In Search of Identity.* New York: Harper & Row.

Schlesinger, A. 1975. *A Thousand Days.* New York: Fawcett Crest.

Scott, G. 1973. *The Rise and Fall of the United Nations.* New York: Macmillan.

Seabury, P. and McDougall, W. 1984. *The Grenada Papers.* San Francisco: Institute of Contemporary Studies.

Seymour, C. 1938. *The Intimate Papers of Colonel House.* Boston: Houghton-Mifflin.

Shamwell, K. 1983. "Implementing the Convention on the Prevention and Punishment of Crimes Against Internationally Protected Persons, Including Diplomatic Agents," *Terrorism.* Vol. 6, no. 4, pp. 529–544.

Sherwood, R. 1948. *Roosevelt and Hopkins.* New York: Harper.

Siekmann, R. 1985. *Basic Documents on United Nations and Related Peacekeeping Forces.* Boston: Martinus Nijhoff.

Simon, S. 1979. "Kampuchea: Vietnam's Vietnam." *Current History.* December.

Sisco, J. "Middle East: Progress or Lost Opportunity." *America and the World—1982.* New York: Council on Foreign Relations.

Smith, G. 1962. *Dean Acheson.* New York: Cooper Square.

Sofaer, A. 1986. "Terrorism and the Law." *Foreign Affairs,* Spring.

Sorensen, T. 1966. *Kennedy.* London: Pan Books.

Spero, J. 1985. *The Politics of International Economic Relations.* New York: St. Martins.

Stalin, J. 1945. *The Great Patriotic War.* Moscow.

Stanley Foundation. July 17–22, 1988. *International Agenda for the 1990s.* Muscatine, IA.

Stern, S. 1988. "World Bank General Capital Increase." *Finance and Development.* June 1958.

Stimson, H. 1936. *The Far Eastern Crisis.* New York: Harper.

Stimson, H. and Bundy, M. 1948. *On Active Service in Peace and War.* New York: Harper.

Stoessinger, J. 1974. *Why Nations Go to War.* New York: St. Martins.

Stoessinger, J. 1977. *The United Nations and the Superpowers: China, Russia and America.* New York: Random House.

Takeuchi, T. 1938. *Amerasia.* July.

Talbott, S. 1984. *Deadly Gambit.* New York: Alfred A. Knopf.

Terrorism, An International Journal. 1983. Vol. 6, no. 4.

Tessitore, J., and Woolfson, S. (eds.). 1992. *A Global Agenda: Issues Before the 47th General Assembly of the United Nations.* Lanham, MD: University Press of America. An annual publication of the United Nations Association of the United States of America.

Truman, H. 1956. *Years of Decision.* New York: Double day (2 vols.).

U.N. Chronicle. New York: United Nations.

U.N. Commission on Transnational Corporations. 1979. Document E/C. 10/45, 11 April. New York: United Nations.

UNDP. 1984. Annual Report of the Administrator for 1983. DP/1984/5. Add. 3. New York: United Nations.

UNDP. 1984. Document (DP/1984) 5/Add. 12. New York: United Nations.

UNDP. 1981. *Promises to Keep.* New York: United Nations.

United Nations. 1970. *Basic Problems of Disarmament.* New York: United Nations.

United Nations. 1972. *Multinational Corporations in World Development.* New York. Document St/ECA/190.

United Nations. 1986. *Everyone's United Nations.* New York: United Nations.

United Nations. 1987. *Annotated Preliminary List of Items to be Included in the Provisional Agenda.* New York: United Nations. Printed annually.

United Nations. From 1946. *United Nations Security Council—Resolutions and Decisions.* New York: United Nations.

United Nations. *United Nations Security Council, Official Records.* New York: United Nations. From first meeting in January, 1946. Later issues do not give verbatim record of proceedings.

United Nations Association of the United States of America. 1991. *A Global Agenda: Issues Before the 46th General Assembly of the United Nations.* New York: University Press of America. Printed annually.

United Nations Association of the United States of America. *Interdependent.* Published monthly.

United Nations Department for Disarmament Affairs. 1991. *Nuclear Weapons: A Comprehensive Study.* New York: United Nations.

United Nations Environment Programme. 1989. *Environmental Data Report.* Cambridge, MA: Basil Blackwell.

Urquart, B. 1972. *Hammarskjold.* New York: Harpers.

U.S. Arms Control and Disarmament Agency. 1980. *Arms Control and Disarmament Agreements.* Washington, DC: GPO.

U.S. Congress, Senate, Select Committee. 1975. *Alleged Assassination Plots Involving Foreign Leaders.* Washington, DC: GPO.

U.S. Department of State. 1991. *United States Contributions to International Organizations: Report to the Congress for Fiscal Year 1990.* Washington, DC: U.S. Department of State.

U.S. Department of State. 1991. *United States Participation in the UN: Report by the President to the Congress for the Year 1990.* Washington, DC: U.S. Department of State.

U.S. Department of State, Bureau of Public Affairs. *Dispatch.* Washington, DC: GPO. Published weekly.

U.S. Department of State. 1954. *Foreign Relations of the United States: East Asia and the Pacific.* Washington, DC: GPO.

U.S. Department of State. 1980. "Soviet Invasion of Afghanistan." Special Report. April. Washington, DC: GPO.

U.S. Department of State. 1981. *Treaties in Force—1981.* Washington, DC: GPO.

U.S. Department of State. 1984. *Foreign Relations of the United States: Korea 1950.* Washington, DC: GPO.

U.S. Department of State. 1986. *Terrorist Attacks on U.S. Business Abroad.* March. Washington, DC: GPO.

U.S. Department of State. 1987. Office of the Ambassador at Large for Counterterrorism. "International Terrorist Incidents, 1968–1987." Washington, DC: GPO.

Von Glahn, G. 1981. *Law Among Nations.* New York: Macmillan.

Wainhouse, D. 1966. *International Peace Observation.* Baltimore: Johns Hopkins Press.

Walp, P. 1931. *Constitutional Development of the League of Nations.* Lexington: University of Kentucky.

Walters, E. 1952. *A History of the League of Nations.* London: Oxford University Press.

Weston, B., Folk, R., and D'Amoto, A. 1980. *International Law and World Order.* St. Paul: West Publishing Co.

World Bank. 1992. *World Development Report—1992.* New York: Oxford University Press. Published annually.

Yoder, A. 1981. "UN Monitoring the Transnational Corporations." *Towson State Journal of International Affairs.* Spring.

————. 1983. "United Nation's Resolutions Against International Terrorism." *Terrorism.* Vol. 6, no. 4.

————. 1986. *World Politics and the Causes of War Since 1914.* Lanham, MD: University Press of America.

Yoshihashi, T. 1963. *Conspiracy at Mukden.* New Haven: Yale University Press.

Index

About the Author

Amos Yoder is Borah Distinguished Professor Emeritus of Political Science from the University of Idaho. He taught international relations courses there from 1974 to 1991. Before then, he was in the diplomatic service of the Department of State for 25 years, assigned to United Nations, Chinese, German, and politico-military affairs in Washington, DC; to U.S. embassies in Thailand and Israel; and to international conferences. In 1986–1987 he taught at the Foreign Affairs College in Beijing, China, as a Fulbright professor, and in 1991 he taught at the L. Kossuth University at Debrecen, Hungary, as a Fulbright professor. He has published articles and books, including *The Conduct of American Foreign Policy since World War II, World Politics and the Causes of War since 1914, International Politics and Policymakers' Ideas, The Evolution of the United Nations System*, and *Communist Systems and Challenges*.